FUNDRAISING STRATEGIES FOR COMMUNITY COLLEGES

FUNDRAISING STRATEGIES FOR COMMUNITY COLLEGES

The Definitive Guide for Advancement

Steve Klingaman

Foreword by Gerardo E. de los Santos

Copublished with

CASE.

Sty/us

STERLING, VIRGINIA

Published by Stylus Publishing, LLC.
22883 Quicksilver Drive
Sterling, Virginia 20166-2102

Library of Congress Cataloging-in-Publication Data
Klingaman, Steve, 1953–
    Fundraising strategies for community colleges : the
definitive guide for advancement / Written by Steve
Klingaman.—First edition.
        pages   cm
    Includes bibliographical references and index.
    ISBN 978-1-57922-730-2 (cloth : alk. paper)
    ISBN 978-1-57922-731-9 (pbk : alk. paper)
    ISBN 978-1-57922-732-6 (library networkable
    e-edition) = - ISBN 978-1-57922-733-3 (consumer
    e-edition)   1. Educational fund raising—United States.
2. Community colleges—United = States—Finance.
I. Title.
LB2336.K65   2012
378.1'06—dc23   2011045139

13-digit ISBN: 978-1-57922-730-2 (cloth)
13-digit ISBN: 978-1-57922-731-9 (paper)
13-digit ISBN: 978-1-57922-732-6 (library networkable
e-edition)
13-digit ISBN: 978-1-57922-733-3 (consumer e-edition)

Printed in the United States of America

All first editions printed on acid-free paper
that meets the American National Standards Institute
Z39-48 Standard.

Bulk Purchases

Quantity discounts are available for use in workshops
and for staff development.
Call 1-800-232-0223

First Edition, 2012

10   9   8   7   6   5   4   3   2   1

This book is dedicated to Dr. C. Ben Wright,
a consummate development professional.

CONTENTS

ACKNOWLEDGMENTS

G rateful acknowledgment is offered to my development colleagues at Dunwoody College of Technology: C. Ben Wright and consultant Mark Davy, of Mark Davy and Associates. Without their insights and investment in my career this book would not have been possible. Together with Mark Skipper, and the Dunwoody development team, we pioneered and tested many of the techniques presented in this work. I thank also my esteemed development colleagues Emily Best and Catherine McGlinch. I thank Julie Schorfheide of CASE, for her valuable insight and perspective at a critical stage of the project and Mary Lynum for manuscript preparation assistance.

I acknowledge with gratitude the organizations where I first implemented the ideas described in the book: Dunwoody College of Technology, Family Caregiver Alliance, Normandale Community College, New College of California, and Sequoia Hospital Foundation.

I thank the following individuals and organizations for permissions granted for cited materials: The Advisory Board Company (www.advisoryboard company.com); *The Chronicle of Higher Education*; Cleveland State University; Laura Cohen; *Contributions* magazine (www.contributionsmagazine .com); James R. Cooper, president, Sales Sense LLC, Plano, Texas; The Council for Advancement and Support of Education (CASE); Mark Davy; Brydon M. DeWitt, DeWitt & Associates; Mark Drozdowski; Dunwoody College of Technology; Kay Sprinkel Grace; Penelepe C. Hunt; Tom Ingram; John Wiley & Sons, Inc.; Mark Skipper; United Way of the Bay Area; University of Arizona Foundation; University of Virginia; and C. Ben Wright.

Thank you to Jim Collins for the quotes reprinted from *Good to Great and the Social Sectors* (copyright © 2005 by Jim Collins, reprinted with permission from Jim Collins). I am indebted also to Mr. Collins and Harper Business for the many ideas from *Good to Great* referenced in this book.

Thank you to Independent Sector for special reprint permissions. Independent Sector "is a nonprofit, nonpartisan coalition of charities, foundations, and corporate philanthropy programs whose mission is to advance the common good by leading, strengthening, and mobilizing the independent sector." (www.independentsector.org)

Thanks also to the Association of Fundraising Professionals (AFP) and *Advancing Philanthropy*, its bimonthly publication. AFP promotes philanthropy through advocacy, research, education, and certifications programs (www.afpnet.org).

This book would not have seen the light of day without the wonderfully creative and persistent acquisitions editor Sarah Burrows, who believed in the project from the beginning. Thank you especially to Stylus Publishing, LLC, for bringing the project to life.

Finally, I would like to thank my wife Barri, without whose loving support this book would not have been possible.

FOREWORD

I n 2003, the League for Innovation in the Community College—the organization for which I serve as president—published a guide to successful approaches to fundraising and development. We asked J. William Wenrich, then chancellor emeritus of the Dallas County Community College District, to write a chapter on how shifts in the fundraising landscape had prompted community college presidents to take a more proactive approach to winning the hearts and dollars of potential donors. Wenrich, who began his illustrious career in community college education in 1968, described his still budding relationship to fundraising as a leader this way: It's not the race I signed up for, but it's the race I'm in.

The economic climate has changed dramatically since 2003, and fundraising at community colleges is no longer an afterthought. If anything, it's become a primary expectation that community college leaders have successful fundraising experiences. And I now have many presidents tell me that they spend between 30 and 50 percent of their time away from campus raising funds.

The dynamics of community college funding are changing dramatically as state support dwindles or even disappears. And if our institutions are going to continue to provide an open door for educational opportunity, we are going to have to find more entrepreneurial ways of raising money through grant-writing opportunities and alumni and corporate giving programs, similar to those found at many four-year institutions.

The good news, as you'll find out in this book, is that it's entirely possible for community colleges to fundraise successfully. And there are some two-year institutions that have been doing it well for years. While community colleges are relatively late to advancement, the idea that these institutions cannot fundraise successfully is a complete farce. Granted, the process is slightly different among smaller suburban and multicampus urban institutions, but there are successful models for how it can take place.

The innovation and entrepreneurship required of fundraising make up part of what community colleges are; these institutions are always adapting and changing to meet the needs of their students. Fundraising is now another need that must be met—and clearly not just a short-term one. Now, it's not a matter of if community colleges can raise money; it's a matter of how they should do it.

Sometimes, however, community college leaders can get caught up thinking about all the barriers and challenges their institution may face when fundraising. They may see success at other institutions, but then counter, "Well, that's not our situation." They may worry that their students swirl in and out so much that they don't have any chances to make true attachments to their institution. They may also worry that their students are already financially challenged enough and won't consider donating.

When you hear these anxieties voiced, that's when you, as an advancement professional, have to turn the tables and ask if the college can afford *not* to fundraise. No one person—neither the advancement officer nor the president—can do this alone. Fundraising has to be imbued in an organization's culture, and everyone has to be responsible for it. This should be the rallying cry on your campus, a recognition that institutional fundraising and advancement requires a team effort.

As you will further discover in this book, those institutions that fundraise well do so because they have strong support from their leadership. Any and all development activity has to be supported by a college's board. And when there's initial success at your institution, it will beget other successes and help to build a culture of advancement.

Fundraising is about relationship building, and community colleges need to be pushing the envelope and looking to the future in that regard. Before you make "the Ask" of a potential donor, you must first demonstrate value and provide assurance that the institution will be a good steward of his or her investment. You have to be perceived as providing donors an opportunity to participate in and contribute to something that is critically important. One of the most important lessons this book will teach you is that there are people out there who want to help and contribute—but often nobody ever asks them.

Depending on various circumstances, however, you may not even be able to make the initial Ask for quite a while. That's why community colleges have to be in the business of fundraising for the long haul. Community college leaders have to think about their commitment to fundraising as being analogous to their commitment to providing lifelong learning opportunities.

Just as students take advantage of our institutions—we hope—for the rest of their lives, we're also going to be establishing a long-term relationship with them. Alumni engagement and fundraising are just part of another way of making that connection and strengthening the opportunity for students to be contributing participants in the betterment of their institution and community.

The League for Innovation has and will continue to support the fund-raising aspirations of community colleges. We're still relatively new to this work; organizations like the Council for Advancement and Support of Education (CASE) have been doing this for years. Our first steps have included publishing about fundraising, and we've dedicated an entire track at one of our conferences to fundraising and advancement. CASE recently refocused its efforts on two-year institutions by launching the Center for Community College Advancement.

The almost 1,200 community colleges around the country are all at different levels of acumen and success when it comes to their advancement programs. While some may be very successful in their fundraising and foundation efforts, others may not even have a foundation yet. Needless to say, there's a lot of learning to be done, and plenty of teachers are eager to help.

But the beauty of community colleges, as I am reminded by this book, is that they are a cohesive community. Our institutions have a rich tradition of sharing. Community college leaders are not about holding their success to their chests and not sharing with their brethren. Community colleges are built upon notions of democracy, citizenship, and service. This goes hand in hand with sharing models of high impact and promising practices. It's part and parcel of what the League for Innovation and CASE were created to do and this book was written for—to share these models and practices. And I'm optimistic that community colleges will maintain this open and sharing tradition into the future.

Gerardo E. de los Santos
Phoenix, AZ

Roughly 1,200 community colleges serve 6.8 million for-credit students in the United States today.[1] This figure represents a significant share of the higher education marketplace, some 43 percent of American undergraduates.[2] The American Association of Community Colleges indicates that "half of the students who receive a baccalaureate degree attend community college in the course of their undergraduate studies."[3] Community colleges nonetheless have suffered from what might be called the Rodney Dangerfield complex—they just don't get any respect. Want proof? Though community colleges serve almost half of all undergraduates in the United States, they probably raise between 2 and 4 percent of all gift revenue made to higher education (Summers 2006, B22).[4]

The period from the late 1960s to the early 1970s marked an explosion in the number of what were then commonly called junior colleges serving American communities. Today, these institutions are entering an academic midlife. Their first-generation faculties are retiring, or have already. Entire careers have transpired within their walls. Their cultures have consolidated into a hardwired firmware of a particular kind of educational machine. Bureaucracy and jargon have grown like kudzu in a shady grove. Most important, countless students spanning two generations have obtained a foothold in the arena of higher education under their tutelage. But the fundamental with which we are most concerned, their funding base, is today under serious and perhaps permanent stress.

In some respects, community colleges are neither fish nor fowl; they are a unique amalgam of the high schools of which they are an extension and the colleges and universities to which they are a gateway. Their funding has mirrored that "tweener" status. These institutions, historically funded via property taxes and state aid, for decades have had the majority of their costs funded by the states—routinely in the range of 60 percent and up. They have enjoyed better funding than high schools, particularly rural and urban schools, while receiving a markedly lower degree of state largesse than public colleges and universities.

In general, the system has worked well. Committed faculties and staff have provided a stable platform upon which to base an educational practicum focused on teaching and learning and on addressing the developmental needs of a student population that often was "not quite ready for prime time."

Over the last ten to fifteen years, inexorable budgetary forces have conspired to reduce state funding from 60 percent of college budgets to less than 40 percent in many cases—and state support continues to fall precipitously even as contractually based personnel costs rise steadily. State-funded, state-assisted—whatever you want to call it, less state funding has caused more of the cost burden to be transferred to the backs of struggling students in ways that conspire to depress their persistence rates. Two-year colleges have yet to document the economic causes for attrition in a quantitative manner, but we know they are there. Community colleges and their governing agencies have responded to declining state support by cutting budgets where they can—given that upward of 70 percent of their budgets is tied to personnel—and holding wages down, making these career positions less attractive to younger academics and managers.

It is amazing that all of this comes at a time when we find nearly universal acceptance of the notion that community colleges are more important to the higher education marketplace than ever before. Yet universal acclaim has largely meant universal lip service in terms of funding, albeit with a few notable exceptions such as targeted federal grant funding and state funding for specific purposes like developmental education.

So what, then, is the answer? Something has got to give, but it doesn't. Until community college cost structure reform and increased state funding are crafted into some new balance, we are left with strategies of working at the margins. One of these margins is nonprofit development for community colleges. In short, fundraising.

The thesis of this book is that by applying the development management perspectives of the four-year higher education sector, community colleges can realize a proportionate share of the philanthropic dollars destined for higher education. I refer to this practice as the *collegiate model of advancement*. Many of these techniques have been adapted and mastered by the practice of a development team at Dunwoody College of Technology in Minneapolis, where $38 million was raised in back-to-back campaigns over the nine years I served as campaign director. Since then, campaign receipts have risen to more than $55 million.

Dunwoody is a private two-year technical college, founded in 1914, that serves sixteen hundred students. The long-term annual baseline performance of the development office is $4 million a year. During the period I served as campaign director, the development operation was led by then–vice president of institutional advancement Dr. C. Ben Wright, who was appointed president of the college in 2002, and became president emeritus in 2009. I formulated the notion that the model and methods that worked so well for Dunwoody could be applied to the public two-year college sector. I had the opportunity to apply and test the application of the model at Normandale Community College in Bloomington, Minnesota, where I served for three years as chief development officer.

While the lessons learned and applications developed at Dunwoody comprise the heart of this book, their practice arises out of a lifetime of development experience with a strong component of grassroots nonprofit experience. What is the ethos of grassroots fundraising? Make every dollar count and leverage modest gifts in ways that outperform the norm, because the need is great and the mission is worthwhile.

I began my career in the private higher education sector at New College of California in San Francisco. New College was, literally, a new college. It was founded just thirteen years before my arrival as assistant director of development. For me, the question of higher education advancement within an emerging institution (read, "no development program to speak of") became a primary strategic issue from the dawn of my development career. Moving through the sectors of hospital and social services development before returning to higher education, I was able to season my practice with practices from wide-ranging realms of the development universe. Many of those applications appear in the pages to follow, tailored to fit the community college milieu. Occasionally I introduce an idea that goes all the way back to The Fund Raising School, taught by the dean of American development professionals, Hank Rosso.[5] I met Hank in 1983, when he was managing The Fund Raising School in San Rafael, California, assisted by his wife, Dottie. I still have my class notes and used them in writing this book.

What I am getting at is that this is not a book that arises out of the community college experience. Instead, this book arises out of mainstream development practice. Furthermore, it arises out of nearly a decade of a most extraordinary campaign conducted at a unique two-year college. As a result, this is not a survey of existing community college development practices. That would be a good survey to have, but this book presents a single, comprehensive method of fundraising. I do not intend that it be taken as a scholarly work, though I have pursued the research component of the project avidly. And though written as if to the attention of the chief development officer, this book is designed to be a valuable resource for the interested college president or board member. It is not intended to be critical of the leadership and established practices of the sector as a whole, or the colleges within it. I am in my present role a presumptive change agent—a *provocateur*.

Interacting with peers working at public two-year colleges through benchmarking, professional conferences, and informal interactions, I was often a little shocked to hear about the state of their fundraising programs, particularly the return on investment they realized. Their development shops too often went through the motions without achieving defensible outcomes. Initially, the only conclusion I could draw was that results didn't much matter in their shops. Over time, in the course of researching this segment of the development community, I learned what, for me, became the truth: this sector of the development community did not believe in itself sufficiently.

These development officers didn't intend to have their shops become the college's Department of Hospitality. They didn't intend to remain largely irrelevant to the power structures within their colleges. They didn't intend that the primary beneficial effect of their college foundation would be a single $150,000 scholarship disbursement to the college once a year. But outcomes like these were too often the hallmarks of their operations. The top fundraising community colleges in the United States are not described here. They achieve impressive results; some of them have for a number of years. But it is interesting that their models didn't "take" in the same manner that fundraising practice spread like wildfire through the public university sector thirty years ago.

So, this book is a "how-to" book. It is not merely a manual, because we consider the philosophical principles that underlie best practices. I refer to the work of some of the best minds in the business as they have advanced theory and practice over the last thirty-five years. In the end, this is the story of what worked for my colleagues and me, and what can work for you, if you are not already where you want to be in your development effort.

I cite Jim Collins's *Good to Great* (2001, 98)[6] as a companion volume to this book. One of his most original notions, the *hedgehog concept*, was used to conceive and delineate the focus of this book. My particular focus is the two-year college market—a market that has not been addressed adequately in the literature of nonprofit development. I hope the approaches addressed to this particular niche, the world of two-year colleges, will resonate, in their particularity and focus, throughout the universe of emerging schools and colleges.

So out of the sum total of the experiences, observations, research, and aspirations of a best-in-class development practice of a tiny two-year college in Minnesota, and the realization that spreading the news of its practice could help to transform the aspirations of emerging colleges everywhere, the idea for this book was born.

Endnotes

1. American Association of Community Colleges. "Fast Facts," www.aacc.nche .edu/AboutCC/Pages/fastfacts.aspx (accessed February 1, 2011). There were 6.8 million for-credit students enrolled in 1,173 U.S. community colleges as of December 2009. They accounted for 43 percent of undergraduates, according to 2007 Integrated Postsecondary Education Data System data. See also note 2.

2. U.S. Department of Education. National Center for Education Statistics. "Participation in Education." Tables: Undergraduate Education, Table 8-1. "Total undergraduate enrollment in degree-granting 2- and 4-year postsecondary institutions with projections, by sex, attendance status, and level of institution: Fall 1970–2016," http://nces.ed.gov/programs/coe/2007/section1/table.asp?tableID = 672 (accessed February 1, 2011). In fall 2005, the numbers were: two-year college enrollment: 6.5 million; four-year: 8.5 million; total: 15 million. The two-year college percentage of the total equals 43.3 percent. This table has not been updated in subsequent years, and doesn't entirely square with other subsequent NCES studies, due entirely to the manner in which the data were collected.

3. American Association of Community Colleges. "Students at Community Colleges," www.aacc.nche.edu/AboutCC/Trends/Pages/studentsatcommunitycolleges .aspx (accessed February 2, 2011).

4. Ann Kaplan, director of the Council for Aid to Education (CAE), maintained, via a private communication with the author on December 8, 2007, that the lack of national data precludes any authoritative estimate from being offered. The 13 percent of all public two-year colleges reporting results to the 2009 Voluntary Support of Education (VSE) survey raise just .0008 percent of the $27 billion reported by participating institutions, but there is no way of knowing how these results reflect the entire universe of higher education (*2009 Voluntary support of education survey* [New York: Council for Aid to Education, 2010], Table 6, p. 9). I think the 2 percent figure is as good as any place to start. Brenda Babitz reports that community colleges raise 3.5 percent of all gifts to higher education, based on a Council for Resource Development (CRD) figure of $34 billion raised by higher education, with $1.2 billion of that total raised by community colleges (Brenda Babitz, *Growing giving: A guide to securing private support for your community college* [Washington, DC: CASE, 2007, 12]). If one extrapolates the average amount raised by the college reporting results to CAE over the last six years—about $1.35 million

a year—that would yield about $1.5 billion raised per year, which more or less validates the CRD number. A definitive number would benefit the national dialogue regarding the efficacy of two-year college advancement programs.

5. Henry A. (Hank) Rosso, CFRE, was the founding director of The Fund Raising School, now a program of the Center on Philanthropy, Indiana University, Indianapolis. He died in 1999. His work has been honored by the creation of the Henry A. Rosso Medal, awarded by the Center on Philanthropy to recognize individuals for lifetime achievement in ethical fundraising.

6. Dr. C. Ben Wright, upon assuming the presidency of Dunwoody College of Technology, introduced this book as a shared text for his management team to use in strategic planning efforts. I have applied the text as a guide to conceptualizing development operations in particular. The hedgehog concept described on page 98 entails determining the particular niche activity at which an organization is capable of excelling to a profound degree.

PART ONE

PLANNING THE WORK

THE CASE FOR FUNDRAISING

Philanthropy begins with a mission. What is the mission of the two-year college sector? Community colleges are the gateway to a college degree, to the middle class and beyond, for millions of Americans. The educational benefits they offer are most essential to underserved segments of society: people of color, immigrants, low-income communities, single-parent heads of household, inner-city kids, and anyone who needs a second chance at higher education. They possess a remarkable capacity to serve the needs of students from all strata of society. In this respect they are the great equalizer of educational benefits in an era in which higher education is important as never before in the face of a challenging employment picture and a widening gap between haves and have-nots. In 2007, Alan Blinder, Gordon S. Rentschler Memorial Professor of Economics at Princeton and former vice chair of the Board of Governors of the Federal Reserve System, warned that 22 to 29 percent of American jobs, roughly 30 million to 40 million of them, are potentially offshorable within ten to twenty years (Blinder 2007). He found that, contrary to what many believe, higher-skilled jobs were more at risk than low-skill positions. Every job that goes offshore is seemingly gone forever, and in the coming decades a new knowledge economy must be constructed on the backs of educated, trained workers who are capable of rising to the challenge.

Community colleges specialize in teaching in ways that outstrip the capacities of their four-year cousins. Their faculty members, even when more glamorous opportunities avail themselves, self-select for a lifelong mission of offering transformational attention to the needs of the student. And those needs are great. Students are underprepared as never before, as the crisis of failing public education outcomes looms larger each year. And we are not talking here about students who fail to graduate. These underprepared students graduate with college aspirations. In math and reading, two-year colleges offer a host of developmental courses to strengthen the basic skills of the students they serve. At the same time, these colleges are held accountable to turn out matriculating students whose skill base is on a par with those who have attended state universities for the first two years of their college education. And this they do, exceedingly well, for the majority of their students, in ways that should be celebrated—and supported—for the profound life changes they engender.

A fundamental definition of *mission* is the ability to change a life. Overcoming language and cultural barriers, offering a place in society to immigrant students who in some cases suffer from a profound sense of dislocation, community colleges do the job, year in and year out. They are the new melting pot of America. This is mission fulfilled par excellence. It is unassailable. It is compelling. It should be shouted from the rooftops. Yet it isn't.

In fact, no one seems to notice. Community colleges receive almost none of the support enjoyed by the major land-grant universities. They are as if invisible, partly due to a funding structure that seems to have been on autopilot for nearly half a century, though state support has been diminishing slowly all the while.

Perhaps the lack of recognition and philanthropic support must be laid at the doorstep of the sector's own leadership. Who better to tell the story, to take tales of missions fulfilled to the boardrooms and living rooms of the nation? Hank Rosso, founder of The Fundraising School and perhaps the preeminent development educator of our time, said, "People give to people with a cause" (Rosso 1983). What he meant when I heard him say these words twenty-five years ago is that people give to *people* with a cause. They give because a real person asked them, an empowered person, a person with a passion for a cause, who possesses the moral authority to ask for the gift. This is the fundamental dynamic of philanthropy. We begin with the cause, the mission. And we begin with the *people* who are the stewards of that cause. We begin with *ourselves*.

Late to the Party—Or Didn't Come at All

Fundraising, development, or advancement, whichever term you prefer, has come late—if indeed in some cases it can be said to have come at all—to the community college sector. The topic has been the subject of a spate of articles in *The Chronicle of Higher Education* (Strout 2006, A25; see also articles referenced from the October 27, 2006, issue). Brenda Babitz, chief advancement officer at Monroe Community College in Rochester, New York, writes in "Strategies for Leveraging a Community College Foundation," "Even today, fundraising at the community college level remains a relatively new and untested phenomenon" (Babitz 2003, 6). Traditionally the least effective segment of the public higher education development spectrum, much community college development has been characterized by underfunded operations, subpar outcomes, and dubious expense ratios. True, there are exceptions, notable ones even, especially in the last decade or so, but the overall observation concerning the relative weakness in fundraising outcomes remains valid and can be documented by referencing the annual Voluntary Support of Education (VSE) survey published by Council for Aid to Education (CAE) (2010a, 2010b).

Historically, the American paradigm of fundraising began with the model of the barn raising—gifts of labor exchanged between neighbors in the expectation of reciprocity. Over the last two centuries, American churches perfected the practice of charitable giving in its grassroots form. In private education, a sector that grew out of the American church structure, the practice is nearly as old as the republic, though not present in its highly organized modern incarnation until the twentieth century.

Fundraising has always been a do-or-die proposition, meaning you only do it when necessary. American private colleges and universities had to do it, to construct their campuses, to subsidize their less fortunate students, and to realize their missions. Jane Stanford, wife of Stanford University founder Leland Stanford, is said to have taken over the financial affairs of the fledgling university during a financial crisis in 1893, just two years after it was established, paying employees out of her own pocket (Nilan, 1979). Public universities, too, engaged in fundraising as early as the nineteenth century. The University of Washington, founded with a gift of land in 1861, received a major gift to keep its doors open just two years later and went on to found an alumni association by 1889 (University of Washington Foundation 2007, 1). This leads to a fundamental truth about development—it is always mission-based, at least when it really matters. In the Reagan years in the 1980s, a huge push toward nonprofit fundraising occurred as government funding decreased, particularly in the social services sector. The loss of government funding as a fundraising catalyst is a hallmark of the contemporary development landscape (Klingaman 1994).

Public higher education joined the fray in a big way during the 1980s, rising rapidly to comprise a new powerhouse sector led by the likes of major land-grant research universities such as the University of California at Berkeley and the University of Wisconsin. State university systems were largely active by the 1990s. San Francisco State University, for example, did not begin an advancement effort in earnest until 1996, yet by 2000 it was raising $20 million a year with a program that included an Annual Fund, grants, major gifts, and planned giving (Johnson 2000). Today, higher education advancement is flourishing and racking up big annual gains punctuated by billion-dollar campaigns. In 2006, Stanford University launched the largest university fundraising campaign ever, with a goal of $4.3 billion, and reached that goal two years early, in 2009 (McFadden 2009). The practice of big-time development within higher education has trickled down to nearly every level of state college systems. Every level, that is, except two-year colleges.

The two-year college sector includes community and technical colleges, in discrete and combined forms. Of the two groups, technical colleges have pulled ahead in some ways, largely by virtue of their strong industry ties and their ability to secure gifts in-kind. These are the gifts of capital equipment and materials necessary to applied education. Nevertheless, taken together, the bulk of neither community nor technical colleges has notably succeeded in establishing effective development programs.

For the purposes of this book, we define a development program as a planned, segmented effort involving development professionals, college leadership, and board leadership to secure private funding in support of an educational mission. Nearly all American community colleges have affiliated nonprofit foundations engaged in development activities. Too many of these development efforts are underperforming compared to the standards of private and public four-year colleges and universities—or nearly any other segment of the development spectrum. The benefits derived from implementing a coherent development program will more than justify the investment of time and energy required for two-year colleges to succeed in the marketplace. And what are those benefits?

First and foremost, the introduction of a productive development program will fund essential activities at the margin. The focus here is on the essential nature of those benefits rather than the margins where they reside. Fundraising revenues will never recover the lost millions from the state. Tuition will never go back to the levels seen in previous generations. In Minnesota, state funding has fallen from about 50 percent of some college budgets to the upper 30 percent range since 2000. Consequently, tuition is rising at rates that many observers view as unsustainable in the long term.

Over the decade from 2000 to 2010, published tuition and fees at public two-year colleges and universities increased at an average rate of 2.7 percent per year beyond the rate of inflation (College Board 2010b, 13). In 2010, the average tuition and fees total for two-year colleges was $2,713 (College Board 2010a, 10), a 13 percent increase over the 2007 rate of $2,371 (College Board 2007a, 10). Tuition rates are highest in New England, at $4,221 (College Board 2010a, 14). Two states, Vermont and New Hampshire, have broken the $6,000 mark, with tuition and fees at $6,250 (The College Board 2010, Table 6C). Twenty-seven states have tuition and fees higher than $3,000, an increase of eight states since 2007 (College Board 2007, 15). But tuition is not the only cost the student bears, making the following fact the most critical in considering the cost of a two-year college education as a component of the case for development. According to the College Board (2007b): "Average public two-year tuition and fees are only 38 percent of the charges at public four-year colleges, but the total student expense budget is three-quarters that of public four-year college students" (7).

Given this level of student expense at community colleges, it is astounding that the two-year college sector receives just a few percent of all higher education philanthropy funds. It is as if the sector were invisible. And what makes up the difference? More and more, student loans. According to another College Board survey, the amount that families borrow continues to climb in the face of increasing costs, with the greatest increase attributed to unsubsidized Stafford loans (2010c, 13).[1] This information should invigorate the case for scholarship aid to students. One reason to increase scholarship aid is the corrosive effect of excessive borrowing as a long-term financial burden on young college graduates, and the utterly destructive effect that borrowing has on students who do *not* succeed in college.

With regard to state support and the cost of tuition, if any are still holding out for a return to the good old days, the pendulum is not likely to swing their way. Norm Nielsen, retired president of Kirkwood Community College in Cedar Rapids, Iowa (a community college that has been notably successful in its fundraising efforts), observed:

> In the past we have been able to remain dependent upon the old primary sources of income: state general aid, local property taxes, and tuition income. But the days of relying on those three sources of income are over. We will not likely ever again experience the kind of state revenue that we enjoyed in the 1970s and 1980s. (Mitvalsky and Hawn 2005, 1)

Why, then, go to the trouble of developing a significant fundraising program if the results of those efforts will never make up for lost state funding and we can never turn back the clock to the days of affordable tuition?

Robert Bruinicks, former president of the University of Minnesota, summed up the limitations of private funding aptly: "Ninety-eight cents of every dollar are dedicated to a particular purpose, and many of these are deferred, long-term gifts. It helps give you the margin of excellence, but it doesn't cover your core costs" (Shelman 2007, 1B).

According to Charles B. Reed, chancellor of the California State University System, "Fees and state funding are no longer enough to ensure quality education. With continued budget reductions and increasing enrollment demands, the need for external support is even greater" (Kaufman 2004, 50). Private funding energizes strategic initiatives, from scholarships to program and capacity enhancements, which involve levels public funding cannot support. Dr. Patricia Simmons, former chair of the University of Minnesota Board of Regents, put it this way: "I believe the increase in philanthropy is an example of people's confidence and high expectations for the University of Minnesota *and very specifically the strategic initiatives* [emphasis added]" (Shelman 2007, 1B).

Second, private giving entails the formation of a group of active stakeholders who sustain community interest and involvement in the mission of the college. These volunteers and donors serve as ambassadors to win the kind of community respect the community college sector so richly deserves. Their involvement is fueled by some fundamental psychological dynamics. A corollary of the theory of cognitive dissonance, as proposed by social psychologist Leon Festinger, holds that once an individual makes an investment in a course of action, the person tends to seek out information that will reinforce that decision, which in turn will cause the individual to view the investment more favorably (Festinger 1957). This becomes a kind of self-reinforcing cycle of involvement; give more, care more.

The search for private support transforms the institution itself. It becomes more responsive, interactive, nimble, and creative in the delivery of education. It serves new populations more effectively. It develops niche expertise in areas that matter to its stakeholders. It becomes more accountable to those stakeholders in fundamentally different ways from the way institutions are accountable to their state funders.

Let's consider that last point for a moment. A significant number of high school educators and a significant segment of the general public have concluded that the No Child Left Behind movement is restricting and impairing public education teaching practice. They contend it's all drill and no thrill. The ability to dive deep into areas of student interest is abruptly cut short as each testing cycle takes precedence. And what's driving it? The mania for accountability. To stay one step "ahead of the law," higher education has heretofore stood on its birthright—independence from state interference and reliance on accrediting agencies. But those agencies are tightening their grip, just as the accreditation initiative known as AQIP, the Academic Quality Improvement Program,[2] asks, in so many words, "How do you know you actually do what you say you do?"

The federal government has considered getting into the act as well. In 2006, the Secretary of Education's Commission on the Future of Higher Education reported "a remarkable absence of accountability mechanisms to ensure that colleges succeed in educating students." In addition, the commission found that "the quality of student learning at U.S. colleges and universities is inadequate and, in some cases, declining" and that they "should measure and report meaningful student learning outcomes" (U.S. Department of Education 2006). In this environment, private funding provides that most precious commodity, research and development money—to improve your college and the programs it delivers as you see fit, as contracted and conceived between you and your donor.

Here is the principle that matters: excellence follows resources. Under-resourced institutions are never at the forefront. They never have the opportunity to dream larger. Access to additional resources of the type that University of Minnesota President Bruinicks espouses, on the other hand, means support for teaching, learning, and the facilities in which these activities transpire. I have always been astounded in my work as a major gift officer at how profoundly enthused faculty members become at receiving external resources—when no personal enrichment follows—to further their mission of teaching. Their morale increases not just significantly, but *transformatively*, as the result of receiving gifts that further their work. Their responsiveness to the philanthropic process has been a source of inspiration to me over the years.

So here is why we do it: private funding transforms institutions of higher learning, inside and out. Private gifts and grants do not replace public funding, nor do they reduce or significantly discount tuition. Instead, they provide the means to strive for excellence in an era of declining public support.

The average annual amount raised by community colleges responding to the 2009 VSE survey is $1.2 million (Council for Aid to Education 2010b, 9)[3] a year, according to the CAE. But that number may be deceiving as it includes receipts from a few megacolleges. Hundreds of community colleges raise $500,000 or less each year. While a few campaigns have gone as high as $30 million, and there are dozens in the $3 million to $6 million range, this is not the common state of development in our two-year colleges.

So let's summarize the case for community college advancement:

1. Community colleges play a critical role as the gateway to higher education and a college degree for millions of students.
2. Community colleges garner only a tiny share of the philanthropic resources devoted to higher education.
3. State support to community colleges has been decreasing at a precipitous rate, while costs rise significantly each year.
4. The tuition rate for community colleges has been growing at a steady rate for well over a decade to make up for the shortfall in state funding.
5. Leading-edge public and private two-year colleges have demonstrated that impressive fundraising results can be achieved.
6. System-wide governing bodies are beginning to mandate improvement in development outcomes in two-year colleges.
7. New models of fundraising practice that have the potential to boost results significantly are being introduced to the marketplace.

Sounds pretty compelling, doesn't it? The question is: What are we going to do about it? When are we going to apply the time-tested principles of development practice to such an essential sector of the educational spectrum? Positive indicators are on the horizon. Milliron, de los Santos, and Browning reported in a 2003 League for Innovation survey of college presidents that the hottest trend was that of interest in private resource development (2003, 89). It is time to ask ourselves whether the promise of that emerging interest has been fulfilled.

For the college that cherishes its mission (and what college doesn't?), the question becomes not why, or if, but what and how and, finally, how much. Having made the decision to engage, let's get started.

Endnotes

1. Prior to the recession of 2007–2009, the greatest increase in loan type was private loans, which peaked at 25 percent of all loans in 2007–2008.
2. The higher education accreditation initiative sponsored by the Higher Learning Commission of the North Central Association of Colleges and Universities, www.hlcommission.org/aqip-home (accessed February 17, 2011).

3. The average amount raised by the 159 public two-year colleges reporting in 2009 is $1.233 million, down 19.9 percent from the 2008 total of $1.527 million. This class of colleges raised an average of $1.385 million in 2005, with 115 colleges reporting.

References

Babitz, B. 2003 (Winter). Strategies for leveraging a community college foundation. In *Successful approaches to fundraising and development*, ed. M. D. Milleron, G. E. de los Santos, and B. Browning, 5–14, New Directions for Community Colleges, No. 124. San Francisco: Jossey-Bass.

Blinder, A. S. 2007 (March). How many U.S. jobs might be offshorable? CEPS Working Paper No. 142, Princeton University Center for Economic Policy Studies. http://www.princeton.edu/~blinder/papers/07ceps142.pdf (accessed January 27, 2011).

College Board. 2007a. Tuition and fee and room and board charges, 2007–2008. *Trends in College Pricing 2007.* http://www.collegeboard.com/prod_downloads/about/news_info/trends/trends_pricing_07.pdf (accessed January 27, 2011).

———. 2007b. Tuition and fees by state. *Trends in College Pricing 2007.* http://www.collegeboard.com/prod_downloads/about/news_info/trends/trends_pricing_07.pdf (accessed January 27, 2011).

———. 2010a. Regional variation in charges, Table 6C: Average published tuition and fees in current dollars, by state and sector, 2004–05 to 2010–11. *Trends in College Pricing 2010.* http://trends.collegeboard.org/college_pricing/report_findings/indicator/Regional_Variation_in_Charges (accessed January 27, 2011).

———. 2010b. Tuition and fee and room and board charges, 2010–2011. *Trends in College Pricing 2010.* http://trends.collegeboard.org/downloads/College_Pricing_2010.pdf (accessed January 27, 2011).

———. 2010c. Types of loans, Figure 4. *Trends in Student Aid 2010*, 13. http://trends.collegeboard.org/downloads/Student_Aid_2010.pdf (accessed January 27, 2011).

Council for Aid to Education. 2010a. *2009 Voluntary support of education.* New York: Author, 59–69.

Council for Aid to Education. 2010b. *2009 Voluntary support of education.* New York: Author, Table 6.

Festinger, L. 1957. *A theory of cognitive dissonance.* Palo Alto, CA: Stanford University Press.

Johnson, D. 2000. *SFSU Academic Senate minutes of November 7, 2000*, San Francisco State University. http://www.sfsu.edu/~senate/documents/minutes/m11-07-00.html (accessed September 16, 2011).

Kaufman, B. 2004. Juggling act. *University Business* 7, no. 7.

Klingaman, S. A. 1994. Repositioning for fundraising. *Nonprofit Management Strategies* 14, no. 4: 8–9.

McFadden, C. (2009). Fundraising effort passes key milestone. *Stanford Daily.* http://www.stanforddaily.com/2009/09/28/fundraising-effort-passes-key-milestone/ (accessed September 16, 2011).

Milleron, M. D., de los Santos, G. E., and Browning, B. 2003 (Winter). Feels like the third wave: The rise of fundraising in community colleges. In *Successful approaches to fundraising and development,* ed. M. D. Milleron, G. E. de los Santos, and B. Browning, 81–93, New Directions for Community Colleges, No. 124. San Francisco: Jossey-Bass.

Mitvalsky, C., and Hawn, S. 2005. Planned giving: Approaches that work for community colleges. *Community College Advancement Series,* electronic file, CASE item #28253. Washington, DC: CASE.

Nilan, R. 1979. Jane Lathrop Stanford and the domestication of Stanford University, 1893–1905. *San Jose Studies* 5, no. 1: 7–30.

Rosso, H. A. 1983. Fundraising 101. Paper presented at The Fundraising School (author's lecture notes), San Rafael, CA, October 23.

Shelman, J. 2007. Fiscal 2007 is rich year for U of M donations. *Minneapolis Star Tribune,* October 13.

Strout, E. 2006. Community colleges struggle when it comes to soliciting private donations. *The Chronicle of Higher Education,* February 10.

University of Washington Foundation. 2007 (September). A history of private support for the University of Washington. https://devar.washington.edu/toolkits/brochures/HofGInside.pdf (accessed September 16, 2011).

U.S. Department of Education. The Secretary of Education's Commission on the Future of Higher Education. 2006 (September). *A test of leadership: Charting the future of U.S. higher education.* Washington, DC: U.S. Department of Education, x, 3, 24. http://www2.ed.gov/about/bdscomm/list/hiedfuture/reports/final-report .pdf (accessed January 26, 2011).

2

"JUST THE FACTS, MA'AM"

Assessing Your Development Program

I retain a vivid impression of a college leadership retreat at which the participants were studying the Jim Collins book *Good to Great*. They were considering his concept of confronting the "brutal facts" (2001, 65). The moderator paraphrased the concept on the whiteboard as "brutal honesty." In later sessions it became apparent that the participants were looking at this issue with a great deal of trepidation about just what the nature of their interaction was supposed to be, as if it might indicate a kind of Esalen-gone-bad, beating each other over the head with brutally honest representations of institutional deficiencies and personal inadequacies. What this little transposition of terms revealed was discomfort with the whole issue of organizational self-analysis. The drive to hold ourselves accountable is fraught with good intentions and caveats. What Collins advocates is a clear, honest look at the facts, just the facts, and the core drivers underlying an enterprise. It can be done with a purely investigative mind-set, as a process of discovery, without the Sgt. Friday attitude.

By the way, if you don't have a copy of *Good to Great*, you might want to buy one. Many of his concepts are useful in considering the function of an advancement program within a college. In his follow-up monograph, *Good to Great and the Social Sectors* (2005, Author's Note), Collins reports that perhaps a third of the readership of the original book came from what he called the social sectors. Such broad use within the nonprofit world intrigued Collins, who had directed *Good to Great* to business practitioners. However, the reasons for its broad popularity within the nonprofit sector are not hard to fathom. This discovery led him to propose in the monograph a number of bridge concepts tailored to the nonprofit sector. We touch on several of those, while referring primarily to the original work, which is more robust in its exploration of the central tenets of approaching greatness.

TIP #1

Perform a do-it-yourself development audit.

In conducting an internal development audit, we ask ourselves, Where are we investing our resources? What are we getting in exchange for those investments? Are we getting sufficient bang for the buck? Let's construct a hypothetical development office. A vice president for advancement, foundation executive director, or chief development officer (CDO) will lead the development office. We use these titles more or less interchangeably. The office includes an executive assistant and one development officer. Table 2.1 provides some personnel and benefit costs and an estimate for program expenses paid by the foundation and the college.

Given that commonly accepted standards in the nonprofit sector hold that the cost per dollar raised should be at or below 25 to 30 percent of fundraising revenue, this development shop or foundation office should be producing at least $875,000 in fundraising revenues each year.

TABLE 2.1* Personnel and Benefit Costs and Estimated Program Expenses	
Personnel:	
Chief development officer	$80,000
Executive assistant	35,000
Development staff	40,000
TOTAL: Personnel	$155,000
Benefits	$47,000
Direct development expenses	60,000
TOTAL	$262,000

*These numbers do not include "soft numbers," such as the cost of public and alumni relations, the college magazine, or college-wide hospitality and community relations events. The Council for Advancement and Support of Education (CASE) is our guide in making these determinations.

This shop raises $500,000. In my consulting practice with community colleges I hear explanations like: "My vice president for advancement is a senior administrator and only works part-time on fundraising." "Nobody in our area is raising that kind of money." "We hit that number once three years ago." "We're a start-up operation." "We don't count it that way." And so on. I often learn that the CDO also sits on several key committees; administers the scholarship program; is responsible for publications, marketing, accreditation team duties, and governmental relations; sits on several more committees; and is responsible for plain old hospitality!

If your community college were a stand-alone charity or a private college development office, these are the metrics that would apply to your return on investment (ROI) ratios. But please, don't put down the book just yet. Think for a moment, "What if?" What if you could raise a million dollars a year in this hypothetical "small-shop" operation? What would that mean to your institution? For the moment, no one is looking at your "all-in" ROI. Your external stakeholders probably only see the fundraising dollars your foundation disburses; certainly they don't see your college advancement budget. It is interesting that no one ever seems to ask for the aggregate total. I can point out college foundation IRS Form 990 statements that show a *zero cost of fundraising*. But we know what the true costs are. And we know that the ROI may be, well, anemic, compared to the standard proposed above.

Let's begin our assessment of your college's development capacity at the beginning, with job descriptions. What does the formal record say your foundation staff members are supposed to be doing with their time? A good job description should spell that out in concrete terms; see appendices A1, A2, and A3 for several examples. The job description should include five to ten broad areas of responsibility, with a number of specific examples for each and, most important, the percentage of time allotment for each.

TIP #2

Conduct a baseline time study of how time is spent.

Calculate how development staff time is spent based on an allocation-of-time audit for a sample week. Have everyone in the office write down, hour by hour, or better, in twenty-minute increments, how they spend their time, as if tracking billable hours for a law firm. We are looking for the *brutal facts*, no fudging allowed. No penalties are assessed. Later, we compare the results of this study to some proposed metrics.

Next, consider the core activities of development—cultivation and fund-raising calls. How many meetings with donors are conducted each week, how many phone calls, grant applications, personal letters, and emails? I will assume your development office is already tracking these actions, but we need real due diligence here to establish a meaningful baseline. If you do not currently record these activities in a systematic fashion, do so for a month, using the capabilities built into your donor database. Then look at how much time these actions take. Don't be surprised if it's miniscule. Seven telephone interactions a week can consume less than one hour.

After this, consider how many dollars you are raising. Look at last year's results, as presented in your audit, donor database record, annual report, VSE report, or reporting provided to your governing agency. We are looking for snapshots here, so use metrics you know and understand.

Break out the results by category:

- Special events (gross and net)
- Annual Fund
- Nongovernmental, private grants
- Major gifts
- Employee annual giving
- Board giving
- Other, capturing the balance of your revenue

Calculate the amounts for each of these categories over the last three years. Identify the trends. What is increasing? What is static? Correlate these dollar amounts with the number of gifts raised by category. What percentage of employees gave to your employee annual giving campaign in each of the last three years? What percentage of the foundation board gives, and how much? How many alumni donors do you have? How many major gifts? What are the number and dollar amounts of private grants?

Calculate your direct, nonpersonnel costs related to each of the programs above. Do you do a "mass mailing"? What does it cost? What is the ROI? How has it measured up over the last three years? If you currently hold a special event, what percentage of the gross is the net? For a phonathon, how much do you spend on student compensation and pizza? Establishing the cost per fundraising activity is a necessary facet of the program evaluation to come.

If we can agree to generalize for the moment, a standard community college development program might look something like this, perhaps even for a descending order in dollars raised:

- Major gifts
- Scholarship giving
- Gala event
- Foundation and corporate grants
- Employee annual giving
- Year-end mailing
- Ancillary event ("fun run" or similar activity)

Lay out these data in an orderly, visually appealing fashion, including data for the last three years. Import the numbers into Microsoft Excel color charts (see Appendix E—it's not that hard to do; get a college software guru to help). This information forms the core of the data you will use to analyze your operation—where you excel and where improvement is needed. The business of development management is largely data-driven, and by making data-driven decisions we reclaim the activity from that of art to science. These are, as Collins says, the brutal facts.

Congratulate yourself upon completion of these exercises; you have just finished a shirtsleeve development audit, something for which fundraising consultants charge big bucks. To be fair, a full-blown development audit, which I believe you should engage in only after completing an informal audit, includes a good amount of interview-derived qualitative data regarding how development staffers (and the president) conduct their affairs and approach their goals and objectives, and the barriers and opportunities they identify in so doing.

We use these data to gauge *institutional readiness*, the overall measure of present, baseline capacity. Institutional readiness most often is assessed in the context of launching a campaign. The issue is imperative to consider in that regard, but institutional readiness should be factored into any plan to take a development program to the next level. Fundraising consultants will introduce additional facets to the development audit, but an internal audit will help to get the effort off on the right foot.

The results of the internal audit establish the groundwork for conversations between the CDO and president and the larger internal community that surrounds your development program. The CDO can be responsible for providing the data for a development audit, but in considering the conclusions to be drawn from the data, others, including the president and a board member or two, should be part of the process. Frank, unhurried discussions need to inform the process so everyone understands the real state of the development program. You will use the information gathered in constructing a prototypical collegiate development program model. Next, we consider the elements of its design.

References

Collins, J. 2001. *Good to great.* New York: HarperBusiness.
———. 2005. *Good to great: A monograph to accompany Good to Great.* Boulder, CO: Author.

3

DESIGNING A
DEVELOPMENT PROGRAM

D espite the variations in community college development programs, they are for the most part *small-shop* programs. We are talking about staff head counts between two and five people. These shops are characterized by flexibility, multitasking, and deployment of development professionals as generalists, rather than specialists. Small-shop development positions can be uniquely rewarding in the variety of activities involved and number of hats to be worn. On the other hand, successful incumbents must have an unerring sense of prioritization and focus to avoid running port to starboard with each new wave encountered.

Let's look at our development program components again with some of the baseline information we've gained as a result of our hypothetical development audit:

- Major gifts: $125,000 last year
- Scholarship giving: $100,000, $125,000, and $132,000 over the last three years, respectively
- Gala event: netted $36,000 on a gross of $70,000
- Foundation and corporate grants: $75,000 per year
- Employee annual giving: 25 percent participation, raised $17,000 last year
- Year-end mailing: raised $5,500, and spent nearly $8,000 on the mailing, which included a color brochure
- Ancillary event (the "fun run"): loses money every year, takes a ton of staff time

Overall, we raised $390,000 last year. This was 8 percent higher than the year before, primarily on the strength of increased scholarship giving and a bump in the gala event. But the brutal fact remains that we spent $262,000 on development operations, giving us a whopping real-world fundraising cost percentage of 67 percent. This meter is deep in the red. The only way to move it into the green is via a fundamental restructuring of the development program.

TIP #3

Introduce a fundraising program based on an adaptation
of the four-year collegiate model.

Compared to the community college sector, four-year colleges and universities have virtually perfected the calculation of fundraising yields. Though there are marked differences between the four-year sector and its community-based cousins, artfully *adapting* their approaches will yield radically improved performance in the community college market.[1] What, then, is their secret?

TIP #4

"Kill" your gala event and replace it with an Annual Fund campaign.

Tips #3 and #4 contain the two central premises of this book, wrapped up in a package fraught with danger that could lead to serious career anxieties. But allow me to make the case for their adoption. Development managers in freestanding nonprofits always make ROI calculations based on the *personnel dollars* expended to raise their funds. That is, they always factor in how much *time* it takes to raise money. Later on, we look at this calculation in terms of strategic planning within the development office. But right now, the demand is for strategic *thinking*. There is a difference. We will begin by applying a little strategic thinking to the issue of basing a fundraising program on special events, as many community colleges do.

A simple cost-benefit analysis will show that special events are an inefficient vehicle upon which to base a college fundraising program. The missing piece in fundraising event reportage is the amount of staff time devoted to the event. First, the case *for* special event fundraising at a community college.

The Case for Gala Events

- Raise money
- Show the flag
- Cultivate
- Recognize
- Involve volunteers
- "Warm & fuzzies"
- People have a good time

And now the contrary . . .

The Case for Focusing on the Annual Fund and Major Gifts, as Opposed to a Gala

1. **A gala event has a low yield as a fundraising vehicle.** Through the use of a hypothetical model, we will show that adopting the collegiate fundraising model without a gala, staffed by a CDO and one Annual Fund director, will yield an additional $200,000 a year. What's more, more of these dollars will be unrestricted. Adopting a more efficient fundraising model will cut your fundraising cost percentage in half and will allow more of the funds raised to support your mission.

2. **A gala saps Annual Fund dollars.** Rarely do event-driven programs coexist with robust Annual Fund campaigns. That is because the number of donor prospects in the pool is limited, and if they are all reserved for the event, you will have few prospects left for an Annual Fund—and those you do have will tend to reduce their Annual Fund commitments knowing that a gala is coming.

3. **A gala preempts other fundraising efforts for a significant portion of the year.** An event generally takes up four critical months of an organization's time and effort. The rule of thumb is that events trump all other fundraising activities, including far more productive ones, like major gift development, in terms of their time drain. A gala, for example, preempts major gift cultivation and Asks by the foundation board.

4. **When staff time is added in, net revenue is too low.** In one study I conducted, total staff time for a gala event amounted to 935 hours, so the labor cost was $30,000. If the organization had used

another fundraising model to raise funds at a factor of three to one, those dollars could be used to raise $90,000. The gala did not.

5. **A gala focuses donor attention on the event rather than the mission.** Selling gala tables and securing auction items is different from talking about the mission of the college. Major gift officers, by comparison, always put the focus on mission.

6. **A gala distracts volunteers from more beneficial involvement.** The use of volunteers to make Annual Fund calls for gifts in the range of $500 to $5,000 is a far better use of their time.

7. **Donors quickly forget a gala.** Once an event is over, guests, volunteers, and board members move on. You can engage your volunteers twelve months a year using the collegiate fundraising model.

8. **A gala is expensive to produce.** Fifty percent of the cost of a $100 gala ticket often goes to pay for the dinner, facility, balloons, and whatnot. You can entertain your donors more cost effectively through a *cultivation event* and still get your message across while capturing 100 percent of their resulting gifts.

Strategic Recommendation

Reformat the gala as a high-end donor recognition event.

Strategic Positioning

- A recognition/cultivation event will address the need for donor recognition, prospect cultivation, community involvement, and an awards platform.
- Invest in the recognition event an amount appropriate to its cultivation value.
- Use the volunteer energy from the gala to launch the Annual Fund.

Table 3.1 reflects a hypothetical event (Klingaman 2005). The net profit: $50,000. Not bad . . . except we forgot to add up the staff time expended on the event. A detailed labor audit reveals that the labor invested in the event was 935 hours worked by 14 staff members. The cost of that labor was $30,000. *The new net is $20,000.* Moreover, the event pretty much occupied the development staff full-time for one-third of the year. (And during the rest of the year they were a little tentative about approaching any gala participants for gifts.) All of which is why I recommend reformatting the gala as a

TABLE 3.1
"Scholarship Safari: Big Game, Big Gifts"
Theme: Gambling, taxidermy, and pith helmets

INCOME

Sponsors	$45,000
Scholarship gifts	13,000
Tickets	7,000
Donations	5,000
Live auction	5,000
Silent auction	2,000
Raffle	1,000
Funds provided by the college to produce the gala	12,000
TOTAL INCOME	**$90,000**

EXPENSES

Hotel banquet cost	$16,000
Celebrity honoraria & expenses	4,000
Services & supplies, video, etc.	12,000
Printing	3,500
Papier mâché rhino heads	1,400
More big-game paraphernalia	1,100
Student servers	1,000
Decoration	500
Meetings	500
TOTAL EXPENSES	**$40,000**
NET PROFIT	**$50,000**

donor recognition/cultivation event to concentrate on the collegiate model of fundraising featuring an Annual Fund. And walk away from the $50,000.

Others agree. Here is Mark Drozdowski, former executive director of the Fitchburg State College Foundation, analyzing a golf tournament:

> When all the dust settles, we net anywhere from $5,000 to $15,000. . . . That irks me for two reasons. First, we dedicate an inordinate amount of time to raising 10 grand. If you calculate the number of work hours

involved, we barely break even. Staff members running the tournament spend months planning every detail, gathering auction items, selling sponsorships, producing brochures, and managing logistics. . . .

Second, we cannibalize our own donors. Instead of asking a small company to contribute $750 for a day of golf, of which only $100 will be added to a scholarship pool, why not just ask them for the $750 outright? (2006, C3)

So why not budget $10,000 to $20,000 for a cultivation/recognition event and put it on autopilot? Replace the gala with repeatable, sustainable, annual support from your primary constituents: businesses, board, friends, employees, alumni, parents, and foundations. With a staff of three, consisting of the CDO, executive assistant, and director of annual giving, this plan should raise $150,000 to $200,000 more a year than a gala would raise. Plan to grow that amount by 4 to 12 percent per year . . . *forever*. With dollars you raise through the Annual Fund, you will easily be able to spend $15,000 on a cultivation/recognition event. Compare the cultivation event versus the fundraising event in the context of the foundation's fundamental role of securing resources to support the mission of the college. The budget for a cultivation event might look like the one in Table 3.2.

I am not against fundraising special events per se. They are essential to the fundraising programs of many charities, including disease-related charities, children's causes, and hospital foundations, to name but a few. It is a professional arena all its own, and high-stakes, special events fundraising can raise hundreds of thousands of dollars and more for a variety of worthy

TABLE 3.2	
Cultivation/Recognition Event Budget	
EXPENSES	
Food and beverage	$8,000
Room rental	1,500
Services & supplies	2,500
Printing	600
Student servers	400
Decoration	500
TOTAL EXPENSES	**$13,500**

causes. They only begin to make sense when the net is greater than $100,000. Event-driven organizations accomplish this through high-powered sponsorship programs, heavy hitters on the organizing committee, and the involvement of celebrities.

Community colleges do not, as a rule, ante in to this rarified atmosphere for a variety of reasons. Even when they manage to net $100,000 on an event, I still contend that they are sapping the potential of their Annual Funds. This is the point that Drozdowski raises. Why not simply ask for the gift? Few colleges consistently net more than $100,000 through a special event–based fundraising program. Those that do will be hard-pressed to let it go. Nevertheless, even they may want to take a second look at their program after we go into strategies for converting special event gifts to Annual Fund support.

Let's say a college reports that its gala has contributed $2 million to the college over twenty years. On the face of it, that sounds pretty impressive, doesn't it? That's an average of $100,000 a year. I predict that this college will have a difficult time walking away from its event. But what other funds were raised and disbursed to the college over the last twenty years? We have already established that a shoestring development operation costs $250,000 a year. Over twenty years that amounts to a cost of $5 million, so, in all cases, a little investigation and context regarding the ROI is necessary.

The special event world can be a bit like Mr. Toad's Wild Ride. Everyone gets excited over, for example, a big name coming to town for a major entertainment event. I recall a board meeting at a hospital foundation where the staff was presenting the credentials of some well-known entertainers of the has-been variety who could be engaged for a mere $35,000 for a gala entertainment event. One of the board members got hold of our entertainment rate sheet and happened to spot MR. REALLY BIG NAME. His services went for $100,000 a night. The board member launched into a passionate speech on how this would really "put us on the map." He began waving his checkbook in the air. "I'll make up the difference," he said. "I'll put down $75,000 right now!" The worm had turned. "Put your checkbook away, Joe," said the others. "You're on. And thank you for your amazing generosity!"

Joe did put the checkbook away, and the staff gingerly followed up for months trying to get that checkbook out again, to no avail. The other board members shied away. When the checkbook did come back out, the check was for only $25,000. And so the staff embarked on a wild gala ride, down $50,000 on day one. Special event fundraising is not for the faint of heart.

Another event that comes to mind was a golf tournament that had been in existence for about five years and was just reaching the $100,000 net mark. The hospital's CEO had just completed a bond issue, and the bond firm that handled it stepped up to offer a $25,000 sponsorship. That year the tournament netted $133,000 and the organization basked in the glow of special event fundraising success. The only problem was that that gift was in no way repeatable. Next year that bond-rating firm would be working on another hospital bond issue and *that organization's* golf tournament was going to get the bonus gift. The staff would have to peddle twice as hard (no pun intended) in the sponsorship department just to stay in place. The problem? Lack of *donative intent.* An Annual Fund program is based on mission; the Ask and the cause remain viable year in and year out. Unless you are soliciting a vendor, you can be pretty sure the Annual Fund gift is just that, a gift.

So how did community colleges drift into the wilderness of special event–driven fundraising in the first place? The answer is simple. As grass-roots foundation boards launched their programs, board members went with what they knew—grassroots events. Development staffers who could not offer an alternate, more strongly held strategic vision never got the chance to say, "Wait a minute, there might be a better way."

Introducing the Collegiate Fundraising Model

The collegiate fundraising model, by comparison, uses events for cultivation. Multiple events are staged each year, including the major recognition event that replaces the gala, a scholarship recognition event, alumni events, a retiree's luncheon, and events related to the life of the campus such as a naming event or the opening of a new facility.

TIP #5

Use events for cultivation.

Cultivation events bring people together and allow the college to tell its story. Event costs are sometimes line items in the development budget but also are funded through other cost centers, such as that of alumni relations, as appropriate to the audience.

Cultivation in a Small-Shop Environment

Cultivation is

- a long-term development strategy based on personalizing the relationship with your donors;
- a linchpin of the collegiate fundraising model; and
- the job of every development officer in a small-shop environment.

The goal in any development operation is to get development officers in front of donors as often as possible to seek advice and to talk about mission and programs. It is essential to develop strategic cultivation plans using a mix of cultivation modes (dinner, note, phone call, email) deployed at intervals of between once a week and once a month to move the donor toward the decision point within a finite amount of time. This focus takes the place of discussions of table sales and sponsorships in an event-driven model.

We discuss how to cultivate prospective donors in detail in chapter 11, but for now it is important to strategize development roles that put a premium on cultivation activities. In development, nothing succeeds like direct, person-to-person interaction. To do that, you have to get out into the community and make every first meeting a prelude to the next. This element of relationship development is something I call the Relationship Key, the combined package of linkage and a message with an occasion that unlocks donative intent.

One of the most important elements of designing a development program is to think about how to create and expand your *culture of cultivation*. If you do this, regardless of methodology, you will achieve many successful outcomes. One of the first ways to do this is to count the number of dedicated, intentional, cultivation interactions you have with external stakeholders. If your primary donor pool is your employee base, you know there is room for improvement. If your development schedules are filled with phone calls and visits with individuals on their turf, you know you are on the right track.

The Annual Fund

Cultivation events are designed to support two development goals, the Annual Fund and the major gift program. The Annual Fund is the core of the collegiate fundraising model. An Annual Fund gift is defined as a *sustainable, repeatable gift*, given annually. Applying this simple definition to new gifts usually will clear up any confusion about how the gift should be booked. Why does it matter? Because the Annual Fund is like a bank account, subject to regular deposits. The donor's intention to give annually is material to the categorization of the gift. The Annual Fund goal should be achievable every year, and the goal should be raised incrementally each year. Under normal circumstances Annual Fund revenues should not reflect a lot of peaks and valleys when viewed over a multiyear period; instead there should be a steady upward progression.

The Annual Fund is composed of a number of what I call *product lines*. Typical Annual Fund products are:

- Board giving
- Employee annual giving
- Scholarship appeals
- Giving clubs
- Board-inspired giving
- Phonathons
- Gifts in honor of/memorials
- Other

These product lines form the building blocks of the numbers you will be putting on the board via the Annual Fund. Manage each product line for its own "profit and loss," or P&L status, to borrow a metaphor from the for-profit sector. This allows you to make accurate revenue projections—a good thing, since you will soon be asking the president, CFO, and foundation board to support increased investment in development operations as we work to ramp up capacity according to a *strategic development plan*.

Major Gifts

The next critical focus of a collegiate fundraising model is the major gift program. Ultimately, this is the more powerful of the two program drivers but is far more difficult to launch—and sustain—unless the Annual Fund is in place first. Community colleges have demonstrated sporadic success in securing major gifts. A few have posted notable successes. Johnson County Community College, in Overland Park, Kansas, which received a $5 million challenge gift from the Victor and Helen Regnier Charitable Foundation, comes to mind. The trick is to launch the effort as a systematic, disciplined program. This effort may well require culture change on the part of the college, which we cover in chapter 4.

Part of that culture change will occur in the development office, where the CDO's job description will change. Part of it happens in the office of the president, because his or her hands-on involvement is required to launch and sustain a major giving program. If this is already the case on your campus, so much the better. Additional cooperation and buy-in is often necessary at the faculty level, certainly among faculty leaders. Beyond the time investment required, and the need for sustained cultivation efforts over time, the college must be receptive to the *ideas* of major gift donors, whose interests often range far afield of scholarship support. The ability to respond to donor interest with authentic program innovation sometimes requires culture change, and increased interdepartmental collaboration is often one element of such change.

In a small shop, the CDO is the college's major gift officer. Now we add the most critical piece of the puzzle: the CDO and the president are going to share equally, albeit with a disproportionate share of time investment on the part of the CDO, the responsibility for the major gift function.

Grant Writing and Planned Gifts

The next leg of our programmatic tripod is the development of a *full-featured fundraising program*. The two essential elements incorporated here are grant writing and planned giving. We define planned giving for our purposes as bequests. The third element of our full-featured program is development of a modest alumni relations program.

Community colleges have long demonstrated a capacity for government grant writing. Federal programs such as U.S. Department of Education Title III, TRIO, the National Science Foundation, and the Fund for the Improvement of Postsecondary Education have long been mainstays of community college government grant programs. Many states offer higher education funding for community colleges through a request for proposal process, as do most authorizing entities that govern community colleges at the state level.

TIP #6

Clearly delineate the activities of government and private grant writing.

Private funders such as corporations and foundations have been a different experience for community colleges, and most have been successful to a lesser degree. Government grant writing is not development; private grant writing is. Regardless of where the activity of government grantsmanship is located within the college, the development office needs to take full responsibility for the private grant-writing function. The primary issues here are identifying a sufficient market of prospective funders and deploying sufficient personnel resources to support the activity.

The nonprofit community widely and falsely regards planned giving as being the restricted and unfamiliar terrain of attorneys, financial planners, and legal gobbledygook. In fact, 80 percent of all planned gifts are simple bequests. Nonspecialists can and do excel at closing planned gifts by the type of cultivation characterized by chatting with longtime donors over coffee.

In back-to-back comprehensive campaigns at Dunwoody College of Technology, millions of dollars' worth of planned gifts were booked. These included exactly one charitable lead trust and only a handful of charitable remainder trusts. No staff specialists were needed and minimal legal fees were incurred. The donor supplied those. What was essential to their success was face-to-face grassroots development work, the kind that any CDO or planned giving officer can perform, given the resolve that planned gifts matter.

Why focus on something that will bring benefits only in coming years, say, the next decade or two? Because bequests are the driver that swings college development programs (think Harvard) into hyperdrive—and if you don't prime that pump, no one will. Again, our focus is not just that of raising funds each year. We are launching permanent programs that will benefit the college in perpetuity.

Alumni Affairs

Alumni affairs is an area largely misapprehended by community colleges. Many think they must reinvent the wheel, finding previously undiscovered vehicles to somehow lure alumni back to campus. The class-year identification that four-year colleges work so effectively doesn't seem to apply to two-year colleges. So what does work? I recommend holding alumni events organized around cohesive career programs like nursing, dental hygiene, law enforcement, etc. Start small, engage a well-liked longtime faculty member or two, a few "spark plug" alumni to help organize the event, and some kind of hook to get people to attend. Events like these can be self-funded by a modest admission fee if necessary.

If you get thirty people to attend the first event, you are not doing badly, even by some four-year college standards. There is no hard sell here, no need to bring the checkbook. (Despite this, you might be surprised by how quickly members of these groups move to the level of proposing establishment of an alumni scholarship.) Instead, we are selling affiliation, loyalty, school pride, involvement, networking, and the opportunity to *give something back*. That last phrase, as unspecific as it is, turns out to be the primary driver of all good development programs. Later on, we explore some basic alumni relations strategies. As in planned giving, we are priming the pump for future success.

The categories defined previously form the core of the collegiate model of development. We cover each in detail later. For now, the most important element in our developmental equation is your ability to believe in, and effectively argue the case for, these strategic changes. Consider your own reservations about the model and jot down. We cover many of these in later chapters, but let's touch on two right now.

Barrier #1: People don't give to community colleges because they are tax-supported.

The four-year college sector proved that this perceived barrier was a nonissue thirty years ago. The fact is, people do give to tax-supported organizations. Education, a large segment of which is tax-supported, trails only religion in attracting private support. The introduction of the college foundation has greatly aided the mechanics of the proposition. The 501(c)(3) status of the foundation clarifies the standing of higher education philanthropy in the spectrum of American charitable giving. Ultimately, people give where they find a real, clearly articulated need.

The decline of tax-based support for higher education has dispelled any previous reservations prospective donors may have had about giving to public higher education. In fact, the next frontier is philanthropic support of public secondary schools. Many of the techniques presented in this book may be adapted by creative practitioners in that nascent sector with the potential for excellent results. Indeed, if the community college sector does not aggressively make the case for support now, it may find itself outflanked by public school system development efforts. If that seems implausible, check out the development efforts of The Chicago Public Education Fund, as just one example.

Barrier #2: Alumni don't give to their community college; they only give to their higher-division alma mater.

I have heard this position expressed as an almost universal truism within the community college sector. But the truth is this: they will give, just not in the same measure as they give to their alma maters. My own experiments have demonstrated a consistent rate of return on solicitations made during a phonathon. This is a predictable rate that can inform reasonable projections for participation and dollars you can expect to raise in the years to come. And the phonathon is only the beginning. Engaged and inspired community college alumni make major gifts. Again, not in the same numbers or measure as they do to four-year colleges, but the sector's prospects (no pun intended) are bright enough to warrant investment in the major gift model. The secret? Encourage prospective donors to honor, celebrate, and support the institution where they began their higher education journey.

Deploying the Development Staff for Success

The chief development officer, whatever the title, will lead the college development effort. By this, we understand the CDO to be a hands-on development officer, rather than an administrator. We also understand that the CDO will be a full-time development officer. If this is not presently the case, we look at some strategies for making it so in the following chapter's discussion of clearing the deck for development. Of course, a foundation executive director, for example, is called upon to perform a wide range of administrative duties. The trick is to dispatch, delegate, and, where possible, offload those, to clear the way for fundraising. The CDO will manage a portfolio of major gifts, planned giving, and, where necessary, grantsmanship. In addition, the CDO can try on another acronym: CCO, or chief cultivation officer!

The executive assistant should be seen as a crucial member of the team. The amount of development-related expertise an experienced executive assistant contributes to the team can make a huge difference in a small shop. These attributes will be sorely missed, and near chaos may ensue, if the executive assistant does not possess these qualities. Cherish the effective executive assistant, because this individual has the capacity to enhance exponentially the performance of the development office he or she administers. The executive assistant position must also be focused 100 percent on the advancement effort.

The next member of the team is the director of annual giving and alumni relations. For this position, I recommend an early career professional, with three to five years of experience in academic fundraising. Annual Fund positions are entry-level professional track positions, and successful incumbents are well positioned to advance within the profession. People who succeed as annual giving officers usually possess two identifying qualities: the ability to track outcomes at a granular level and the ability to follow up on every transaction they begin.

For many shops, this will conclude our staff inventory. A variation for better-funded operations is the introduction of another development officer. (Mega-colleges have even more personnel power.) In this case, hiring a grant writer, a major gift officer, or a planned giving officer becomes a viable option. Some small shops have, in addition to the executive assistant, another person whose job description is largely administrative. In the small, emerging shop, that will need to change. In the "real world" of nonprofit development, shops raising a few hundred thousand dollars a year do not have two administrative positions.

The smallest shops, particularly those in small or rural communities, may not even have the wherewithal to support a director of annual giving position. You can get by without the grant writer, but without the annual giving director, your prospects for success will be limited. In the most severe case, the two-person shop, the CDO gets yet another acronym, this one somewhat foreboding—the ODO, or only development officer. However, even in this case, there is cause for hope that early successes will foster increased funding in the future.

Before you book some conversation time with your president, take another look at the personnel budget all of this might entail. Recall for a moment the hypothetical three-person office salary budget of $155,000 discussed in chapter 2. We're going to tweak that because if the second development officer is an experienced director of annual giving and alumni relations, that position will cost you $50,000 a year. So, the budget looks like the one portrayed in Table 3.3.

TABLE 3.3	
Small-Shop Personnel Budget	
Chief development officer	$80,000
Executive assistant	35,000
Director of annual giving & alumni relations	50,000
TOTAL: Personnel	$165,000

Of course, you, as a vice president for institutional advancement, might be making $90,000, $100,000, or more. And your executive assistant (especially if he or she is in the Teamster-affiliated clerical union and has twenty years of experience) might be making $50,000. Either way, it adds up. Funding additional personnel either will or will not be a battle, depending on a variety of factors. To some, it is a fait accompli, to others, seemingly impossible. (We have already noted that you might be destined to be an ODO.)

So far, we have the *what*, the *who*, and some ideas about the price tag. To flesh out direct costs, let's go back to our hypothetical budget in chapter 2 and increase our direct development expenses from $60,000 to $90,000, allowing that we may charge some small part of that to the foundation. Remember, this is a composite of college and foundation costs covering fundraising expenses, management, and administration, without frills like college magazines. So, all in for development, we are talking about investing $300,000 in a three-person shop. Here we pause, take a deep breath, and firmly but gently introduce the concept that this little operation is someday, say three to five years from now, going to raise over a million dollars a year.

Endnote

1. For more on the topic of adapting the practices of four-year colleges, see Bass, D. 2003 (Winter). From the foundations up: Contexts for change in community college advancement. In *Successful approaches to fundraising and development*, ed. M. D. Milleron, G. E. de los Santos, and B. Browning, 20, New Directions for Community Colleges No. 124. San Francisco: Jossey-Bass.

References

Drozdowski, Mark J. 2006. Teed off. *The Chronicle of Higher Education*, October 27.

Klingaman, Steve A. 2005. All that glitters is not gold . . . special events and the annual fund. Paper presented at Minnesota Schools Colleges and Universities Fall Development Conference, St. Paul, MN, October. (Published subsequently as Klingaman, S. A. 2007. All that glitters is not gold . . . special events and the annual fund. *Successful Fund Raising* 15, no. 3.)

4

CULTURE CHANGE

C ulture change is at the heart of this book. Unless your development shop is already performing at a high level, with a robust Annual Fund, a major gift track record, and a respectable private grants record, culture change is a prerequisite to developing these capacities. The primary question here is whether development will become a top institutional priority, because if it does not your prospects for success are limited.

Clearing the Deck

You have probably heard the adage "Culture trumps strategy." I would amend that to "culture trumps strategy unless the strategy is to change the culture." Culture change is amorphous. It is paradoxical. It is immensely frustrating. It tests, and often unnerves, experienced practitioners. Culture change, like fundraising, is not for the faint of heart. But if you want to get where you want to go, it will be necessary. That makes you, the CDO, a certified change agent.

TIP #7

Culture trumps strategy unless the strategy is to change the culture.

Becoming a change agent comes naturally to few development professionals. I was fascinated by an exercise conducted at the Executive Leadership Institute at the Indiana University Center on Philanthropy. The participants, all senior development officers, completed the Myers-Briggs Type Indicator (MBTI). They were strikingly similar in their profiles; 60 to 70

percent of them registered as "ENTJs." That stands for Extroverted, Intu-
itive, Thinking, and Judging. The workshop leader commented that this
finding was remarkably consistent with each group of development leaders
that took the survey.

The term *ENTJ* describes a classic executive mind-set: outgoing, sober-
minded, rational, analytical, critical, objective, and judicious. Myers-Briggs
describes members of this group as "practical, realistic, matter-of-fact."[1] You
could also call them cautious. This is not the profile of a change agent. Given
that ENTJs are rational risk takers by nature, they need to be involved in a
process through the consideration of a case for action that can be backed up
by facts and the demonstrated plausibility of success. This is laudable, very
much in keeping with the *Good to Great* methodology. It is an important
methodology to keep in mind, given that you, the CDO, may be playing
against type when acting in the role of change agent.

One way in which the development profession has institutionalized the
role of change agent is through use of the development consultant, who is
by definition a change agent. Nobody brings in an expensive consultant to
maintain the status quo; yet the demeanor and presentation style of this type
of professional falls well within the boundaries of the ENTJ universe. The
decision to use a consultant can be a critical determinant in the success of
the endeavor. Often, the organizations that most need fundraising counsel
are the first to dismiss the option. I recommend that you keep the option
open throughout the planning process.

Efforts to promote culture change in the interest of empowering development must be purposeful, incremental, and permanent. There is no end
point at which you exclaim, "There, we did it!" Fundraising is hard, hard
work, and the temptation for a community college to put it on autopilot
after an initial focus for a year or two is immense. A change in leadership at
the top, the succession of a new board chair, a misfired early effort, and
board members who let you know there is "no way in hell" they are going
to give up "everything they've worked for on the gala" can skew your plan
in unforeseen and downright frightening ways. It can even lead to a new
development title acronym, the "ECDO," for ex–chief development officer!
But take heart; institutional change in favor of advancement has successfully
transformed the public four-year college sector. And history, as in the relentless ratcheting down of state support for higher education, places inexorable
forces in your corner.

A Plague of Meetings

A favorite fundraising consultant of mine is Mark Davy of Mark Davy and Associates[2] in Minneapolis. Mark served as fundraising counsel to Dunwoody College of Technology for over ten years. He has a favorite saying. When told that presidents, or chief development officers, just cannot seem to find time for fundraising due to all the important meetings they have to attend, he'll tease, "Give me their calendars. I'll clear those meetings!" The will and capacity to bulldoze meetings can come in handy in clearing the deck for development. The fact is we don't raise a dime on time spent in internal meetings. Staff meetings, shared governance meetings, accreditation meetings, informational meetings, meetings about meetings (I suppose those would be meta-meetings) are a real barrier to working directly with donors. We first have to look at our own calendars and determine whether we are part of the problem. Small-shop development executives do not have the luxury of figurehead attendance at a slew of meetings in which their active involvement is not required.

I know one vice president of advancement who proposed to his staff "standing meetings." That's right, no one gets to sit down. He did so to make the point that the business of a one-hour meeting could be boiled down to fifteen minutes if only we didn't get so comfy. In practice, I believe that could be a little awkward—you might strain your back taking notes—but the proposal makes the point.

Meetings are not "free" either. For a meeting of six staff members making an average of $50,000 a year, the aggregate hourly rate is $300 (*NonProfit Times* 1995, 32).[3] Therefore, it is up to us as development officers to make our meetings as businesslike and efficient as possible—and to request the same of our colleagues. Nearly every CEO I encounter requires that meetings begin and end on time.

It seems that bureaucracy begets bureaucracy, just as one meeting leads to another; and in my experience the community college sector is rife with bureaucracy. Bureaucracy and development do not mix particularly well. The former, at its worst, is process about process, while the latter is about closing the gift. Yet the practice of development flourishes in large research universities, whose governance machinations are even more arcane than their community college counterparts'. So the two realities can coexist.

One difference between two-year colleges and large universities is that research universities are more competitive, top-down, and driven by strong leaders, whereas the community college process tends to be more about building consensus. The dominant leadership style in community colleges is, in Collins's terms, *legislative* (2005, 11).[4] Development functions quite well in the competitive climate of a large university, characterized by strong leadership and well-articulated strategic imperatives. Consensus, especially to the degree that it reinforces the status quo, can, on the other hand, make it more difficult for an institution to commit to a course of action such as ramping up development investment to reap big gains later.

Presidents in the Hot Seat

Whatever the leadership style or culture of an institution, leadership begins with the president. To advance advancement, we must first engage the president. One party that can easily gain the ear of the president is the system chancellor. That approach to culture change can safely be described as top-down, and system leaders increasingly are starting to mandate better performance in fundraising. The trouble is that influencing presidents is a bit like herding cats. I have personally heard community college presidents in a group setting protest that they simply have no time for fundraising. (And to the intrepid college president reading this book I say, "I feel your pain!")

The intention here is not to disrespect presidents—far from it; the crux of the matter is how community college presidents conceive of their jobs. Community colleges, as we noted earlier, suffer from the neither-fish-nor-fowl syndrome. Their presidents tend to conceive of their position as that of an executive administrator. That is not how it works at four-year colleges. As one friend of mine says, "College president? That's a sales job." At the four-year level, I believe few would argue the point, but at the community college level it is a different story.

According to Donald C. Summers (2006, B22), "The failure of community colleges to raise significant amounts of money is partly a result of their organizational culture and their leadership." He attributes the lack of performance to "weak presidents and system heads." Community college presidents are almost never selected for their fundraising abilities; this would be unthinkable in the four-year college setting. Going forward, this will probably change. John Sellars, former president of Drury University, says, "Whether you are president of a private or public institution, you have growing pressure to raise money and build external constituencies" (Pulley 2007, 35).

Sellars estimates that college presidents "spend 50 to 70 percent of their time on external relations and relationship building." Attenuating this level of external commitment to an appropriate level of commitment for two-year college presidents is an issue around which consensus has not been achieved, if even seriously considered. We can be reasonably sure, however, that change is coming to the definition of what it means to be a community college president.

G. Jeremiah Ryan, former president of Raritan Valley Community College in North Branch, New Jersey, articulated this vision of the presidency as far back as 1994: "The president must be the one to jet off to the Big City to confer with the major corporation or foundation executive; the president must be the one to 'make the ask.'" In 2005, he advanced a platform of "Eight Rules for Active Fund-Raising Presidents" that parallels the ideas advanced here. His rule #1 speaks to the issue of culture: "The president should create the atmosphere under which successful fund raising can occur" (Ryan 2005). Robert H. Greenwood, president of the Greenwood Company, a San Francisco consulting firm, concurs: "This is an axiom. If the CEO of any nonprofit doesn't hold the development program as one of the most important things the organization does there won't be an effective development program" (Tepperman 1995, 22).

TIP #8

Offer your president a glimpse of "dollars on the horizon."

My suggestion is to begin by engaging the president in a series of conversations offering a vision of significant new resources available to the college. These are dependent on increased investment in capacity and more leadership involvement with the development function. Explain how the development office will ramp up production and how the foundation board will be strengthened to support the mission of the college. Share your aspirations for significant private support and how implementing them will require that the president become more involved in reaching out to the community.

Explain your plans to introduce specific new capacities that replace existing areas of focus because of their demonstrated potential for significantly greater yields. Draw analogies between this arena and the college's attempts to grow its corporate training department. Seek advice about how to best implement such strategies and in what time horizons. Correlate increased development capacity to the college strategic plan. Explain how you expect to personally take on the task of major gift fundraising.

If you are working for a metropolitan area community college of average size, focus attention on an Annual Fund goal of $300,000 and a major gifts and grants program that will raise $300,000 in the near term if you are not at or beyond this level already. If your college differs from this profile, adjust the amounts up or down as necessary. All of this is essential to move the conversation toward a partnership between the office of the president and the office of advancement.

Engaging College Leadership

Senior leaders, including the vice president of academics, the deans, and the CFO or chief administrative officer (CAO) will need to be brought on board if you are to succeed in becoming a best-in-class development shop. I assume you are already a member of the college's top-level leadership team. If not, you are at a serious disadvantage—tagged with the unfortunate "middle manager" stigma. If that is the case, your only recourse may be to engage an external consultant who can advocate elevating your position in the hierarchy.

Meet with academic officers and invite them to share their aspirations for their programs. What ideas worthy of significant private support can you collaborate on to bring to the attention of the college leadership team? Are there any doable projects the foundation could fund to demonstrate tangible early success? A demonstrated instance of early success can be instrumental in furthering culture change within this group as well as with the faculty.

I am no social psychologist, but I believe that community college leadership cultures are characterized by high recognition and image needs that are linked to a collective sense of low self-esteem. This leadership culture covets nothing more than ink in the metropolitan daily or a positive mention on the local television news. These leaders perk up whenever national political discourse turns to workforce development. They pepper the local media with press releases about their good works. They love it when the governor, or any government official, shows up on campus. Chalk it up to the Rodney Dangerfield complex.

One prescription for this syndrome is to launch a well-conceived major initiative linked to private funding. As a sector we excel when we dream larger and look beyond the classroom door to see ourselves as full partners in the higher education arena. A successful advancement program can transform an institution. There is nothing like a million-dollar gift to boost institutional self-esteem. We need to acknowledge that a few well-positioned community colleges are raising million-dollar gifts, and that every college can be a contender in the race for private support. No one is saying that it will be easy, or that it will happen overnight. High-functioning development operations are among the most intentional and deliberate of all institutional endeavors.

Moving fundraising to the top of the priority list in a community college is foreign to the culture. It is not going to happen overnight, but it will never happen if you don't lay the groundwork now. A bottom-line-oriented conversation with the CFO can demonstrate your sensitivity to his or her world of competing priorities. Priming the pump is imperative to the launch of a significant development initiative, and you will need to have the CFO on the side of the effort. The trump card you hold with a CFO is ROI, which a well-executed development plan provides.

Expect resistance, but expect also that it will be veiled. In *Good to Great and the Social Sectors*, Jim Collins perceived a "culture of 'niceness' that inhibits candor about the brutal facts" (2005, 32). It is not that in advancing the case for making development a top priority the CDO is adopting an uncompromising position, rather that development itself is an uncompromising endeavor. Indeed, Collins writes that all aspirations to greatness must be uncompromising endeavors, referring to leaders who have "the will to do whatever it takes to make good on that ambition" (2005, 11). The ambition to which he refers is the ambition to fulfill the mission of an organization.

Development officers are all carrot and no stick, although few would deny having felt the urge to use their carrots as sticks at one time or another. Coming on board as a new development officer, for example, one might feel the urge to "fit in" first, because "fitting in" in many community colleges is a paramount concern. And in most cases, as a new executive leader, the CDO has about a year to push through transformational change before your peers decide you are just another schmo and roll over and go back to sleep! I poke only gentle fun here, and only because the tacit resistance to prioritizing development can be as real as the urgency to do so.

Engaging the Board

I was tempted to call this section "Transforming the Board," but before the board can be transformed, it must first be *engaged*. That is, the CDO must garner the members' attention and must telegraph that change is needed. My own experience, as well as insight gained via extensive consultation with peers, suggests that you may be experiencing some, for lack of a better term, *imbalances* in board performance. My interactions as a consultant with community college development officers have revealed some situations that can best be called board horror stories.

Boards tend to perform in accordance with the rules of their formal structures and the habits of their informal ones. Their formal structures are composed of their bylaws, policies, and procedures. The informal structures are those of tradition, history, and habit. The degree to which boards follow their own bylaws, policies, and procedures is one of the first determinations consultants make when analyzing board performance. Informal attributes must also be understood, although these are often hidden. In contemplating culture change at the board level, one must first get a handle on these two facets of the life of a board. They reveal the fundamentals of board culture.

Board performance can be distorted by personalities, lack of direction, inertia, or all of the above and more. The responsibility for upholding the board charter lies with the president; the CDO; and, most important, the board itself, especially its officers. Before we look at some specific techniques for board transformation, we're going to concern ourselves with involving board leadership members in an informal advise-and-consent capacity to enroll their support as stakeholders in the process.

TIP #9

Form a board "kitchen cabinet" to discuss
your emerging proposals informally.

You may want to begin by organizing an ad hoc "kitchen cabinet" of handpicked members to serve as your sounding board over the course of your planning process. Begin by bringing up some of your ideas for change as trial balloons. As the CDO, you must position yourself as the expert to prevent knee-jerk "let's do this, let's do that" thinking. This is crucial to success. Boards tend to founder without strong executive leadership. If the board does not perceive the CDO or president to be in control of the process, it will attempt to seize the reins.

Why presume that the development executive should even have the authority to aspire to transforming the board? After all, the board is the authorized governing body of the organization. This depends on your out-comes. Rarely does a weak, inefficient board govern a high-functioning fund-raising foundation. Conversely, few high-functioning boards preside over weak, inefficient fundraising programs. The litmus test is whether the board is fulfilling its mission of providing resources to the host institution. If that is the case, all is well. If not—if the outcomes are unacceptable from an ROI perspective—then change, even transformation, is needed. The case for change that you present to the president and the board is one and the same, but targeted to the different functions they serve within the college structure, and with sensitivity to the differing forms of dysfunction to which their respective offices are subject.

Scrutinize College–Foundation Relations

Whatever your starting point in evaluating the relationship between the col-lege and the foundation, you probably have inherited some baggage. Many community college foundations are now around thirty years old. That is a fair bit of history, enough to have created seemingly indelible precedents of culture, tradition, and practice. Chances are, in the area of development, it is a history of underperformance compared to nonprofit sector norms. That fact does nothing to strengthen the foundation's position in relationship to the host college. The fundamental philosophy behind the relationship between the two entities should be that the college invests in developing the fundraising capacity of the foundation in order to receive far greater value in return in the form of private gifts, be they scholarship funds, endowment funds, gifts in-kind, or restricted-purpose grants.

The relationship between the college and the foundation may be spelled out in contractual form somewhere. In Minnesota, the Minnesota State Col-leges and Universities (MnSCU) system codifies the relationship between the two entities in a document known as the Standard Contract. This document applies to all the schools within the system. Though the agreement can be amended to suit a particular college, the amendments may not contradict the basic arrangement.

The Standard Contract spells out that the college is responsible for administrative support services on behalf of the foundation and will "make employees available to the foundation to provide services pursuant to this agreement." The college is also to provide accounting and bookkeeping ser-vices to the foundation under the contract.[5]

The foundation is bound to return each year

an amount, at a minimum, sufficient to cover the value of the facilities and equipment used by the FOUNDATION and of time and related fringe benefits that would be earned by State employees performing services for the FOUNDATION.

Note that the minimum ROI is a ratio of one to one—a return of the amount invested. This is far short of the nonprofit norm.

Beyond the legalese, a whole body of practice has grown up around the relationship between the college and the foundation. One of the most interesting questions is, "Who pays for what?" Another interesting area of investigation is the question of disbursements to the college. Does the foundation fund only scholarships? Is it sitting on a balance of cash, a corpus of funds, or does it disburse a reasonable percentage of revenues annually? Is there an aura of trust and communication between the foundation and the college, or are transactions conducted under the shadow of suspicion and entitlement?

Occasionally the opposition can go so far as to delineate an area of *college* development in presumed opposition to *foundation* development. This flies in the face of the integrated private college model that says, "Hey, we're all family here." There are no hard-and-fast answers regarding the imperfections of history and habit encountered here. Nevertheless, to advance on our proposed course we will need to introduce an atmosphere of flexibility, give-and-take, and mutual partnership.

TIP #10

Position the foundation office as "the college's development office."

Focus efforts to promote culture change within an established time frame. After all, if you just keep saying the same things over and over and nothing changes, you will just be considered a nag. When Saint Norbert College of De Pere, Wisconsin, attempted to create a new culture of accountability and stewardship in its advancement program, its development leadership concluded that the college needed two years to achieve success involving culture change (Rickards 2005, 10). Concrete demonstrations of good intent can go a long way toward bridging any gaps. For example, if scholarship disbursements to the college have been flat for a couple of years, ask the board to commit to, and deliver, a noticeable increase in scholarship disbursements to the college. Then make sure your faculty and staff hear about it.

TIP #11

Ask the foundation board to commit to incremental, annual increases in scholarship disbursements to the college.

Transforming the Development Office

Referring back to the results of our internal development audit, and beginning with your own position, plan to increase the amount of time you spend on external relations. Keep in mind that cultivating prospective donors is not just contact; it is contact with a purpose. Remember, in our small-shop scheme, you are the major gift officer. If you haven't been frequenting your local region's Council for the Advancement and Support of Education (CASE) conference, do so. Talk to the CDOs of four-year colleges and learn how they quantify the cultivation arc leading to a major gift Ask. You might be amazed at how targeted it is. Are you already an experienced major gift officer? If not, if you are a development generalist, I recommend you attend one of the many reputable major gift workshops offered around the country, such as those offered by The Sharpe Group.[6]

I suspect that some foundation executive directors or VPs for external relations do not even consider themselves to *be* development officers! If you are a college administrative leader who recently moved into the CDO position by virtue of your leadership skills in other areas, I would suggest that there is no real substitute for actual development experience. Many of the most respected practitioners in the profession have come out of a higher education background but have toiled for years perfecting the craft before rising to top-level positions.

In the case of a recent move into development, I would recommend a sequenced training plan consisting of The Fund Raising School offered by the Center on Philanthropy at Indiana University, followed by a major gift workshop and then the Executive Leadership Institute offered by the center.

Such an investment in professional development will transform your professional life.

Identify the administrative activities that prevent you from engaging in development. Give up unnecessary committee assignments. If your foundation office currently manages the scholarship award process, transfer that to the financial aid office. Development offices raise money; they do not award scholarships.

TIP #12

Clear the decks for development activities by transferring ancillary
functions such as awarding scholarships to other offices.

How many face-to-face donor cultivation visits have you completed in the last month? How many solicitations did you complete? Were they related to Annual Fund or major gift accounts? Were you selling tables to the gala? Going forward, the job of the CDO will be that of regular and consistent donor contact, setting the stage for the gifts to come. Ten to twenty donor contacts per week are necessary to achieve success.

Next, take a frank look at your staff, beginning with your executive assistant. Here are some questions to consider:

- Does the assistant understand development?
- Does the assistant know your donors?
- Are there any underlying performance issues?
- Does the assistant possess the necessary skill sets?
- Does the assistant have command of the hundreds of details for which you will be held accountable?
- Is the assistant proficient in using all of your software platforms?
- Do acknowledgment letters go out within twenty-four hours of receiving funds?
- Can the assistant perform data entry into your donor database, construct queries, and run reports efficiently?
- Are gifts entered daily?
- Are bank deposits made at least once a week?
- Do complex assignments seem to get put off indefinitely?
- What training does the assistant need?

- Are the assistant's job duties reflected in an accurate job description (see Appendix A3)?
- Is the assistant responsible for your accounting? If so, plan to change that. Include the transfer of accounting functions to the college in your development strategic plan. You have two options here: either a college business office employee performs the accounting function, or you will need to engage a bookkeeper as an independent contractor.

Your executive assistant is your best ally or weakest link. The answers to the previous questions are critical to your success and, indeed, your survival. If your answers to these questions are mostly positive, ask yourself, "How have I rewarded or thanked my assistant recently?" because if these indications are positive, your assistant is priceless.

Next, look at the other positions in the office. If you already have an experienced professional development officer serving as director of annual giving, give yourself an "A" on this one, because you are way ahead of the pack. If you have a staff member who is not a trained development professional, you may want to find money in your budget right now to send him or her to The Fund Raising School. Jim Collins's dictum of getting the right people on the bus, and getting them into the right seats, should be your guide here (2001, chapter 3). You may need to confront the brutal fact that you do not have the right person on the bus, and in your little vehicle, you may have only a single seat to fill. Perhaps you will need to find another position within the college where the staff member would be a better fit. The reason is obvious. An amateur with little experience or aptitude will not be capable of launching an Annual Fund.

Finally, do you have a *development mind-set* within your team? Does everyone know what that is? Can you promote its adoption? It is at once an ethos, a way of working, an esprit de corps, a devotion to mission, a shared discipline, and a dedication to the work at hand.

TIP #13

A high-performance development office
functions like a well-oiled machine.

Achieving Tip #13 is the goal of our process. A dedicated team effort, from president, to staff, to board, working at an optimal level for five to ten years can expect to achieve the goal of functioning like a well-oiled machine if they are resolute and avoid any pitfalls along the way. Collins calls this the "resource engine" (2005, 18).[7] The state of becoming, of aspiring—the launch and the ramp-up—can be some of the most engaging, even fun, development experiences on the planet. So fasten your seat belts; culture change is coming!

Endnotes

1. The Myers & Briggs Foundation. "The 16 MBTI® Types." Entry for ENTJ. http://www.myersbriggs.org/my-mbti-personality-type/mbti-basics/the-16-mbti-types.asp (accessed February 17, 2011).

2. http://www.markdavyfundraising.com (accessed February 17, 2011).

3. The calculation cited is based on the calculation that appeared in the article.

4. "Legislative leadership relies more upon persuasion, political currency, and shared interests to create the conditions for the right decisions to happen."

5. Minnesota State Colleges and Universities. "Standard Contract." Sections 1.a. & 1.b. http://www.docstoc.com/docs/3000096/STANDARD-CONTRACT-AGREEMENT (accessed January 13, 2011).

6. http://www.sharpenet.com (accessed February 17, 2011).

7. Collins addresses the mechanism of the "resource engine" of the organization as a whole. I use the term to refer to the resource engine of the advancement effort.

References

Collins, J. 2001. *Good to great.* New York: HarperBusiness.

Collins, J. 2005. *Good to great and the social sectors.* Boulder, CO: Author.

NonProfit Times. 1995. At organizational meetings, talk isn't cheap. 9: 32.

Pulley, J. 2007. The same but bigger. *CASE Currents* 33, no. 1: 35.

Rickards, B. 2005. Creating a new culture of efficiency, accountability and stewardship in your advancement program. Presented at CASE V Conference, Chicago, December 12.

Ryan, G. J. 2005. The role of the president. *Community College Advancement Series*, electronic file, CASE item #28253. Washington, DC: CASE, 3–4.

Summers, D. C. 2006. Why are community colleges so slow to jump on the fundraising bandwagon? *The Chronicle of Higher Education*, October 27.

Tepperman, J. 1995. AHP Conference Report: Starting at the top—development officers are senior management. *NonProfit Times* 9: 22.

5

BUILDING THE BOARD

As we prepare the launch of a new development model, we encounter a plethora of chickens and eggs, so to speak. The question arises, "Which comes first?" when, in fact, the many fronts of the endeavor occur simultaneously. We devote some time here to building the board; partly because this process takes some time and, if you will forgive me . . . these are some valuable chickens.

The optimal format for board assessment is that of a knowledgeable CDO in tandem with a sympathetic board chair. There are many board development publications and resources on the market to assist your review. Two of my favorites are *The Ultimate Board Member's Book* by Kay Sprinkel Grace (2003) and *Fundraising Responsibilities of Nonprofit Boards*, published by BoardSource (Greenfield 2003). Appendix B contains a simple board self-evaluation template used by Cleveland State University. When we consider that the foundation board governs only itself, as opposed to the college, we are forced to conclude that the better part of its *raison d'être* is to further advancement. But sometimes this fact gets lost in the shuffle of board meetings, college events, and staff reports.

Here is a checklist of board-improvement questions to consider:

1. Are your board members actively involved?
2. Are your bylaws in order?
3. Do you follow your bylaws?
4. How do board members assist your development efforts?
5. Is your committee structure functional?
6. Do you have a leadership succession plan in place?
7. What is the decision-making culture of the board?
8. Do you perceive imbalances such as the dominance of one or more members?

9. How many open seats do you have?
10. What does your board care about?
11. Are your meetings engaging?
12. Do you seek board input on topics that matter?
13. Does the chair "run the show"?
14. Does your board meddle in staff affairs?
15. Are there cliques?
16. Does the board evaluate the executive director annually?
17. Do you offer a board orientation?
18. Do you have a job description for board members?
19. Do you have formal terms of membership, and if so, do you follow them?
20. How does your board recruit new members?
21. What is the relationship of the board to the college president?
22. What formal resolutions has your board passed this year?
23. What events does the board sponsor?
24. How much money has the board disbursed to the college over the last three years?
25. Does your board give?

Let's take them one by one.

1. Are your board members actively involved?

Commencing with the adage that the world is ruled by those who show up, you might take a look at your board and committee meeting attendance records for the last two years. I will assume you have those. If not, get a work-study worker—I will assume you have one—to construct an attendance chart from your minutes on file. You might consider those who have not shown up at all for the "dead wood" file. Board members are often reluctant to confront peers on this score. In fact, no confrontation is necessary. Check to see that the terms of membership clauses in your bylaws are relevant. For chronic "no-shows," consider a "presumptive removal clause."

According to Collins, a corollary of the *Good to Great* rule of getting the right people on the bus is getting the wrong people off (2001, 41, 63). With board members, this can be a delicate matter. Here is a technique that has worked repeatedly for me. Create an honorary President's Council, an honorific affiliation that entails no duties whatsoever. The council can meet for lunch once a year (if anyone shows up). As executive director of the foundation, you can call the no-show members of the board and feel them out

---

TIP #14

Move inactive board members "upstairs"
to an honorific President's Council seat.

---

about their board membership status. Tell them that you have missed them at recent meetings and you wonder how their calendar looks going forward. Inform them about the option of the President's Council and ask whether that might be a fit. Tell them that it is up to them, of course. Chances are they will jump at the opportunity. Send a confirming, official-looking letter, signed by the president and the chair, followed by a certificate of appreciation for services rendered as voted by the full board. Mission accomplished!

Some companies require senior executives to serve on nonprofit boards. One board member's executive assistant asked me whether President's Council membership would fulfill his board membership requirement. I informed her that, sadly, it would not, but she still, *on behalf of her boss*, took me up on the President's Council offer on the spot. So, when recruiting board members, caveat emptor.

2. Are your bylaws in order?

I put this question near the top of the list because having a living set of bylaws can solve many of the problems boards face. Here are a few "bylaw upgrades" to consider:

- Increase the voting membership to around twenty-five.
- Reconstitute the Nominating Committee as the Board Relations Committee and expand its scope of duties to include membership performance reviews. It can meet three times a year.
- Missing four consecutive meetings will trigger a membership review by the Board Relations Committee.
- Create a Governance Committee of the chair, past chair, and chair-designate to evaluate or offer input on the performance of the executive director and manage bylaw changes. This committee meets twice a year.
- Create an Executive Committee if none exists and define the membership to include the chairs of the standing board committees. This committee meets quarterly, *not monthly*, prior to board meetings.

- Make the Executive Committee responsible for strategic planning.
- Recast the Development Committee as the Annual Fund Committee.
- Create a Major Gift Committee.
- External groups *nominate* rather than *appoint* ex officio members.
- Limit the maximum number of consecutive terms to three with an easy override clause upon recommendation of the Board Relations Committee.
- Limit the number of ex officio members to one faculty and one staff representative serving staggered three-year terms. You do not need spectators on a board. A student representative (if already mandated in the bylaws), nominated by the executive director, serves for a one-year term.
- Consider making the term of the chair a two-year term or make the one-year renewable by a onetime, one year extension.

TIP #15

Update your bylaws.

---

3. Do you follow your bylaws?

This one is easy. Do you or don't you? Make a list of the items that are honored in the breach and bring them to the attention of your new Governance Committee.

4. How do board members assist your development efforts?

This is a biggie. How many times have I heard a prospective board member say, "I would be happy to serve on the board but I don't do fundraising." The line to take is this: board members are our *ambassadors*. Their job is to open doors and help us with access to resources. Solicitation may or may not be involved. Of course, board members have to give. Tell them you will not ask them to do something with which they are uncomfortable. Then repeat the word *ambassador*. See Appendix C for a board member job description.

5. Is your committee structure functional?

Participation via active committee work energizes the board and generates areas of expertise on the part of board members. The Finance Committee often develops such expertise, for example.

> # TIP #16
>
> Replace the Development Committee (we all do development) with Annual Fund and Major Gift committees.

Here is a list of committees I recommend:

- Annual Fund—meets quarterly, staffed by the director of annual giving
- Board Relations—meets twice a year for recruitment, once for board review
- Executive—meets quarterly
- Finance—meets quarterly
- Governance—meets twice a year, once for executive review, once for bylaw review
- Major Gift—meets quarterly

The committee structure above represents a total of twenty meetings a year, sixteen of them staffed by the executive director. Given the significant amount of staff time they require, it may be a good idea to spread them out a bit, rather than schedule them all in the week before the quarterly board meeting. The time demands are daunting, but the board lives through its committee life. Even a small committee composed of three members can generate impressive competence in its area of focus. My advice is to recruit well, deploy well, and select good chairs.

6. Do you have a leadership succession plan in place?

I have seen even strong, well-functioning boards get caught short on this one. Consider the suggestion to make the term of the board chair renewable for an additional year to offer some flexibility in this area. A renewable one-year term may well be preferable to an automatic two-year term. The trick here is that the term renewal not become automatic. The Board Relations Committee and the Executive Committee should work together on this one. It should also be a top priority of the sitting chair to cultivate a successor. Leadership comes from involvement, and a strong committee system should establish a line of succession. Deal with this issue using a two-year horizon. Gentle reminders from the executive director and especially the college president can help facilitate transition planning.

7. What is the decision-making culture of the board?

Is it ad hoc? Is it sloppy? Or do recommendations percolate up from committees to the Executive Committee for presentation to the full board? Does the Executive Committee too often usurp the full board's prerogatives and merely seek ratification of what is, in effect, a done deal? The board that decides together abides together and is more likely to own the outcomes of its actions. Major issues, such as the adoption of a new fundraising initiative, should be the subject of full-board presentations and may even need to be considered over the course of two or more meetings. In short, formal is better.

8. Do you perceive imbalances such as the dominance of one or more members?

This is a hard one, is sometimes unavoidable, and is often indicative of a board that is out of whack. James M. (Bo) Hardy addressed the issue as follows:

> If we want boards to be active rather than passive, vigorous rather than lethargic, to provide leadership and thrust rather than coast, then we must provide for real, genuine, and meaningful involvement of all members. This, in essence, is the job of the CEO and the board chair. (1995, 4)

My prescriptions include creating a robust committee system; adopting the Board Relations Committee recommendation; following the bylaws regarding terms of membership; sticking to board meeting agendas; rotating committee chairs; and, sometimes, having quiet, one-on-one "come to Jesus" conversations among members. Avoid factions such as old guard–new guard through continuous membership renewal.

9. How many open seats do you have?

Some are good, many are bad. Having a few open seats allows for quick action when you recruit a hot prospect. Having more open seats than that simply means that your Nominating Committee is not doing its job. See the recommendations for #2, concerning bylaws. The board recruitment and nominating functions are prerogatives that are often closely held by the members themselves, who sometimes exclude the foundation executive from the party. That is, after all, an aspect of their rightful prerogative as a board. It is a question of balance. One way for the executive director to influence the process is to present "warm" candidates who are eager and qualified to serve. Just ensure that the nominating thrust comes from a board member who has adopted your prospective candidate. Above all, beware of snap judgments that arise from the lack of a true nominating process. A board can be a clubby culture. "Oh, by the way, Bill Bigbucks said he might be willing to join the board." "Yeah? Great, call him, let's do it!"

TIP #17

Beware of electing members to the board
without first performing due diligence.

---

10. What does your board care about?

Say, the gala, for example? The bottom line? Couldn't care less about the bottom line, you say? One board's preoccupation can be another's nonstarter. However, much of the information the board receives, or doesn't receive, comes at the discretion of the executive director and the president. If you want the board to care about what you care about, take the time to make a compelling case for your vision and the initiatives that back it up. If you leave board members in a vacuum, they will be sure to fill it. You hope and expect that they care about your mission. So sell the mission at all times. If you get students in front of them telling their stories, they will care about students.

11. Are your meetings engaging?

It is incumbent on the CDO to present compelling content at board meetings. Student and faculty presentations can expand awareness of the educational mission of the college. Deliberate real questions. Ask what fundamental role the foundation plays in meeting the need for scholarship support, and at what rate that level of support should grow. PowerPoint presentations presented by the executive director based on a CASE conference session on innovative development practices from the four-year college sector can expand board horizons. At Dunwoody College of Technology, the board sometimes uses the mechanism of a *consent agenda*, by which it collapses the standard agenda to devote time to a particular topic or an on-campus field trip. At such a meeting, the entire board might take a walking tour to witness a hands-on demonstration or review progress on a construction project.

12. Do you seek board input on topics that matter?

If you want real answers, ask real questions. When you get board members alone, offline, it is amazing how precisely they can hone in on the fact that in many meetings there's no "there, there." If you want meetings that matter, introduce topics that matter.

13. Does the chair "run the show"?

According to Cyril Houle, a seminal thinker in nonprofit management, the primary task of the chair is "helping diverse personalities merge into an effective social whole" (1979, 11). A strong chair is a double-edged sword. With a strong chair, you seem to get things done, but gradually the board just sits back and lets the chair run the show. And that is a bad thing. You want to encourage buy-in, multiple perspectives, and cross-pollination of ideas. If your chair runs the show, start looking for a co-star, or stars.

14. Does your board meddle in staff affairs?

It is not uncommon for foundation boards to disregard the rules about micromanaging the staff. Weak executive directors, unclear ground rules, and underfunded development operations lead to board interference in the day-to-day operations of the office. I have seen development staffers take their private issues directly to board members. That is never appropriate. The classic structure is the board makes policy and evaluates the executive director. The executive director manages the staff, and together they carry out the Action Plan that fulfills board policy. Of course, when this is not the norm it can be difficult to restore the balance, to get the board out of the kitchen, so to speak. Appropriately defending staff-level prerogatives is not out of bounds.

15. Are there cliques?

Where cliques exist, try recruiting new members who are untainted by these divisions. Cliques often arise along the lines of old guard–new guard; gala–no gala; corporate money–private money; disburse it all–keep it all; likes the executive director–not so much; Republican–Democrat; and the classic, risk takers–risk averse. There is no magic bullet for dealing with cliques, but a board process that encourages the airing of multiple perspectives can help to mitigate the problem.

16. Does the board evaluate the executive director annually?

If the executive director reports to the college president, there should be a dotted line reporting relationship to the board chair. The governance committee should conduct an interview with the executive director and provide input to the president for the formal review. An executive director who does not meet the legitimate expectations of the board is not performing his or her assigned role.

17. Do you offer a board orientation?

If not, it is easy enough to do. Offer a couple of sessions per year so you can orient a couple of new board members at a time. The executive director should take the lead on this with assistance from the board chair and the president. New members appreciate receiving an orientation—and may bring it up if they don't receive one.

18. Do you have a job description for board members?

This one is simple. If you don't, refer to Appendix C.

19. Do you have formal terms of membership, and if so, do you follow them?

The bylaws spell out the terms of membership; I recommend time-specific terms. The standard length of a term is three years, but following your own rules is another issue. Some boards do not. Following the rules is a prerequisite for fulfilling the board governance mandate. Point out bylaw infractions to the Governance, Board Relations, and/or Executive committee. In an era of increased IRS scrutiny of the nonprofit sector, your auditors will thank you.

20. How does your board recruit new members?

The correct answer is . . . *strategically*. It should be noted that casual is common, formal is better. Maintain an active list of board prospects and cultivate them as if they were major gift prospects. Do your best to make sure the nominating process operates through the designated committee structure. Do you tell prospective board members up front what is expected of them? Prepare talking points listing your expectations of them as board members. Show them the job description. Give them examples of the activities of current members. Offer a commitment menu from which to choose areas of involvement (see Appendix D).

Evaluate each prospect on each of the following criteria:

- Ability to give or leverage significant gifts
- Desire to "give something back"

- Willingness to fulfill the ambassador role
- Reputation and personal integrity
- Leverage within the individual's corporate structure
- Strength of the individual's network
- Sufficient time to devote to the organization
- Special skills or training

Of these attributes, the first four are the most important. When considering a prospective member, I always ask myself whether the individual or the company the person represents could realistically be expected to make or leverage a multiyear pledge of $25,000 to $50,000 at some point. If not, they usually don't make my cut.

TIP #18

Instill a shared organizational discipline to recruit board
members who have the capacity to give, or leverage,
major gifts of at least $25,000 to $50,000.

---

21. What is the relationship of the board to the college president?

A close relationship between the college president and the board chair is ideal. Encourage the two to meet regularly, facilitate three-way meetings to consider issues at hand, and keep them in the loop by sending out emails addressed to the two of them.

22. What formal resolutions has your board passed this year?

Your auditors might pose this question. Collecting this information demonstrates to what extent your board actually makes decisions. Many boards spend a substantial portion of their meeting time hearing what a great job the staff is doing, all the wonderful things the college is doing, that the admissions open house was a smashing success, and so on. In the end, all these things may mean a great deal to the staff and president but not so much to the board. It will be instructive to share with the board a list of all the resolutions it passed in one year. My prediction: most foundations will have little to show other than disbursement resolutions. If that is the case, it would not be surprising for them to feel like they are only "the bank."

23. What events does the board sponsor?

Here you have the gala, soon to be the recognition event, right? Also, the Scholarship Recognition Event, a joint meeting with an advisory group, the chair's social for board members, and so on. Publicize the board's sponsorship of these events as a way to let your other stakeholders know the board is actively engaged.

24. How much money has the board disbursed to the college over the last three years?

Every board member should know these statistics. Benchmark these numbers against those of comparable colleges and inform your board of the results. Publicize disbursement totals to the community, and to the faculty and staff, in an annual report. Disbursements to the college demonstrate the board's commitment to support the mission of the college. It does no good to raise money only to sit on it, yet some boards do. The board should learn to be more concerned with funds disbursed than with net assets. It should also have some kind of strategic focus on how to increase the amount disbursed to the college over the next several years. If the amount has been static for the last three years, that should tell you something.

25. Does your board give?

If the answer to this question is, to any extent, "No," then do not pass Go, go straight to fundraising jail and ask the members to bail each other out. Giving is the alpha and omega of foundation board membership and must be understood as a prerequisite to board membership. How much should the board give? Hank Rosso said each board member should give an amount that would be considered generous by a peer (1983). This applies to annual and campaign gifts.

It was at Rosso's The Fund Raising School where I first heard the phrase, uttered by one of the presenters, "Give, get, or get off" (The Fund Raising School 1983). It is telling that this phrase contains the germ of Collins's notion of getting the right people on—and the wrong people off—the bus. I have the feeling that both concepts are taken as being a tad confrontational, yet there they are, as proposed by best-practice thinkers spanning twenty-five years. There must be something to it. Let's refer back to our culture change principle: the endeavor itself is uncompromising. This point needs to be underscored, particularly in the movement toward culture change in two-year colleges. The phrase "Give, get, or get off" should, with due respect, be held up to the board as a mirror. After all, for foundation boards, what other justification for membership could there be?

As much as we have looked in-depth at some specific questions here, we've just scratched the surface of the tricky and rewarding business of board relations. That is why so many high-level consultants are out there working with nonprofit boards of every description. Consider it an option. You may also want to consider resources such as *Self-Assessment for Nonprofit Governing Boards*, published by BoardSource (Slesinger 1999).

Community-based leadership of our precious nonprofit resources is a uniquely American phenomenon. It goes all way the back to the time of Alexis de Tocqueville, who marveled at our chaotic and seemingly ungovernable system of voluntary association governance. Yet, it is a blessing, if sometimes in disguise. It is the "secret sauce" of American nonprofit life.

References

Collins, J. 2001. *Good to great*. New York: HarperBusiness, 41, 63.

Grace, K. S. 2003. *The ultimate board member's book*. Medfield, MA: Emerson & Church.

Greenfield, J. M. 2003. *Fundraising responsibilities of nonprofit boards*. Washington, DC: BoardSource.

Hardy, J. 1995. Board wise. *Contributions* 9, no. 5.

Houle, C. O. 1979. *The effective board*. New York: Association Press.

Rosso, H. A. 1983. Fund raising 101 (author's lecture notes). Presented at The Fund Raising School, San Rafael, CA, October 23.

Slesinger, L. H. *Self-assessment for nonprofit governing boards*. Washington, DC: BoardSource, 1999.

The Fund Raising School. 1983. Annual giving (author's lecture notes). Presented at The Fund Raising School, San Rafael, CA, October 24.

6

A MESSAGE TO
BOARD MEMBERS

The previous chapter established how the chief development officer can partner with the board to improve its operations, but the real power lies with the board itself. How boards choose to use this power determines their reputations within the communities they serve. As the fundraising pioneer and educator Brian O'Connell said over twenty years ago, "Fund raising is hard work" (1987, 3). Despite the efforts of your talented development staff, the heart and soul of your advancement program lies in your board. It is the magic of volunteerism that imbues boards with their influence. And influence differs from clout. One sometimes uses clout to exert influence within the community, but influence can also be achieved by walking very softly.

Many, if not most, new board members assume their positions of leadership feeling ill equipped to engage in fundraising. Yet the dynamics of fundraising may be the most businesslike of all nonprofit operations. Yes, there are distinct differences, but as I maintain in this book, fundraising is sales with a mission. And it is the selling of a mission. But fundraising is not sales per se. That is to say, the techniques of selling in the commercial sector differ from those of the nonprofit sector. If it can be said we use any prescribed model at all, we tend to use the consultative model. This is the model used in selling the capacities of a law firm to a potential client, or in selling one's expertise as a financial planner. The product is often intangible, and the selling is never something done *to* someone, but rather *with* someone.

The cultivation curve is essential in selling the good works of a nonprofit to a potential donor. What is the biggest mistake solicitors make in asking for a big gift? They ask too soon. Relationship development is essential in most cases. In nonprofit development, approach trumps technique. The initiative, relationship development, and matching of solicitor to prospect are all in some respects more important than the "close." That said, I encounter many development officers (and presidents) who shy away from asking for the order. A board member with sharp business instincts can bolster a campaign with his or her hard-won commercial resolve, but a board member can also rush things. Turning a cultivation call into a sales call rarely lands a big gift.

Getting Ready to Serve

Volunteer fundraising begins with *commitment.* Every board, and every member of a board, must commit to engaging in the organizational processes that lead to gifts. People give to people with a cause. But to be more precise, people give to *people* with a cause. You are the person who matters, the person who represents the cause. The passion and commitment you bring to the cause you serve count for everything in this equation.

As a board member, you are valued for your record of achievement, your standing in the community, your volunteer experience; but beyond those attributes, you are valued for your commitment as a board member. Once an organization has your commitment, everything else falls into place, including the so-called techniques of fundraising.

Confronting Reluctance

I mentioned in the previous chapter the condition of would-be foundation board members who attest that they will do *anything* as long as it isn't fundraising. This is a curious but not uncommon position to take as one assumes a volunteer leadership role that essentially involves securing resources for a good cause. This reluctance often springs from two propositions:

1. We confuse the status of asking on behalf of others with asking for something for ourselves.
2. We sense how uncomfortable we would be if we were asked out of the blue for a substantial amount of money for a cause with which we do not identify.

The truth is, when we enter into the covenant of fundraising, we enter a cherished tradition of community support for the qualities it values. Those we seek to serve, students, or any other group, are not in a position to address the community on their own behalf. That is why you, a person of some standing in the community, can represent that cause—these people— far more effectively than they could themselves. When we ask on behalf of those in need, we don't seek anything for ourselves. Our only reward is the inner satisfaction of having done well for others. And what a substantial reward it is.

As to the second point—the lack of comfort—board members must learn to trust the process. New members will find many allies in this endeavor among peers and staff. The board, development staff, and college leadership converge to develop relationships over time. It is the application of attention over time that creates the opportunities for a board to raise big gifts. Just as you would be quite rightly *surprised*, if that is the correct word, if a peer were to ask you out of the blue for $10,000 to support her favorite cause, it is useful to trust that the nonprofit team will come together to create appropriate opportunities for people to give. No one will be asked until that step is appropriate and entirely warranted by the circumstances at hand. When I interact with experienced board members, I am struck by the fact that familiarity with the process breeds comfort with fundraising.

I have come to believe that fundraising reluctance is the biggest factor holding back boards that have been unable to make their mark in the fund-raising arena. I have heard dozens of reasons why organizations are un-successful in the fundraising arena, and at every turn I can find similar organizations or boards that have achieved notable successes in the face of similar challenges. It boils down to commitment and faith. We make a com-mitment to the process and then have a little faith that the process will develop a momentum and expertise that leads to gifts. As a board member you have to push that process along; it is a central role of the board member.

How Much Do You Need to Know about a College to Represent Its Mission in the Community?

You don't need to know all the details about a college, its programs, or management structure to talk about *mission*. Study the mission of the college and foundation. Understand the difference between the two and your role in supporting each. You need to know something about the students, their demographic profile and enrollment patterns. You need to know the top three initiatives of the administration and president. You need to know somewhat more about the foundation: its history, financial profile, initia-tives, and a thing or two about the profile and culture of the board. An executive who has received a reasonably detailed board orientation can master these elements in short order. Consider the knowledge base required to be on a par with what you would need to know as part of a new client profile.

Board members, especially new ones, sometimes feel they need to be around a while before they ante in. While that can be a wise course of action in terms of discussions at full board meetings, there is no reason why relatively new board members cannot begin to contribute after just a few months of getting comfortable with the position. In most community college environments, the core issues for a foundation board are students and scholarships. The foundation exists to garner resources to support students, and scholarships remain the top priority at most two-year college foundations.

The Difference Between "College Time" and "Business Time"

This distinction refers to the perception on the part of business professionals that "things," that is, decisions, launches, *changes*, take too long in academia. This is more or less true from the business perspective, yet it isn't likely to change anytime soon. Community colleges especially rely on a consensus model of decision making. The advantages of this model include better, deeper buy-in by faculty and staff, but the trade-off is that change comes more slowly. Rather than react against the model, many board members find that firm, constant pressure—and consistency—are the most effective approaches to speed things along.

You may be shocked to find that tasks that would take weeks in your business might take months in an academic environment. Even then, major changes have a way of getting postponed so that the tortuous route to success can take years. But if staff and leadership know that they are going to be asked about a particular initiative *each and every board meeting*, it will rise to the top of their agendas. And, of course, one of those board preoccupations should be: *How much money are we raising?*

Initiative and Initiatives

High-functioning boards need both. They need initiative in the sense of becoming proactive centers of change and improvement on behalf of the college. Your job as a foundation board member is to secure resources to further the mission of the college. If you find yourself enduring meetings that lack substance, offer feedback to that effect and introduce substance. Ask your peers what the board is doing to increase scholarship support to students. Ask questions about the special event's return on investment. Ask the board to consider how it can assist the advancement staff and president in reaching out to the community, because reaching out is the core element of your fundraising responsibility on the board.

Beyond becoming a proactive board, a board with initiative, your board needs to develop several initiatives—concrete, high-profile activities that embody your mission. Here are a few examples:

- Launch and develop a phonathon.
- Double scholarship disbursements over five years.
- Host a cultivation event.
- Support a particular program or activity.
- Construct or refurbish a lab or building.

These initiatives should answer the question, What does your board do? Unless you can answer that question with concrete examples, your board will not be viewed as a body with initiative and initiatives.

Support the Annual Fund

College fundraising begins with the Annual Fund—repeatable, sustainable gifts that support core programs and the expenses of the foundation. Your first encounter with actual fundraising will probably occur in relation to the Annual Fund. Although your first exposure to these perpetual cycles of advancement activity may not inspire you, try to give it your all, because, in general, as the Annual Fund goes, so goes the entire program. You may be called upon to offer up peers to be solicited in your name. *Worse yet, you may be asked to ask them for a gift.* I jest only to highlight that being asked to ask for money can feel a little threatening.

But here's why it matters: Let's consider an Annual Fund initiative through which each member of a twenty-six-member board is asked to produce just one new $1,000 donor every other year. At the end of the first year, you raise $13,000 in scholarship dollars. The next year, the first group again donates $13,000 (because these are sustainable Annual Fund gifts) in addition to $13,000 in new money, $26,000 in all. In the third year, the first group of board members produces a second donor each, for a total of $39,000 raised over the initial baseline. Do you begin to see how powerful this resource engine is, and, by extension, how essential those Annual Fund dollars are? For an average small-shop college foundation office, these advances are transformational over time. And this hypothetical example comes down to each member producing just one new loyal donor every other year.

TIP #19

Members of effective boards actively support the fundraising activities of the Annual Fund and make it a priority for personal involvement.

Your Own Gift

In considering your role as a foundation board member, the rule is: give an amount that a peer would consider to be generous, and, I would add, make that peer a generous, well-informed, philanthropic peer. Your first gift will be your Annual Fund gift. It goes without saying that every member of the board will give—otherwise why would you be there? Another way to think of your giving level as a board member is that you should give as if this were your favorite charity. That can help frame the amount. I think a thousand dollars is a good psychological "floor" for board members. Circumstances vary, but I know faculty members who give that amount to the Annual Fund, so, even if it is a stretch, it is a good place to start.

Make your gift willingly and quickly. Don't make development officers chase you around over the course of a year. Make your pledge, express your payment preference, and pay the very first invoice you receive. This frees up your annual giving officer to work with the external community. Moreover, it allows the advancement staff to announce 100 percent board support early in the fiscal year. Such announcements bolster efforts such as Employee Annual Giving.

You may want to give some thought early on to your role as a major gift prospect. A major gift is sometimes thought of as a commitment of funds from your asset base, rather than income, and is often paid off over three or five years. Unless you have a longstanding record as a generous donor, your moment in the sun as a major gift prospect may not arrive for some time. But it doesn't hurt to begin saving, if only psychologically, now. Not every college foundation actively solicits its board for major gifts, and not every board member is capable of making a "major" major gift. But if your college is aggressively engaged in advancement, or is planning a campaign, your day probably will arrive. The best way to think about this potential commitment is to think about what you could do over five years and then "round up" by 10 or 20 percent to ensure that you have arrived at your "stretch goal."

And remember, until you give, it's still your money. You have every right to hold out until the college leadership arrives at a gift proposal that inspires you. No one suggests that just because you are a board member you *have* to give to an unrestricted campaign fund (although someone must). Your philanthropic priorities can be reconciled with college priorities in nearly all cases.

One caveat here: if your college embarks upon a campaign, it probably will look to the board for lead gifts. These are large gifts closed early in the campaign. While not every board member needs to step up at the very outset of a campaign, some must.

If you read the last chapter, you will no doubt recall the maxim "Give, get, or get off." Actually, it's worse than that. It's "Give *and* get, or get off." In a major gift or campaign situation, it's a little more nuanced, though. Board members who may themselves be able to give only relatively modest major gifts may be able to leverage much larger gifts from the corporations, businesses, or private foundations they represent. That is perfectly fine. It is, however, an element of your corporate or philanthropic life that you will want to plan well in advance. And once again, you have every right to expect that the college will jump through whatever hoops as are normally required by the giving program of the organization or business you represent. So, to update our maxim, we might say that board members give generously, and they sometimes leverage really large gifts from others.

TIP #20

Board members should give an amount that
would be considered generous by a peer.

Strategic Recruitment

While your board has a nominating committee, being on the lookout for outstanding potential members is every board member's responsibility. The first principle here is to *recruit strategically*. I am not talking about a sense of recruiting one accountant, one lawyer, and so on; that approach is old hat. I am talking about recruiting beyond the impressive resume. To build a better board we need to look at people, not resumes. Beyond wealth, beyond reputation, the personal attributes of a potential board member are the most important elements in the equation. It doesn't matter how much clout people have if they refuse to use it on behalf of your mission. Never just put a "name" on a board. This, too, is outdated thinking. That is why it is important to recruit people you know, at least professionally.

There are some exceptions to this rule, but they are rather rare. It is true that some people who are invited onto a board before they make a commitment to the organization sometimes grow into their commitments, but you never know which ones will do so—and you can be sure some won't. This leaves you with the significant problem of having *dead wood* on the board—and that can be a problem that inhibits your entire momentum.

Another case is one in which you have a corporation that preselects the individual who will represent it on your board. In this case, corporate culture and traditions may help predict your outcomes. If you had a dynamic corporate representative last time around, that culture may help to provide you with a new member who will strive to fill the shoes of a predecessor. Then again, maybe not—vetting prospective members is always the best policy.

Avoid Clubby Cliques

Boards that to a reasonable degree reflect the diversity of a community tend to make better decisions and raise more money. Though most boards tend to represent affluence to the detriment of diversity, they can still approximate the character of a whole community if you address the issue of diversity in the nominating process. If you have a purely homogeneous board in that they are all CEOs or senior VPs, try to broaden the representation with entrepreneurs, professionals, retirees, socialites, and others with deep pockets. Wait, I'll take that back. I would have no issues with a board consisting entirely of *philanthropists*!

Balance Renewal and Longevity

In the world of philanthropy, I have a problem with any board that says, "Two terms and out." It takes some people many years, more than ten even, to make the gift of a lifetime. If they are on that track, you want them around—as active members, of course—for the entire time it takes to gestate a major gift. At the same time, boards require new blood, so they need to think about balance in this regard. By opening up just a few slots at a time, you create a natural quality filter. Boards should be exclusive in terms of membership requirements. Nonprofit organizations can lay a stronger moral claim to this imperative than country clubs, where the culture of exclusivity is deeply ingrained. Strong, effective, somewhat exclusive boards are ones that people *want* to join. Although a community college foundation board may never have the same social cachet as a symphony board, you can work together to build a board with significant clout *and* cachet. If one's volunteer legacy is to have helped to build "the best little board in Texas," one has done a great service to the community.

It All Comes Down to Mission, and Stewardship

Mission and stewardship are the alpha and omega of a board member's concerns. If you keep these values close at hand you are bound to remain pretty close to the right track. A focus on mission keeps you engaged in things that matter—and away from those that don't. Essentially, you are there to provide resources to students with needs. There are many ways to waste time on a board, but boards that are busy securing resources are generally too busy to get sidetracked.

Stewardship is the process of using your resources wisely. That includes people and relationships as well as money. Stewardship encompasses the issues of governance you will address. On a foundation board with a strong focus on mission, those issues should remain manageable. If your board is like most, stewardship comes down to how you deploy the resources you raise. There are "bang for the buck" issues to address as well as challenges in leveraging your impact as a foundation. This sometimes boils down to a commitment to grow to meet future needs. The organization that stays in one place falls behind. Perhaps that is why *advancement* was chosen as a euphemism for fundraising.

Governing Boards That Also Raise Funds

Most two-year colleges in the United States are part of a system and do not have their own governing boards. Some comprise a district with a district board. Most of these boards are appointed; a few are elected. Even most of these have spawned foundation boards to assume the fundraising role. But in those cases where governing boards bear some responsibility for fundraising, they find themselves squarely positioned in a strong nonprofit tradition. Even among all the responsibilities of governance, fundraising remains a top priority.

If that is the case with your board, then all the references to foundation boards pertain to your fundraising mission as well. If your governing board does not have a tradition as a fundraising board, then there is no better time than now to begin the journey. The model presented in this book will provide you with a viable blueprint, but commitment precedes action. For the board that wishes to change course, I recommend three steps:

1. Convene a board retreat around the issue of fundraising.
2. Engage a fundraising consultant.
3. Develop a strategic plan for fundraising.

For the board that wishes to succeed in fundraising, the directive is clear. *Prioritize fundraising*, and then measure your outcomes. Elsewhere in this book you find two related propositions: *what gets measured gets done* and *what gets noticed gets done*.

If fundraising were easy, we wouldn't need boards or fundraising professionals. The fact that it is difficult, and that organizations engage in it only as necessary, offers us the opportunity to celebrate the brave men and women who put their personal values on the line to do good works for good causes. Having done the work is recognition enough, but you will also find a recognition that runs deep and wide when you succeed as a trustee. Yet, as with so many things in life, the doing is the real reward.

A Final Word About Asking for Money

It should be said that most board members only rarely make direct solicitations, or Asks. Granted, a few assume roles in which they make many Asks, but most don't. That doesn't mean that you shouldn't learn everything you can about the process. But it also means you shouldn't worry about it too much as you develop and refine your skills as a board member. Working with a development professional takes a huge load off your shoulders. And in development models like mine, most big Asks do not occur until the odds are in your favor. Instead, you will spend much more of your time cultivating people. For most people, this is a pleasant, self-reinforcing activity, and it is one that most business professionals have mastered in one form or another. So if you feel that you are not "ready," don't worry! When you care deeply about a mission, and make a commitment to the greater cause, things have a way of falling into place in their own good time. Lead with mission; follow up with stewardship.

Reference

O'Connell, B. 1987. Fund raising. *Nonprofit Management Series* 7. Washington, DC: Independent Sector.

7

YOUR STRATEGIC PLAN

Quality movement thinking has permeated parts of the two- and four-year higher education sectors over the last decade. For example, the Higher Learning Commission's Academic Quality Improvement Program (AQIP) "infuses the principles and benefits of continuous improvement into the culture of colleges and universities" (n.d.) that seek reaccreditation through this alternative. Could it be true that higher education is under invasion by the language and philosophy of commerce, of lean manufacturing, with its emphasis on continuous quality improvement? If so, development was the first frontier, because this line of thinking is in no way foreign to the development professional. I had the opportunity to write a section of an AQIP accreditation portfolio for a college, and it was one of the hardest writing assignments I ever encountered. The reason is that one has to stick to substance, process, and outcomes in a highly compressed format. And one has to provide evidence at every turn, while sticking to the brutal facts.

The value of strategic planning is widely recognized within the culture of the quality movement. You might consider joining the Continuous Quality Improvement Network, or CQIN, to facilitate the introduction of quality-movement thinking into your strategic planning process. CQIN is a group of community and technical colleges, and a few four-year colleges, like the University of Wisconsin-Stout, the first Malcolm Baldrige National Quality Award recipient in higher education.

As director of strategic planning for Dunwoody College of Technology, I found benchmarking with other CQIN participants to be of substantial benefit to strategic plan development and deployment. I was able to further my education in this area by becoming certified as a member of the CQIN

Board of Examiners, for the Trailblazer Recognition and the Pacesetter Award for Quality in Education programs.[1]

The fundamentals of quality-based thinking in a higher education system can sometimes be as simple as: *Are we doing what we think we are doing, and how do we know?* This single question underlies the entire AQIP accreditation process. It starts out with *quantifiable* goals and objectives. In development, we are at an advantage compared to our academic counterparts, because many development outcomes are inherently quantifiable in dollars and cents, number of donors, legacy gifts on file, and so on. This simplifies the construction of a strategic plan for advancement.

We'll start with mission. Take a moment to review the mission of your college foundation. It might look like this:

Mission

The mission of the Foundation is to secure charitable resources from the stakeholders of the college to allow Our Town Community College to achieve its full potential in educating youth and adults in the community.

Next, we might consider a vision statement for the foundation:

Vision

The vision of Our Town Community College Foundation is to achieve fundraising results in the top 10 percent of all community college foundations located in our state. We will endeavor to achieve this status within three years of adoption of our five-year advancement initiative.

Your mission statement is your anchor in a turbulent sea. It prevents you from being tossed about by the winds of whimsy, fad, and personal inclination. For example, it does not say that you will advance public relations for the college, or that you will become the Department of Hospitality. Instead it focuses attention on securing charitable resources—a fairly clear statement.

Your vision statement expresses your aspirations. Note that we avoid simply saying that you will be "the best." That is way too easy and ultimately means little. Instead, the vision statement expresses a clear benchmark, "to achieve fundraising results in the top 10 percent of all community college foundations located in our state." It is specific in terms of class, geography, and time frame. We convey by this statement that we are embarking on an ambitious program, and that we are willing to be held accountable for the outcomes we achieve.

Before we move on to the topic of goals, let's take a short digression to consider the meaning of strategic planning (Klingaman 2004). Strategic planning begins with strategic *thinking*. But what is that? Strategy is a plan to expend resources to achieve a goal in an orderly, managed way:

> **Strategic** *adj.*—highly important to or an integral part of a strategy or plan of action; "a strategic chess move;" or "strategic advance."

Strategic thinking is the capacity to identify and deploy those elements of a plan that will have the greatest impact on advancing the cause toward the desired outcome—those few things we might do that really make a difference. We employ strategic thinking in the development of a strategic plan to make sure our plan really matters.

The purpose of strategic planning is to *manage change*. To do this, we must have a vision, a strategic vision, derived from the sum total of our research, experience, broad input, and best thinking on the subject. And what is the difference between a *plan* and a *vision*? A plan is a vehicle to achieve a vision. To succeed in promoting the institutional change we seek, we must create a clearly stated strategic vision that all constituencies understand and that provides a framework for the plan. The vision is backed up by a plan to transport us from where we are to where we want to go. The plan will:

- provide a decision-making framework;
- respond to changing market conditions;
- create a sustainable framework for growth;
- promote continuous quality improvement;
- promote the achievement of desired performance; and
- allow the institution to thrive financially.

Our process will include the following elements:

- Stakeholder input
- Use of data to make decisions
- Recommendations to the board and college leadership
- Board and college ratification
- Formulation of objectives that flow from our goals

- Development of an Action Plan
- Linkage of individual work outcomes to our common vision
- Creation of annual updates to the plan
- Documentation of work on the plan
- Documentation of the annual and multiyear outcomes of the work

We have incorporated the notions of vision, plan, and process. Let's formulate a goal:

Goal 1: Launch an Annual Fund.

The substance is clear, given that we define its components via subordinate objectives, which we will. It is strategic, by virtue of all the considerations we have brought to the discussion so far. It is simple. The board should "get it." But it would remain a little vague without the use of objectives. We'll use a few to define the goal:

Objective 1: Raise $250,000 from eight Annual Fund categories by 6/30/13.

Objective 2: Launch a board-inspired giving campaign to raise $20,000 by 6/30/13.

Objective 3: Launch a phonathon to raise $8,000 by 11/15/12.

Objective 4: Raise $250,000 through the Annual Fund in two fund categories:
Scholarships—$150,000.
Annual operating support—$100,000.

Objective 5: Double alumni giving participation to 250 donors by 6/30/13.

Now we have some useful parameters. We have the activity, the dollar amounts, and the delivery dates. But we're not done yet. Now we introduce an excerpt from the *Action Plan*, the document that *cascades* the planning down to the staff level:

Action Plan

Goal 1. Launch an Annual Fund

Objective 1: Raise $250,000 from eight Annual Fund categories by 6/30/13.
Objective 1a: Breakout of the Annual Fund goal by components (see Table 7.1).

TABLE 7.1		
Breakout of Annual Fund Goals by Component		
Position	*Monthly*	*Annual*
Director of Annual Giving and Alumni Relations	$13,333	$160,000
Grant writer: working 50 percent time on Annual Fund	7,500	90,000
Total	**$20,833**	**$250,000**

Objective 1b: Breakout of the Annual Fund goals by product line for the director of annual giving and alumni relations position (see Table 7.2).

Objective 2: Launch a board-inspired giving campaign to raise $20,000 by 6/30/13.

Objective 2a: Launch program at October 2012 board meeting.

Objective 2b: Complete twenty team-based Annual Fund Asks by 12/31/12, sixty by 6/30/13.

Objective 2c: Raise $20,000 by 6/30/13.

Objective 3: Raise $250,000 through the Annual Fund in two fund categories:

Scholarships—$150,000.

Annual operating support—$100,000.

TABLE 7.2	
Breakout of Annual Fund Goals by Product Line	
Activity	*Goal*
Board of Directors giving	$30,000
Employee annual giving	25,000
Phonathon	8,000
Giving clubs	20,000
Board-inspired giving	20,000
Scholarships	50,000
Other	2,000
In honor/memorials	5,000
Total	**$160,000**

Objective 3a: Director of annual giving raises $70,000 from letter, phone, and personal solicitations by 12/31/12, $160,000 by 6/30/13.

Objective 3b: Grant writer raises $40,000 from Annual Fund grant proposals by 12/31/12, $100,000 by 6/30/13.

Objective 4: Double alumni giving participation to 250 donors by 6/30/13 (director of annual giving).

Objective 4a: Acquire 160 alumni donors via the phonathon.

Objective 4b: Acquire forty alumni donors through appeals related to alumni functions.

Objective 4c: Acquire fifty alumni donors through all other appeals.

These objectives supply the necessary detail to ensure that we can measure the attainment of the larger goal. These are its metrics. This comprises a segment, a single slice of our strategic plan as it cascades down to the individual staff level. No one can doubt that we are serious about the enterprise. This will be crucial as we attempt to sell the plan to the president and foundation. But how did we come up with all of these numbers? By data-based decision making and by using our best judgment where no preceding data were available, such as in the case of our proposed board-inspired giving initiative. (This is a launch, after all.) But let's assume you called a colleague or two and *benchmarked* your estimate.

Now we'll go back and discuss the issue of goals in some detail. The amount of attention focused on a particular goal exists in inverse proportion to the number of goals you have. Goals are the means by which we communicate to our stakeholders the challenges that really matter to us. Institutions are not designed to carry out a large number of strategic imperatives all at once. A handy rule is the *Rule of Three*, which states that any list of possible messages should be distilled down to three simple points. I assume this axiom is part of common management practice, but in my own practice it was developed by two colleagues and myself—Mark Davy and Ben Wright, former president of Dunwoody College of Technology. We were discussing the need for order and focus in institutional priorities, and we figured that in terms of messages, initiatives, goals, or whatever, the Rule of Three would be a good place to start when prioritizing actions. "For good measure," I added, "make numbers one and three the same."

Note the degree to which U.S. presidential administrations attempt to adhere to this rule. Staying "on message" is the discipline of focusing attention on the two or three priorities of the day. Colleges, on the other hand,

> # TIP #21
>
> Use the Rule of Three to focus attention
> on a limited number of priorities.

are prone to want to do everything at once. I once saw a college president enumerate six strategic priorities for the college and move effectively in all six directions simultaneously. It was an impressive display of will and focus. I do not expect this paradigm to be the norm in higher education administration, however.

At a conference entitled "Understanding Outcomes," which I attended back in 1995 (Northern California Community Services Council, Inc. 1995, 7–9), the presenters identified the four elements of a plan:

- Inputs: The ingredients
- Process: The interaction
- Outputs: The units of work
- Outcomes: The impact

The most important element here is the discrimination between Outputs and Outcomes, because nonprofit planners are forever confusing the two. An *output* is "to deliver sixteen hundred hours of academic counseling" or "to telephone forty-five hundred alumni." An *outcome* is:

- To increase the retention rate of students engaging in academic counseling by 2 percent over the 2011–2012 academic year
- To raise $10,000 in gifts from new alumni donors through the phonathon by October 31

Mastering the difference between outputs and outcomes is a required skill for strategic planners. As Jim Collins says in *Good to Great and the Social Sectors*, "What matters is not finding the perfect indicator, but settling upon a *consistent and intelligent* method of assessing your output results, and then tracking your trajectory with rigor" (2005, 8). (Collins's use of the term "output results" translates to "outcomes" in our system.) In the end, the ability to master and apply the concept of outcomes delineates the difference between good intentions and good results.

In considering most advancement programs at community colleges and emerging institutions, try as I might, I can think only of four or five goals that truly make a difference. Remember, we are talking about those programs that are in a developmental state, raising less than $500,000 or $600,000 a year. For them, the most important goal is launching the Annual Fund. This also applies to colleges that land occasional big gifts yet still do not have a proper Annual Fund.

Then there is the goal of launching a major gift program. You will also need to make time in your work plan to introduce the essential elements of a full-bodied program—elements such as bequests, grant writing, and alumni relations. And then there is the need to run the foundation in a businesslike manner. Most anything else seems to be means to an end. Launch a college publication? Means to an end. Hire staff? Means to an end. Have we missed anything? Don't suggest "launch a capital campaign" until you have mastered the four above!

In relation to the final goal listed above, the need to run the foundation in a businesslike manner, this advice is a specific tenet of the consulting practice of consultant Mark Davy. He defines the concept in opposition to running a nonprofit organization "like a business." Nonprofits, he posits, are not run like a business but they *are* run in a businesslike manner. I merely applied his concept to the operation of community college foundation offices. Could it be true that every community college foundation in the nation would reap benefits by being run in a more businesslike fashion? Are 20 percent of them already there? Perhaps a standardized survey, along the lines of the VSE survey, is needed. IRS Form 990 is moving in this direction in this era of Sarbanes-Oxley, but it still falls short in measuring the efficiencies with which we are concerned.

With the benefit of our discussion above, go back and fill out the objectives and Action Plan entries for the remainder of your (preferably few) goals. I keep my goal statements short and simple to make them more memorable and put my outcome parameters in the objective statements. This is in keeping with the logic behind the Rule of Three—keep it simple! This approach is validated in a classic handbook, *Fund Raising*, by Brian O'Connell (1987):

Develop a fund raising plan.
   a. An identification of the type or types of fund raising to be undertaken . . .
   b. Establish a realistic goal for the first year . . .

    c. Determine exactly how many board members and other campaign work-
ers you need to make the contacts necessary to raise that amount of
money. *Here, too, be coldly realistic* [emphasis added] . . . (6)

Saint Leo University in Saint Leo, Florida, offers an excellent example
of how these types of objectives are used in a mature program. Saint Leo's
Division of University Advancement 2005–06 Institutional Objectives
include the following metrics (Rose and Peirce 2005, 8):

- Secure $5 million in new commitments.
- Secure 6.5 percent alumni participation, 2,177 donors.
- Secure 2,488 donors.

It is easy to see the clarity and accountability that flows from such metrics.
They don't have to be complex to allow the overall program to be measured
against its goals.

    We maintain a strong annual focus because that is our primary measure
for tracking results. In strategic planning for mature development programs,
we would tend to favor multiyear goals. Collins describes really large strategic
goals as "BHAGs" (pronounced "BEE-hags"), or "Big Hairy Audacious
Goals" (Collins 2001, 198–204; Collins and Porras 1994, 90–114), and that is
exactly where mature development programs should be setting their sights.
That is where the campaign goal enters the picture. But for the emerging
program, everything in the future depends on achieving the desired results
in the launch. Indeed, for many development offices, establishing an Annual
Fund will be a multiyear goal. To sell the program to the college and the
foundation board, we will need to propose some multiyear projections,
which should also be formally expressed as goals.

The Three- to Five-Year Window

The difference between the three- and the five-year window is demonstrating
solid progress and entering the threshold of maturity, respectively. For an
organization raising $200,000 to $300,000 a year in private gifts, the
million-dollar-a-year goal may be five years off. For the college foundation
raising a million dollars a year right now, two million a year may be three
years off. And we're not talking about campaigns here. Campaigns are a
different animal entirely. Prematurely rushing into a campaign can do more
harm than good.

We are talking about bankable future revenue, which arises from a demonstrated record of performance. Take the Annual Fund as an example. Dunwoody College, serving sixteen hundred students, raises a little more than a million dollars a year through its Annual Fund. It raises more than some public colleges five times its size. Its program is mature. Given that, it really has to go some to achieve a 10 percent annual increase in revenues. All the *low-hanging fruit* (that unfortunate cliché!) has been picked. So it is more vulnerable to economic downturns and potential shortfalls caused by the loss of larger Annual Fund gifts.

Based on my long acquaintance with that program, I concluded that a mature community college Annual Fund campaign should be able to raise $500,000 a year. (Colleges with very small enrollments may raise less.) The only question is: How long to maturity? For the college currently raising $300,000 through its Annual Fund, I propose a five-year window for achieving that goal. Discount the number for small colleges, double it (or more) for mega-colleges.

In projecting the growth of an Annual Fund over five years, we must factor in the flattening curve of a maturing program. To counteract this tendency, we must outperform the average in the middle years to accommodate the glide path of the last year or two. In addition, though you would like to project $300,000 for Year 1, your baseline de facto annual support over the last three years is only $175,000 when major gifts are factored out. So we will project $270,000 in Year 1. The projection looks like Table 7.3.

And what of Year 6? Who knows, it could be a 4 percent increase for a total of $520,000. Mature Annual Fund programs grow incrementally; they may even lose ground in an off year. And just as your retirement account

TABLE 7.3		
Annual Fund Projections		
BASELINE:	$175,000	
Year 1:	$225,000	(Aggressive)
Year 2:	$300,000	(Still learning)
Year 3:	$400,000	(*Flywheel*[1] has started to turn)
Year 4:	$455,000	(Leveling off)
Year 5:	$500,000	(Flattening has increased)

[1]Collins 2001, 14, 164–178.

falls, it is a lot easier to lose money than it is to make it back. But the bottom line is this: a $500,000 Annual Fund, composed of *sustainable, repeatable gifts*, not including grants and major gifts, is a beautiful thing to behold.

A major gift program is a different endeavor entirely. First, the flywheel is harder to turn. That is due to the longer cultivation curve inherent in major gift work. Second, major gifts do not come in annually, so it's more like a roller coaster than a rocket launch. Unlike your Annual Fund projections, the curve is not going to flatten toward Year 5 and beyond. In fact, it may just be taking off.

Start by counting your major gifts and grants received over the last three years. Discount any really big gifts you received by 50 percent and divide the total by three. This is your rolling three-year average baseline performance. For an example, see Table 7.4.

It may be that in arriving at your three-year average you counted some gifts that you had difficulty classifying as annual or major, such as a renewable three-year grant. But you applied the sustainability test, and that left you with an annualized average of $175,000 per year for all other giving (your de facto Annual Fund). So your overall baseline performance, all in, was $465,000 ($290,000 + $175,000), when annualized over three years. If your major gift baseline is lower than the amount shown, don't worry about it. True, the major gift pipeline is an unforgiving element of development practice. You might be able to jump-start it for a year or two, but you need a prospect pool and practice of cultivation in place to sustain a major gift *program*.

For the purposes of this exercise, let's assume you are going to hire a grant writer, and 50 percent of that position will be devoted to securing major grants. You estimate that in the first year, that investment will result

TABLE 7.4 Annual Major Gifts and Grants, Years 1 through 3		
FY1	$290,000	
FY2	$120,000	
FY3	$460,000	($610,000 but with a $300,000 gift discounted by 50 percent)
TOTAL	$870,000	(divided by 3 = $290,000)
BASELINE	$290,000	(per year)

in new grant monies in the range of $70,000. Your first year of an intensified major gift focus is not necessarily going to yield many pledges due to the requisite cultivation curve. You will have to evaluate how "warm" your prospects are at the outset. I have seen cultivation environments where prospects were "stone cold," even a little alienated. So our major gift projection might look like Table 7.5.

The results of Years 3–5, a total of $1,780,000 divided by three, yields an expected *trailing average* of about $600,000 a year for Year 6. Now, to put it all together, see Table 7.6.

There you have it—a five-year projection that puts your college ahead of the national average as computed by the Council for Aid to Education (CAE), well over a million dollars a year (CAE 2010, 9).[2] Later, since we are building a programmatic capacity, you should be able to surpass that total

TABLE 7.5
Major Gift Projections

BASELINE:	$290,000	
Year 1:	$390,000	(Small increase, plus new grants)
Year 2:	$420,000	(Still learning)
Year 3:	$480,000	(Flywheel has started to turn)
Year 4:	$350,000	(Not necessarily a linear equation)
Year 5:	$950,000	(Jackpot, but still no million-dollar gift)

TABLE 7.6
Composite Five-Year Projection

Year	Annual	Major Gifts	Total
BASELINE:	$175,000	$290,000	$465,000
Year 1:	225,000	320,000	545,000
Year 2:	300,000	420,000	720,000
Year 3:	400,000	480,000	880,000
Year 4:	455,000	350,000	805,000
Year 5:	500,000	950,000	**$1,450,000**
TOTAL Years 1–5:	$1,880,000	$2,520,000	**$4,400,000**

every year. However, before you get too confident, as you consider Year 6, you now have a mature Annual Fund growing at between 3 and 7 percent per year, and your three-year trailing average for major gifts is $600,000. Therefore, a safe bet for a Year 6 projection might be a figure in the range of $1,120,000. Yes, that amount is *lower* than your actual Year 5 results. Year 5 was a banner year for major gifts. You can count on the trailing average only for the purposes of strategic planning. Even with a Year 6 decline, you have developed a solid million-dollar program.

How hard is your college going to have to work to achieve this goal? *Very hard.* And though it may surprise both parties, much of the burden for attaining this goal is going to fall on the backs of your board and your president. It simply can't be done with a staff-only effort. Board development, board education, and gaining the commitment of your president to spend at least 15 percent of his or her time on development are the requisite leadership resources for a rollout like this. If the board members buy your proposal, they may conclude that you have a $5 million–plus *comprehensive campaign* here. (A comprehensive campaign is a campaign in which you just count everything.) Heck, just throw in another "half a mil" and you are there. I caution, however, as your capacity is unproven, *that decision would be very ambitious* and would require immediate recourse to fundraising counsel. We cover comprehensive campaigns in chapter 16.

Alignment of Resources

Alignment of resources is a term used in strategic planning that refers to aligning budget expenditures to support the attainment of strategic goals. It refers to investing in the few things that will make a difference in outcomes. So how much is it going to take to accomplish this BHAG transformation? It all begins with personnel, which accounts for 80 percent of your costs.

We're going to adapt our personnel worksheet from the development audit for this exercise, using revised numbers, as shown in Table 7.7. There you have the brutal facts. The first year will cost more than $400,000. And this is a *bare-bones* budget. It may even contain cuts in some line items compared to what you are used to.

To calculate revenue over expenses see Table 7.8.

The net of $161,000 is pretty low, but let's put the number in context. This is the number the CFO of a private college or nonprofit would want to see. And if you stand back a moment and look, it does reflect reality—one

TABLE 7.7 Year 1 Expense Budget	
Personnel:	
Chief development officer	$94,000
Executive assistant	$47,000
Director, annual giving & alumni relations	$52,000
Grant writer	$50,000
TOTAL: Personnel	**$243,000**
Benefits @ 30 percent	**$73,000**
TOTAL: Personnel & Benefits	**$316,000**
Direct development expenses	$70,000
Direct alumni relations expenses	$43,000
TOTAL: Direct Expenses	**$113,000**
TOTAL: Development & Alumni Relations	**$429,000**

TABLE 7.8 Total Revenue and Expenses, Year 1	
Year 1 Revenue	$590,000
Year 1 Expenses	**(429,000)**
NET REVENUE	**$161,000**

all too close to your baseline budget if you were to rerun it with your current revenues and expenses plugged in. However, we have several tools at our disposal to mitigate the effect. *CASE Management and Reporting Standards*, the definitive guide for cost and revenue reporting in higher education, says pull alumni relations out of your cost-of-fundraising equation.[3] You can allocate those direct costs, $43,000 in Table 7.7, to your alumni relations activities and to cover part of the cost of your beautiful, four-color, flagship college magazine. (If your CDO is responsible for editing the magazine, too, you'd

better add something to the salary above—and allocate it to alumni relations.) We are also going to allocate 15 percent of the salaries of the director
of annual giving and alumni relations and the executive assistant (for maintaining the alumni database) to alumni relations (see Table 7.9).

The net is still low. If you were working in a private college, this would
never fly. This is how those colleges analyze the cost of fundraising, and this
is, at the bottom line, what drives the imperative to succeed. But we have
some public–private magic to work. Let's say the college covers all of the
salaries, as most do. In addition, the college covers all of the direct expenses
except for those where sound management practice or convenience dictate
that the foundation assume the expenses. I'm thinking of the audit here.
Let's say the college covers all but $25,000! (See Table 7.10.) "Holy cow!"
you say. "That looks great!" And, indeed, it does. That is the reality of what
we as a sector report to the public. And because private funders almost never

TABLE 7.9 Alumni Relations: Year 1	
Allocated personnel & benefits: 15 percent of two positions	**$21,000**
Alumni relations direct costs	12,000
College magazine	31,000[a]
NET COST	**$64,000**
Now we have a new equation:	
Year 1 revenue	$590,000
Year 1 fundraising expenses (less alumni relations)	**(365,000)**[b]
NET REVENUE	**$225,000**

[a]This amount does not include the cost of editorial, which is allocated to the public relations budget.
[b]Reducing personnel/benefits by $21,000 and cutting out the alumni relations expenses line item yields
a cost savings of $64,000.

TABLE 7.10 Net Revenue, Year 1	
Year 1 revenue	$590,000
Year 1 fundraising expenses	(25,000)
NET REVENUE	**$565,000**

look behind the curtain, no one is likely to ask you about it. But we know. If you think I exaggerate, one glossy, four-color annual report produced by a two-year college in the Midwest reports gifts of $3.3 million against management expenses of just . . . *$13,000*! (That would be their audit.) How do they do it? We know how they do it, because we do it. Now, in their defense, with revenues like that they'd have to spend over a million dollars a year on fundraising to get into trouble with an organization like charity-watch.org.[4] Freestanding nonprofits have much less wiggle room, as they need to keep their fundraising expenses below 30 percent of funds raised. But, as you develop your fundraising capacity over the next five years to the point where even the *brutal-fact* expenses are justified by the revenues you report, you'll know that institutional viability *and integrity* are growing with each passing year.

TIP #22

Don't budget a full year of revenue if the
position will be filled after only six months.

Your aggregate costs should grow at two different rates. You might keep your personnel cost increases to 3.5 percent a year, just a tad over a long-term rate of inflation, but your benefit costs will go up by about twice that rate. Therefore, personnel and benefits might increase at a composite rate of 4.4 percent per year. For the sake of a simple projection, we'll forecast your direct costs at the same rate. We can make some broad projections based on your 4.4 percent overall rate of growth in expenses (see Table 7.11).

So, at long last, here is the message for the board and president: if we adopt this course of action and execute it faithfully, five years from now we will spend $416,000 on fundraising per year to make over a million dollars, possibly as much as $1.4 million! (As opposed to spending 60 percent of that now to make a measly $465,000.) Granted, this may not be the yield of a private college, but it is vastly superior to the status quo. Moreover, in the years to follow, the ratios are only going to improve. Admittedly, this has been a lot of math. But multiyear projections are essential to selling the plan. When you make firmly grounded projections, you are speaking the language of the businesspeople on your board.

TABLE 7.11 Fundraising and Alumni Relations Expenses, with Allocated Salaries, by Year			
Year	Fundraising	Alumni Relations	Total
BASELINE:	$255,000	$45,000	$300,000
Year 1:	$365,000	$64,000	$429,000
Year 2:	381,000	67,000	448,000
Year 3:	398,000	70,000	468,000
Year 4:	416,000	73,000	489,000
Year 5:	434,000	76,000	510,000
TOTAL: Years 1–5	$1,994,000	$350,000	$2,344,000

High- and Low-End Variations

If your college is already raising a million dollars a year, you may want to set your sights on two million. In that case, you will need to add a major gift officer to the plan. According to *The Chronicle of Higher Education*, the median salary for this position is $63,000 (2010). The rationale for adding the major gift position rather than an alumni relations position is that small-shop development programs must be driven by development considerations over those of alumni relations. In a larger shop, you might add the alumni relations position next, and it might be a half-time position at first.

According to CASE, "The primary intent of this activity is to inform alumni of the plans and activities of the school, college or university; to maintain their contact with it and their fellow alumni; and to involve them in its efforts to carry out its mission" (Netherton 2004, 151).

Alumni relations activities, although necessary, are secondary to the bottom-line imperatives of development activity and must remain secondary until the college deems it worthwhile to invest sufficiently in alumni relations based on the logic of long-term payoffs.

The low-end variation of this plan is a very different scenario. In it, the college elects *not* to fund the director of annual giving and alumni relations position. This option seems to be preferred by underdeveloped or financially challenged colleges. It may also be suitable for newly incorporated foundations set up to support public primary and secondary schools and districts. In this option, we have a "one-professional shop," the ODO, staffed only by an executive assistant. When this option is adopted, the CDO becomes the de facto director of development and alumni relations.

The development professional in a one-professional shop is charged with many lower-level tasks such as managing the phonathon, sending out scholarship solicitations, and running the employee annual giving campaign. It is a less-than-desirable option but, if artfully implemented, can yield sufficient results over a year or two to justify a strategic review of the investment side of the equation. In this option, it is even more crucial to let go of the gala event and concentrate on the basics of the collegiate model. Schools electing this model, however, will tend to be the most resistant to letting it go.

A half measure on the low end is to hire a half-time or shared-time director of annual giving. But development is never really a half-time job, and in the case of a shared-time position, the incumbent will encounter the irresistible temptation to put development on the bottom of the to-do list. Similarly, the grant writer position could be half-time, perhaps shared with a government grants position, or an independent contractor could perform the work. Both arrangements, though problematic, can be made to work in a pinch.

College–Foundation Cost Allocation

There is one more issue, a thorny one, that should be considered here, because it may arise in the course of selling the plan. That is the question, speaking of the college and foundation, "Who pays for what?" We noted previously the example of the college foundation that reported raising $3.3 million on a foundation expenditure of $13,000. Not all college–foundation relationships are constructed on that understanding. Some colleges prefer to have the foundation pay for fundraising operations, and that tradition is firmly entrenched in their relationship.

I know of one group of state community college presidents that has openly considered the question of how to move their foundations to "pay their share." This formulation of the relationship is unfortunate given that college funding of a foundation is a generally accepted practice. Shifting costs to the foundation will tend to put it at a relative disadvantage in terms of donor relations and public disclosure. For some, the cost-shifting question becomes one of college disinvestment in development, while simultaneously expecting more from the foundation-based development effort. Which brings us to an ironclad rule: *you cannot simultaneously disinvest and ramp up production.*

The best alternative to cost shifting is to have the foundation provide greater unrestricted support to the college by way of increased disbursements. Such disbursements reinforce the case for the Annual Fund. Plan to increase the amount disbursed every year. The proposed solicitation methods presented in Part Two will yield sufficient unrestricted income to fund the increases.

There are a few exceptions to this rule. First, the foundation may choose to assume certain costs, say for the recognition event, or for printing, to allow the engagement of vendors outside of the rules of procurement to which the college is bound. You can offset these by *pass-throughs*, a GAAP (Generally Accepted Accounting Principles)–approved category of fund transfers from the college to the foundation. This accounting technique effectively removes those costs from the cost-of-fundraising equation because you recoup them by the offsetting reimbursement from the college.

Second, after the college and the foundation reach a basic understanding on cost sharing, the two partners may decide that an additional position, such as a major gift officer, will be funded jointly. Some state college–affiliated foundations currently engage in this practice. It is even possible for the foundation executive director position, the college's chief development officer, to be funded jointly. This practice, unlikely as it may seem, allows the executive director the option of being a foundation employee. It may be considered because of constraints inherent in the college hiring practice: salary caps, hiring methodology, and so on.

Shifting personnel costs to the foundation is a risky practice, and I do not generally recommend it. First, the practice increases foundation-funded fundraising costs beyond those of comparable foundations unless pass-throughs offset personnel costs. Second, the dual reporting and dotted line reporting relations can get sticky. Third, the college leadership may not accept the standing of the foundation executive director as a full partner in leadership and may even attempt to deny the incumbent the normal prerogatives of leadership team participation, staff supervision of college employees, budgeting, encumbering funds, and so on. Finally, unlike the college governing board, a foundation board has no experience, and no systems in place, to supervise and evaluate a chief executive officer.

Conflicts arise if there are disagreements between the foundation and the college on the question of executive authority. The president may not accept a foundation with operational capacities. In my research I came across a lawyer's brief from 1981, an era when hospitals were establishing foundations. On the topic of potential pitfalls of interorganizational reporting relationships, the attorney wrote:

Many hospital chief executives resist corporate restructuring because the development of new organizations/corporations diminishes direct CEO control over operations. The traditional pyramid management structure (prevalent in most hospitals today) is interrupted and middle management becomes more visible and responsible. Many CEO's will actively resist this loss of operational control.

College–foundation partnerships can institute practices such as formal dual-reporting responsibility and CEO input on performance evaluations to minimize such anxieties. The arrangement of a foundation-employed executive director can work, but the president's commitment to the deal must be unequivocal and actively supported by the college administration at all levels.

The employment of development officers is another matter. Without higher-level management responsibilities, they constitute far less of threat to the management prerogatives of the college. In many community colleges, they are not exempt employees, but are instead members of a collective bargaining organization. A unionized development officer is a virtual oxymoron, yet the arrangement exists in some public colleges. Development professionals at traditional nonprofits would just shake their heads upon hearing that the college development officer is a Teamster!

Some college unions, especially in four-year universities, have a fairly strong professional orientation. For example, the employee may be able to work more than forty hours a week without requiring compensatory time or overtime. Still, these concessions to a true professional-grade position are incomplete. In two-year colleges, the union options are sometimes even more restrictive, choking the development process in significant ways. In some, employees "bid" on development positions for which they are presumptively qualified via broad classifications such as *program director 1*. Or the executive assistant must take an hour break after attending a paid, catered luncheon if business is discussed!

These conditions give rise to the proposition that college-funded positions hired through the foundation can allow true "at will," exempt employment status. On the other hand, relinquishing control is not a prospect that most colleges undertake lightly. However, with new positions, collaborative opportunities may arise. If a deal is struck for the foundation to hire the development officer, it becomes necessary for the foundation to find a way to implement administration of the position. This can be a huge challenge. One solution is to find a company that specializes in temporary placement of professional employees to administer the position. The company may impose a rate structure that charges several percentage points above the cost of salary and benefits to cover its profit margin. Even costs in the range of $5,000 a year per position represent a good deal in lieu of devoting foundation staff time to HR administration. This is *not* a core competency of a college foundation. If that arrangement proves elusive, the foundation can try to affiliate with a nonprofit umbrella group. Count on this arrangement to leave large gaps in the fabric of seamless personnel administration desired by the foundation.

Whatever the result, the public college sector needs to advocate system-wide for changes in the employment status of development officers in a unionized environment. The arrangement is uniquely detrimental to the status of the profession in public colleges. Development officer positions need to be true at-will, exempt, professional positions.

Endnotes

1. CQIN Board of Examiners training, cosponsored by the Continuous Quality Improvement Network and the Center for Institutional Effectiveness™, Datatel, Inc., Fairfax, VA.

2. The national average for public two-year colleges is $1,233,000, based on 159 colleges reporting. This sample represents 13 percent of all colleges in this class and is not necessarily representative of the universe of all public two-year colleges. (See Editors, *The Chronicle of Higher Education*. 2010. Median salaries of faculty and administrators. *The Chronicle of Higher Education, Almanac Issue 2009–2010* 57, no. 1, 22–22.) Actual median salaries for these positions in a two-year public college as of 2009–2010 are chief development officer, $93,812; executive assistant (shown as coordinator, resource development), $47,050; director, annual giving and alumni affairs (shown as annual giving officer, entry level), $52,019; grant writer (shown as director, corporate/foundation relations), $77,978. The table also includes director, annual giving, $63,330.

3. To best understand the discussion that follows, read first "Appendix Q: Expenditure Guidelines and Definitions" in Netherton 2004, 147–154.

4. You'll do okay with a cost-of-fundraising percentage below 30 percent according to the Minnesota Charities Review Council, 25 percent according to charitywatch.org.

References

Chronicle of Higher Education. 2010. Median salaries of faculty and administrators. *The Chronicle of Higher Education. Almanac Issue 2009–2010* 57, no. 1, 22–22.
Collins, J. 2001. *Good to great.* New York: HarperBusiness.
Collins, J. 2005. *Good to great and the social sectors.* Boulder, CO: Author.

Collins, J., and Porras, J. 1994. *Built to last*. New York: HarperBusiness.

Council for Aid to Education (CAE). 2010. *2009 Voluntary support of education*. New York: Council for Aid to Education, Table 6.

Higher Learning Commission. n.d. Academic Quality Improvement Program (AQIP). http://www.hlcommission.org/aqip-home/ (accessed February 18, 2011).

Klingaman, S. A. 2004. Strategic visioning: Process to plan. Presented to Dunwoody College of Technology, University of Minnesota Carlson School of Management education series, Minneapolis, MN, October.

Netherton, R. (ed.). 2004. *CASE management and reporting standards* (3rd ed.). Washington, DC: Council for Advancement and Support of Education.

Northern California Community Services Council, Inc. 1995. *Understanding outcomes*. San Francisco: NCCS/United Way of the Bay Area.

O'Connell, B. 1987. Fund raising. *Nonprofit Management Series 7*. Washington, DC: Independent Sector.

Rose, J., and Peirce, S. 2005. Applying the discipline of "execution." Presented at CASE V Conference, Chicago, December 12.

8

SELLING THE PLAN

Whether you are new to the college or have held your position for years, selling the plan will be a challenging assignment. You are asking the leadership to commit significant new resources to what historically may have been a low-yield activity. Some risks are involved, for both the college and the foundation. The CFO may be especially wary about spending more on development. You will be asking the college to commit to this investment based on comparison with results achieved at other schools. Some colleges are resistant to the practice of benchmarking, figuring no college is really a valid comparison, or *comp*, especially if the comps are raising a lot more money than your college.

You have already involved your president and CFO in conversations related to planning this initiative. The president has already acknowledged that development, at least in theory, could become an institutional priority—and the CFO has heard the message. You have involved your board "kitchen cabinet" in planning meetings, during which they offered their opinions on the ideas you presented. We will assume you have identified and cultivated several influential board members as believers in the plan's potential. In this phase, you will need to muster all of the early stage capital you have amassed to lead the board and the president to a decision to launch.

First-Round Deliberations

Once you have completed the strategic plan and the case for support, it is time to produce the collateral materials needed to sell the plan. Less is more; think business presentations. Board members appreciate data presented in the form of color charts and graphs (see Appendix E for examples in black and white). These are relatively easy to produce using Microsoft Excel templates. The kit should include:

- a case statement;
- a strategic plan with goals and objectives, in outline form;
- color charts and graphs containing baseline performance and projected outcomes;
- a Year 1 summary budget;
- a multiyear revenue and expense chart; and
- a PowerPoint presentation of these items.

Plan to take roughly six months to sell the plan, including two board meetings, one to present the initiative and one to decide on a course of action. Get the president's feedback on draft-stage presentations. Ask for advice. Ask when you should brief the leadership team on the plan. This is a strategic decision, because leadership team support is crucial to internal college acceptance of the plan. Make sure you have obtained broadly communicated *support in concept* from the president before publicizing the initiative.

Next, complete the process of benchmarking and soliciting external input. Create a *lunch summary*, less than ten minutes in length, that summarizes the entire endeavor. Meet with development professionals you respect to solicit their input. You might want to avoid peers from underperforming development shops. Instead, use the VSE survey to identify comparable institutions that raise more money than yours. Ask a CDO from one of these shops to act as a *benchmarking buddy.*

Make a list of ten comparable schools that have raised more money than your college. Base your comps on similar enrollment, college budget, and geographical characteristics. Check out colleges that belong to the Continuous Quality Improvement Network (CQIN), because adherents to quality improvement methodology tend to embrace the concept of benchmarking. Plan to take a trip to visit a benchmark college for a day, and then follow up with phone and email conversations.

Seek out a local consultant with extensive grassroots fundraising expertise. Consider a low-cost, limited-term engagement consisting of personal consultation with you and your board, materials review, and the option of a consultant presentation to a board committee and the entire board. Use the consultant sparingly at this stage of the process; this is your initiative and you are the driver. Make this clear to your prospective consultant. Part of a consultant's business is to *improve* development officers, but at this point you must be perceived as the leader.

Explain to potential consultants that upon adoption of advancement as a top college priority, the consultant involved with the initiative could be engaged to provide board development and fundraising training. This may help you secure a more reasonable bid for the initial engagement.

Meet with the chair of the board and the college president to hash out the details of the proposed development initiative. Request their approval of:

- strategic goals and objectives;
- timelines;
- personnel recommendations; and
- resources required.

Regardless of how the details are decided, I recommend that the chair and the president agree in advance that the development initiative will become a *top five priority* (I actually prefer *top three*) for the college and the president.

Convene a wrap-up meeting of the kitchen cabinet to seek unanimous informal approval of the plan. Do this before submitting it for consideration by other appropriate committees, as indicated by your board structure. This should include the Development and Finance committees. The final committee presentation should be a formal one to the Executive Committee.

Ask the Executive Committee to approve the proposal in concept—as a viable direction for the foundation—for formal review and consideration by the full board at the first of two meetings devoted to the topic. The Executive Committee itself may need to devote two meetings to the topic, one convened as a special-focus, single-agenda-item meeting. Consider inviting a consultant to present an expert's perspective on the initiative to the Executive Committee. By this point, your board cheerleaders for the initiative will need to secure the support of the chair, who presumably will drive the board's consideration of the proposal.

On the internal front, ask the president to host a meeting with the CFO to hear your presentation. Having a board presence at the meeting could be useful to reassure the CFO that the board will step up to the plate on this issue. Consider presentations to other leadership structures within the college to vet the proposal more thoroughly, but don't advertise the proposal all over town. This is a strategic leadership imperative sanctioned by the office of the president, as opposed to an initiative subject to consensus at every level of college advisory mechanisms. What's more, the proposal could be controversial in its demand for additional college resources, particularly if the foundation's record is a little spotty. Ask the president to help you set the tone regarding the importance of the initiative to the college.

Winning Board Support

Chances are you will be asking the board to change a longstanding pattern of participation to that of far greater support and commitment. Rest assured that you are within your rights as a steward of the college's mission. *The Handbook of College and University Trusteeship*, a classic in the field, states, "Obtaining resources is a basic responsibility of board members" (Radcock and Jacobson 1980, 265). But that doesn't mean it will come easily, especially if you spell out what will be expected of the board in the new regime. You may consider a consultant for this role. Classic development theory abounds with tradition and precedent emphasizing the fundraising role of the board. We sugarcoat it from time to time; we talk about being ambassadors and "opening doors," and that is all true. Nevertheless, in an aggressive major gift program, your board is your first pool of prospects.

Consider these words of wisdom from Brian O'Connell in *The Board Member's Book*:

- "One of the greatest problems with fundraising and within nonprofit organizations generally is the confusion between the fundraising roles for board and staff."
- "The campaign . . . is always a board function."
- "All trustees should be expected to contribute and to raise funds within their means and contacts."
- "The board is accountable and the board leads." (1985, 8–9)

This wisdom is not new. O'Connell wrote these words in 1985. The organization that aims to excel in fundraising enters a time-honored tradition of board ownership and responsibility. We cannot sidestep the importance of board acceptance of this responsibility.

At the board meeting, the chair should summarize the planning process to date. The chair should invite a board advocate for the initiative to introduce the topic. You have a choice of two, maybe three, possible presenters. The preferred format is to have a kitchen cabinet member deliver a twenty-minute PowerPoint presentation. I have seen this work to powerful effect. It requires that the board member *get it*, believe in it, want to sell it, and possess strong presentation skills.

In some colleges, the president may be the best choice. If the president is a believer, half the battle is won. If neither a board member nor the president is the right fit, consider the stature and presentation skills of the

CDO. If these are all high-caliber, let "the expert" do the job. But I still prefer a board presenter. If the board presenter is the chair, so much the better—*if* he or she is a strong presenter who believes in the strategy. Whatever the choice, be it president, board member, or development executive, someone must *own* the initiative. That individual should be prepared to be accountable for managing the deliberative process in its entirety. An involved chair is an invaluable ally in this effort. On the other hand, passive or lukewarm support is deadly support.

After the presentation to the full board, expect a litany of questions followed by spirited discussion. This may turn out be one of the best discussions the board has had in a long time. Engage in the process without defensiveness, in an open and engaging manner, acknowledging reservations, in the spirit of open inquiry. *Let the process take its course.* Don't talk too much; listen instead. At the end of the day, it will be the board members who will sway each other. This is not something that can be railroaded through to approval. The board's first reaction may simply be that of trepidation, of not knowing. That is why we are going to let these ideas percolate for a while before requesting board approval.

To conclude the discussion, have the board chair formally summarize the consensus, or lack thereof, listing areas of agreement, areas where members have requested more information, and areas of nonagreement, should they exist. *The chair should conclude by stating the expectation that the board will reach a decision on the proposal at the next meeting.* Otherwise, consideration could go on forever. The chair should enumerate a few of the decision steps that will be taken in the interim, such as additional meetings with the president, reconvening the kitchen cabinet, another meeting of the Executive Committee, and so on.

After the board meeting, follow up on the questions and reservations that arose. Summarize the proceedings in an email and send it out in the chair's name. Avoid sending any long documents as attachments, especially anything with a lot of numbers on it. You want the board to focus on the big picture, and sharing too many details may well be counterproductive.

Above all, debrief with your board partners and the president, preferably with the chair and the president in the same room. This is necessary to instill a shared sense of what transpired, and where the board stands in its deliberations. Seek specific commitments of follow-up calls the president and chair will make to privately address the concerns of those whose opinions matter the most, especially those who are waffling.

The goal is to create a sense of inevitability to the whole endeavor, because individual members nearly always defer to a perceived inevitability of support in the end, even if they hold private reservations. They want to know that the leadership will take responsibility for the ultimate course of action and will actively work to achieve success. Upon hearing that commitment, they will usually rally behind the initiative and even begin to speak as if they were believers all along. Board thinking at this level is usually *groupthink* of the most amorphous kind. Never assume you know what they think.

Second-Round Deliberations

In the intervening months strengthen the case and build consensus with individual members. Address the substantive questions they raised. Did the "Who pays for what?" question come up? Was there notable dissension? Were your numbers credible? Do they seem to want to do this if perceived barriers are removed, or are you more or less dragging them along? Are they, or is the college, reluctant to invest? This is quite common. Prepare a second PowerPoint presentation of five to eight minutes that specifically addresses those discussion points upon which the board spent the bulk of its deliberations. A skilled board presenter will deliver this presentation at the next meeting.

Here is the optimal outcome: the college commits to funding the plan and the board commits to raising the funds. Chances are the president and the CFO have not yet committed; they are waiting to see what the board will say. Now is the time to "close" them. "*If* the board will commit to raising the funds," you ask, "then will the college agree to fund it?" If the answer is "No" or "Maybe," you have arrived at the most sensitive moment of the selling phase. Ask what level of stretch commitment the college would be willing to make. Take that information to your consultant and solicit his or her advice.

Do you scale the initiative down, putting off hiring the grant writer for a year, and reduce your revenue projections accordingly? Do you consider asking the board to fund half of a position? These questions depend on the facts that bear on your program. If you raised $100,000 in unrestricted funds last year, could you possibly commit 30 percent of that amount to a position? That seems unlikely. Is the board sitting on an unrestricted reserve? If so, how does it regard those funds? Understand that any precedents you set here will probably come back to haunt you in the future. Creative thinking is required.

Assemble the best final proposal you can and put it in front of the president and the Executive Committee for a decision. Ask the committee to formally recommend it to the full board for adoption. It is time for the CDO *to ask for the order*, backed up by the board leadership. Assemble the launch dates, and the dates by which you will hire for new positions. An implementation delay caused by this occurring at the "wrong time in the college budget cycle" could set you back a year. Let's assume you get the two decisions you need, one by the president and one by the Executive Committee. Now it's back to the full board.

The chair frames the discussion, the PowerPoint presentation conveys the proposed plan, and the motion is presented for discussion. The president will express the college's definitive stance on the project. The discussion leads to the motion and a vote is taken. With any luck, you win. That is to say, the college wins, and, ultimately, the students you serve win. Pat yourself and your colleagues on the back. A tectonic shift in the future direction of the college has occurred.

After the Decision

In the aftermath of a decision by the board, expect to address some final questions posed during its deliberations. The CDO will assume responsibility for addressing those and for bringing the solutions to the attention of the Executive Committee.

Devise a modified presentation for the leadership team and other leadership groups within the college apprising them that the new initiative has been adopted. Even if middle-management support for the initiative is passive, it is far superior to apathy, or worse, opposition. Opposition differs from quiet griping. There will always be those who are unsympathetic to the development function. The key is to allow the voices of those who are sympathetic to the plan to be heard. They are sure to outnumber the naysayers.

Colleges and their foundations can be extremely reticent to take what are perceived to be major financial risks when the future rewards are as yet unknown. Building this type of consensus takes time. You cannot rush the deliberative process when the proposed course of action is such a departure from past practice.

It all comes down to building a compelling case for the proper role of advancement within a two-year college. If the case is compelling, eventually most boards and college leadership teams will embrace it. Keep attention firmly focused on the process over a matter of months to increase your chances of success. And remember the Rule of Three. Make sure the launch of a major new development initiative remains the top priority within your own office while you formulate and sell the plan. Sometimes the process is the product. This is one of those times.

References

O'Connell, B. 1985. *The board member's book*. Washington, DC: Foundation Center.
Radcock, M., and Jacobson, H. K. 1980. Securing resources. In *The handbook of college and university trusteeship*, ed. R. T. Ingram. San Francisco: Jossey-Bass.

PART TWO

WORKING THE PLAN

9

LAUNCH!

With an institutional commitment to the plan in hand, the real work begins. We'll begin by filling the seats on the bus. You might want to consult *Good to Great*, chapter 3, to establish the proper mind-set with which to fill those seats. In *Good to Great and the Social Sectors*, Collins offers notable insight:

> In the social sectors, where getting the wrong people off the bus can be more difficult than in a business, early assessment mechanisms turn out to be more important than hiring mechanisms. There is no perfect interviewing technique, no ideal hiring method; even the best executives make hiring mistakes. You can only know for certain about a person by working with that person. (2005, 15)

Personnel

Hiring a Chief Development Officer

This book has been oriented primarily toward the CDO as the driver of the bus. But it is possible that a board chair or college president has been driving the process in the absence of a CDO, so we'll take a moment to examine the skill set needed for the top development position. If the position needs to be filled, I recommend looking for candidates with four-year college experience. Given the case we have been making for basing the two-year college program on the four-year model, that is a logical choice. Staffing the position from another department within the college is a nonstarter. We need an experienced development officer, and chances are that you do not have a viable internal candidate.

Familiarity with the collegiate model of advancement is a basic requirement of the CDO position. Your prospects of recruiting a CDO from a community college with a robust program already in place are limited. You may be able to find a viable candidate from a private school or college. Your primary candidate pool might include an experienced academic development professional, major gift officer, associate foundation director, or perhaps an experienced Annual Fund director with some major gift experience, all of whom view this as a step-up move. A secondary target profile might be that of an experienced development officer from elsewhere in the nonprofit sector, preferably with educational advancement experience indicated somewhere on his or her resume. A health care fundraising executive *might* suffice but would probably bring a strong pro–special event bias to the mix, and that is not our model. (You probably could not afford the health care professional anyway.)

Use of a search firm is highly recommended. Viable candidates whom you can afford may be hard to find. The salary range should be enticing— $90,000 to $100,000 is a good place to start. The preferred job title, assuming the college is doing the hiring, is vice president for advancement/foundation executive director. This title properly elevates the status of the position and most closely resembles that of four-year colleges and universities.

The ideal candidate should be experienced, possess a real passion to attempt a start-up or turnaround, confident, personable, persuasive, somewhat driven, and politically astute. Major gift experience is a must since this CDO will be your major gift officer. Strong systems thinking, strategic thinking, and a thorough familiarity with how development offices operate are required to ensure that the office work flow is managed in an efficient, businesslike manner. Familiarity with donor databases and experience in managing an audit are important for the same reason. You may want to consider that someone coming from a large shop may not have hands-on familiarity in all of these areas.

Experience in managing board relations is another necessity. Associate directors, for example, work actively with their boards. Experience with publications and marketing communications as it relates to development is a plus. The list could go on and on. Most job descriptions for this position usually do, for pages and pages, until, in the end, the strategic focus of the position is lost. Codify the requisite skills into a concise job description with seven to ten broad categories containing five to ten detail entries for each. Then, and this is crucial, weight the activities with percentage of time guidelines, as shown in Table 9.1.

TABLE 9.1
Responsibilities of Chief Development Officer

Responsibilities	*% of Time*
Conduct the major gift solicitation program.	30

1. Implement the major gift program as described in the Action Plan.
2. Make a minimum of ten personal cultivation visits per month.
3. Make fifteen major gift Asks per year.
4. Co-host two president's cultivation breakfasts.
5. Maintain a prospect list with seventy-five qualified major gift prospects.
6. Develop major gift strategies and proposals.
7. Support the president's major gift interactions.
8. Generate reports, documentation, and projections.
9. Manage production of collateral materials.

TIP #23

Assign realistic percentage-of-time calculations
to each category of job description responsibilities.

Hiring processes have an inherent tendency to become beauty contests, especially in an educational bureaucracy. Putting each finalist in front of a group of twelve hiring committee participants only exacerbates the syndrome. The candidate who dazzles the most gets the nod. The hard questions that actually mean something are usually asked only in interviews with no more than three interviewers. You want to elicit dialogue. You want the applicant's guard down. You want thoughtful, nuanced answers to your questions. You want to ask follow-up questions that ferret out the real person behind the suit. This approach may be foreign to the usual search process staffed by a college middle manager who nominally heads a large committee.

The search process should belong almost entirely to the president and the board. The rest is window dressing.

You want someone with an actual track record—a demonstrable, multi-year record of landing gifts and building programs. You want someone who can offer a compelling narrative concerning how a particular development initiative grew over a period of years, including the culture surrounding the effort, the obstacles overcome, the leadership dynamics, the dollar amounts involved, and the ultimate effect of achieving the goal. You want that candidate's references to back up the candidate's accounts with corroborating information. By the way, don't assume you will be able to talk to the candidate's current supervisor. Career explorations can be a death knell for career advancement within a nonprofit organization.

Senior development officers from private schools and colleges may have an incentive plan in place, which may allow for the payment of up to 15 percent of salary in the form of a bonus if a parcel of goals is achieved. These incentives could be institution-wide and/or dependent on overall development outcomes and personal performance. In a public college, this form of compensation probably is prohibited, even if the foundation pays it. Figure that your candidate will ratchet up salary demands to replace some part of what might be expected in income from such an incentive plan. This type of consideration sometimes precipitates a look at having the foundation act as the hiring agency, as problematic as that can be.

Due Diligence on the Part of the CDO Candidate

A successful hire is a two-way street, and mutual due diligence is required to create a viable match. The prospective candidate may not have previous experience within a community college or public education foundation setting. The candidate should perform the following due diligence prior to accepting a position:

- Review the foundation and college annual reports for the preceding three years.
- Review internal fundraising reports for the preceding three years.
- Review the foundation audit for the preceding three years.
- Review the most recent Form 990.[1]
- Review the college advancement and foundation budgets.
- Review the college and foundation strategic plans.
- Research external data such as the VSE report or guidestar.org entry.
- Meet all development staff for a question-and-answer session.

- Determine what development experience the staff possesses.
- Determine what formal development training the staff has received.
- Meet with the members of the Executive Committee of the board.
- Ask about recent consultant engagements by the foundation.

Let's assume the college successfully negotiates all these steps and hires a gifted executive. An outsider coming into the fold, especially one from a private college or school, will face some real challenges dealing with culture and bureaucracy. This will cause problems for almost any Type A development officer with that background. Even an import from a university program may be perplexed by your culture. Why? Because university programs are more ambitious, aggressive, demanding, and institutionalized than the fray the new hire is about to enter.

The president should carefully consider how to pave the way for the new CDO to succeed. The CDO will need generous amounts of the president's time during his or her first months on the job to build a relationship and learn exactly how to execute the plan within an unfamiliar culture. Whatever you do, don't leave a new CDO hanging out there to dry in the new culture. Bureaucratic obstacles to deployment can be deadly—especially anything that smacks of bait-and-switch. The last thing you want is a new CDO with buyer's remorse.

The Incumbent Chief Development Officer

This circumstance is the norm. We discussed earlier some of the actions related to "clearing the deck" that might be necessary. Reviewing percentage-of-time allocations and introducing them into the job description is the first order of business. The object is to reduce the time spent on administration in order to spend it on development activities. The CDO should engage in a self-assessment against the criteria presented in the preceding chapters to establish a firm self-awareness of preparedness to do the job.

CDO percentage-of-time allocations might look like this:

- Major gifts   30%
  - Initiative development
  - Cultivation
  - Solicitation
  - Proposal development

- ○ Prospect identification and qualification
- ○ Working with the president
- General development responsibilities   25%
  - ○ Annual Fund
  - ○ Planned giving
  - ○ Cultivation events
- Management and administration   25%
  - ○ Strategic planning
  - ○ Board relations
  - ○ Reporting
  - ○ Office administration
- Staff supervision   10%
  - ○ Development office meetings
  - ○ Coaching development officers
  - ○ Executive assistant supervision
  - ○ Performance reviews
- College affairs   10%
  - ○ Leadership team
  - ○ Committee work
  - ○ College events

The Executive Assistant

It goes without saying that the CDO has a full-time executive assistant. We discussed the essential nature of this position to development office and executive performance in chapter 4. Let's look at the requisite skills for the position. (Appendix A3 contains a sample job description.) The major categories are:

1. Support of the chief development officer
2. Office management functions, systems, and processes
3. Donor relations activities
4. Database and financial management
5. Development team activities

The job description presents a clear outline of the job, with percentage-of-time allocations attached to each category. Assess current performance in each category and plan for desired improvements. The biggest questions are: Are you staffed as an executive should be? Are you consistently offered assistance with the myriad details you manage, or are you the one supplying reminders on calendar items, calls to be made, checks to be written, and minutes to be ready when needed? If you are making the arrangements, your executive assistant has turned the tables on you and it is your responsibility to realign this relationship. If these things are covered consistently, count your blessings. Thank, praise, and reward your assistant, because you are highly dependent on this person's ability to do the job well.

Inadequate database applications are a common drag on efficiency. In your small shop, this task falls largely to the executive assistant. The demanding nature of database administration is item number one in my case against executive assistant responsibility for the accounting function. Asking a generalist to handle both is almost always untenable. Consider database training. Nothing eats up hours like attempting to perform database functions without sufficient training.

Another critical area of responsibility is that of managing relations with board members and donors. The executive assistant must know everybody and must maintain appropriate, regular communication with the board and donors on your behalf. In addition, the executive assistant must be adept at managing event logistics.

Hiring a Director of Annual Giving and Alumni Relations

There is no substitute for a qualified professional in this position. The recommended profile is that of an emerging career professional with about three years of experience in an academic development shop. (See Appendix A1 for a job description.) An associate director of annual giving from a larger shop would be ideal. Expect a fair bit of position-to-position movement in the work history of the entry-level development professional. Employers don't always show these development officers the love they deserve. People move on and up in the hopes of achieving greater success, recognition, and experience. Burnout is a career hazard in these positions, experienced in the face of unrealistic goals and the fact that the meter always goes back to zero at the beginning of each fiscal year. A secondary target might be an annual giving specialist from elsewhere in the nonprofit sector, but there is no substitute for experience in a school or college. Occasionally you might find an alumni relations coordinator who wants to break into the development side of the business.

Look for a demonstrated record of measurable growth from year to year, from 10 to 20 percent in emerging programs, and 4 to 10 percent in mature ones. Look for formal development training. The requisite personal attributes include persistence, likeability, drive, intelligence, communication skills, writing ability, and the ability to work the plan. Basic aptitudes should include personal solicitations, written appeals, targeted mail appeals, short proposals, phonathons, and employee annual giving. Direct mail experience is less of a focus in our model, but it can't hurt.

Expect qualified individuals to be in high demand. Assume they will have other offers. Sell them on the nature of the experience they will gain: access to the board, being part of a launch, staffing the Annual Fund Committee, organizing an alumni association board, and the career benefits they will derive from taking an Annual Fund from modest beginnings to maturity.

The alumni relations component of this position comprises a relatively small portion of the job description, perhaps 15 percent. The development officer will spend this time primarily on organizing and managing the alumni association board, managing an alumni relations initiative, and staging several alumni events each year.

Here is a key to closing the deal with a desirable candidate: offer the individual personal attention and the ability to try new things, devoid of micromanagement. Make it clear during the interview that a comprehensive strategic planning process has transpired and that it will be the job of this development professional to work the plan.

Advertise online through existing nonprofit channels such as the Association of Fundraising Professionals (AFP) and through the job listings in your local metropolitan paper or online. Expect to spend two to three months on the search. Plan to encounter a number of "tire kickers"—Annual Fund specialists appear to fantasize a lot. If the process takes longer than that, reevaluate your salary range.

The Incumbent Development Officer

This circumstance is trickier, especially if you, the CDO, are new. The first question is: Is this a development assistant with an administrative focus or an actual development officer? The second question is: Is this an effective development officer? If the incumbent is primarily an administrative assistant and you already have an executive assistant, you have a problem on your hands. Using Collins's rules about the bus, use reclassification of the job description as justification to transfer the individual to another position within the college that can make better use of the person's administrative talents. The revenues of your small shop cannot begin to justify the luxury of two administrative staff members. If you are a new CDO, you may "use up a bullet" or two on this objective.

If the answer to the second question is an unqualified yes, we have a different equation altogether. In this case, even if the development officer has not previously been successful in terms of the bottom line, that could be due at least partially to a defective plan. And we know who bears responsibility for the plan. The development officer may have run an event like clockwork, selling tickets and tables like there was no tomorrow, all of which would be a good sign. He or she may have obtained mediocre results on a first try at a phonathon. If a deficient phonathon plan was well executed, mediocre results may not be the development officer's fault.

The central question is: Can this development officer close gifts, deal with any constituency, and manage multifaceted programs independently? Can this development officer run an employee annual giving campaign or phonathon *on his or her own*? If not, you don't have what you need. For the incumbent with demonstrated potential, I recommend formal training such as that provided by CASE, AFP, and especially The Fund Raising School. For the incumbent with nothing but potential, a training plan should be the first order of business.

Hiring a Grant Writer

In considering the hire of a grant writer, you might begin by reviewing the job description in Appendix A2. It tells you pretty much everything you need to know about what is required for the position. Verify writing samples and ask that funders and coworkers be included on the list of references. Request a detailed list of grants secured. Explore how the candidate feels about the need to produce a relatively high volume of proposals. You need a grant writer who is not above submitting a large number of small scholarship proposals to local businesses in addition to the big, prestigious grants you hope to win.

Determine whether the candidate has the skills to write master templates for big grants, or whether you will need to write those yourself. The grants officer is charged with managing the ongoing process of submitting a large volume of tailored proposals to foundations, corporations, organizations, and businesses. We are mostly talking about the need for a strong output manager in this position rather than a proposal development genius. An individual who is astute at recognizing compelling programs within the college and matching them to a well-researched funding base is ideal. A minimum of three to five years' experience is recommended.

It may be advisable to make this a one-year, renewable position if you do not know your foundation and formal corporate markets that well. Not every college can sustain this position. You want grant writers to raise roughly twice the amount of their salaries in grants during the first year. That should escalate to three to four times the salary over the course of the next couple of years. Anything less makes it a position you can't afford.

Major Gift Officer

Maybe your strategic plan calls for a major gift officer, because you believe the grant writer option is not for you, or you have already achieved significant success with major gifts and you want to take it to the next level. I would expect that you have identified a pool of major gift prospects that will justify this investment, knowing these may not pay off for a couple of years.

Here is the secret for major gift officers. Get them out of the office and keep them out of the office. Determine whether they will be calling primarily on corporate or individual prospects. Coordinate their duties with your own major gift portfolio. (You will always remain a major gift officer, as will the president.) I am going to save considerations related to a "by the numbers" approach for the chapter on major gifts, so refer to chapter 12 for considerations that will help you refine your search and develop interview questions.

Do you want a major gift officer who is also a grants expert? Don't count on it. The skill sets are independent, and you may find that your "grant writer/major gift officer" is always in the office working on proposals.

Alumni Relations

Unless you are already raising a bundle, hold off on hiring an alumni relations specialist. When ready, you can augment the efforts of the director of annual giving and alumni relations with a half-time alumni relations specialist. Often, you can hire a recent college graduate for this position.

The current thinking in many community colleges is that they have to somehow get a large number of alumni back on campus to "do something" or somehow be engaged, and only then will they begin to give. Not so. You can do a lot to engage alumni, but drive it from the development side. The key to affordable, doable alumni relations in a small shop is focus, focus, focus. This is the approach to alumni relations employed at Dunwoody College of Technology—even when it was raising $5 million a year. Before you invest money in untested alumni relations activities, try a little reunion experiment to gauge alumni interest.

TIP #24

Invite alumni who give to the phonathon to a special
reception with the president. *Invite them by phone.*

Budgeting

The key to strategic budgeting is aligning resources to goals. To construct a
detailed budget, you have to examine the nature of your actual activities. To
emphasize cultivation in your mix of activities, spend less money on mailing
things to people and more on engaging them—less four-color, more food
and drink. To budget your gala cultivation event, establish how much you
will spend on high-end catering. To budget your phonathon, recognize that
part of getting students to show up every day at 5:30 p.m. is to *feed them*.
This costs money. The CDO and president, particularly the latter, will need
an entertainment budget, and your board committees will need refresh-
ments. Food and beverages are the social lubricants of a good development
operation. Table 9.2 illustrates how two different line-item budgets might
look.

Activity by activity, consider the actual parameters of the work and
assign costs that will give you the resources you need to get the job done, as
shown in Table 9.3.

Areas of special focus within the budget include travel, training and
development, conferences, professional memberships, and meals. Early stage
programs need to keep costs in line with revenue. You can't afford (and
don't need) four-color brochures for every program you pitch. You can't

TABLE 9.2 Line-Item Budget for Phonathon	
Food for 10 people: $60/night × 3 nights × 3 weeks	$540
Compensation: $10/hr × 3 hours × 3 nights × 3 weeks × 10 people	2,700
Cash bonuses	150
Premiums	350
TOTAL	$3,740

TABLE 9.3 Expenses for Recognition Event for 220 Guests	
Catering	$13,500
Hall rental	1,400
Invitations: quantity = 1,200; mail through college at no charge	1,000
Insurance	1,000
Signage	300
Awards	150
Miscellaneous	650
TOTAL	$18,000

afford every subscription, online research service, donor capacity analysis, or donor recognition wall that you might like. Those things, to the extent that they are necessary, come later.

You will need to allocate costs to the college or foundation and determine what pass-throughs might offset foundation costs. With any luck, the budgeting you did as a part of your strategic planning took this into account, establishing firm policies to which each party will adhere.

TIP #25

To emphasize cultivation in your mix of activities, spend less on mailing things to people and more on face-to-face engagement.

Action Plan

If you have already cascaded your strategic plan down to the level of an Action Plan, you are ahead of the game. In this case, all you have to do is plug in the actual dates related to your launch. If you have been authorized to fill positions for which you do not have Action Plan objectives in place, now is the time to create them. If the president or chair drove your strategic planning process and you only have the broad outlines of a plan, now is the time to flesh it out. The Action Plan will keep you on course in launching the programs described in the chapters that follow.

Endnote

1. Form 990s for more than 850,000 organizations can be found at www.guide star.org, sponsored by Philanthropic Research, Williamsburg, Virginia.

Reference

Collins, J. 2005. *Good to great and the social sectors.* Boulder, CO: Author.

10

THE BLUEPRINT OF
AN ANNUAL FUND

This chapter is the heart of Part Two, "Working the Plan," because the Annual Fund is the bedrock on which the advancement program is built. We walk you step-by-step through the various product lines of the Annual Fund that we identified in the strategic plan. These are portrayed in Table 10.1.

We begin by constructing an annual calendar of activities for each activity, based on a July 1 to June 30 fiscal year, as shown in Table 10.2. The calendar months listed indicate those in which the activity is a primary focus.

TABLE 10.1 Annual Fund Product Lines	
Director of Annual Giving: Activities	*Goal*
Board of Directors giving	$30,000
Employee annual giving	25,000
Phonathon	8,000
Giving clubs	20,000
Board-inspired giving	20,000
Scholarships	50,000
Other	2,000
In honor/memorial	5,000
Subtotal	**$160,000**
Grant writer: Grants (annual)	$90,000
TOTAL	**$250,000**

TABLE 10.2	
Annual Fund Calendar	
Director of Annual Giving: Activities	*Calendar Months*
Board of Directors giving	July–October
Employee annual giving	August–September
Phonathon	September–October
Giving clubs	November–June
Board-inspired giving	October–June
Scholarships	July–June
Other	July–June
In honor/memorials	July–June
Grant writer: Grants (annual)	
Grants (annual)	July–June

Planning and residual efforts expand the parameters of each. Why the calendar focus? Because it helps prevent the director of annual giving from trying to do everything at once. Focused activity trumps scattered activity. If you like, you can represent this as a color-coded calendar or a color-coded Gantt chart.

Unrestricted Operating Support Versus Scholarships

Let's dispel one community college fundraising myth right now. That would be the tendency for community college programs to restrict their Asks exclusively to funding scholarships. I am not sure how the practice originated, but it is pervasive today. It probably arose from the perception that the state funded everything else. Perhaps it relates to a fundamental self-doubt about having a viable philanthropic case. In any case, I have seen system documents that equate scholarship support with the term *disbursement,* as if there was no possibility of even considering any other type of support!

The mania for scholarships is strange given that community college tuitions are much lower than those of their four-year counterparts. I have heard financial aid officers make the case that community college scholarships should reach the threshold of 50 percent of tuition just to attract student interest. The case for scholarship support was made with far more emphasis at a community college that charges $4,300 a year than at a private two-year college that charges $14,000, though the student bodies of both institutions were demographically comparable.

Scholarships are *not* synonymous with the mission of a college foundation; they are merely one option for support to the college. Here is a corollary: if you ask for unrestricted support you will receive it. Unrestricted dollars are precious. They are essential in helping the foundation to fulfill its mission. They allow flexibility of purpose. They allow the foundation to disburse funds in support of a variety of initiatives that may be more strategic than scholarships. This includes ramping up development activities.

Knowing when and how to request unrestricted annual support through the Annual Fund is an essential capacity to develop if it is not already in place. Knowing when and how to ask for unrestricted support is an art that comes with experience and practice. As Jim Collins points out in *Good to Great and the Social Sectors*, "Restricted giving misses a fundamental point: to make the greatest impact on society requires first and foremost a great organization, not a single great program (2001, 25).

Armed with an awareness that unrestricted dollars trump scholarship dollars, the development officer must evaluate the following to arrive at a judgment regarding the nature of the Ask:

- Giving history
- Prospect type
- Degree of "warmth" toward the cause
- Degree of identification with the overall mission
- Degree of identification with the circumstances of students
- Experience with fellow donors
- Motivation toward named gifts

If a prospect has given to a scholarship program in the past and is not sufficiently warm to the overall mission of the college, but instead displays a direct emotional connection with students—or if the prospect represents a business that might value the recognition—I would pitch the scholarship. I know I can sell scholarships by focusing on the financial plight of students. But I can also sell the overall mission of the college. And I can sell the unique benefits I have built into Annual Fund support to the college.

By making an annual operating grant to the college, the college foundation can claim credit for:

- overall support of the mission;
- support for student activities;
- support for faculty; and
- support for student services.

This approach allows the college foundation to expand its horizons to address a greater range of college needs.

The foundation may want to fund specific initiatives such as an emergency support to students fund. In Minnesota, one such fund, known as Random Acts of Kindness, has become the specific focus of one family foundation. This fund provides emergency assistance grants to keep students enrolled when they need a cash grant to deal with a hardship such as the loss of housing, a car repair, or emergency child care.

Some operating support is restricted by department yet is not restricted to scholarships. This arrangement is most common in four-year programs and technical colleges. Restricted support is fine, but do not restrict gifts unnecessarily. Do so when you need to in order to land the gift. Some development officers think that a scholarship pitch trumps an operating support pitch and will lead to a larger gift. This is not necessarily the case. Most of the $5,000 Annual Fund gifts I secured were unrestricted because the Ask was unrestricted.

TIP #26

Have the dean of the department receiving a significant restricted gift send a second acknowledgment on departmental letterhead.

Still, scholarships comprise the lion's share of the Annual Fund. The percentage should be around 60 percent of funds raised. Yes, only 60 percent—if you ask for unrestricted support. This is a demonstrated, transferable rule. Don't assume this will leave your scholarship fund short. The foundation board can always disburse unrestricted funds as scholarships. The board can even target these funds as scholarships for those hard-to-get scholarships, such as those for part-time or adult students.

Colleges that do not ask properly for unrestricted operating support can get into a bind, forcing them to impose "levies" on scholarship Asks. I know one state university that informs its donors that a certain percentage of each scholarship gift will be directed to unrestricted operating support. That is not a clean Ask. It creates an accounting headache and detracts from the scholarship Ask itself. A scholarship donor wants 100 percent of the gift to support the student. Even disbursement gets messy. A $1,000 gift that yields a $900 scholarship is a nonstarter in my opinion. And asking the donor for $1,100 to fund a $1,000 scholarship seems like a tax, like overhead, to the donor.

TIP #27

Secure unrestricted operating support by
asking the right prospects for it.

In my experience, a number of Annual Fund product lines will yield each of the three types of support in various proportions. Results will vary depending on the amount of emphasis put on restricted departmental gifts and on special initiatives such as emergency assistance grants. Table 10.3 includes some sample results you can achieve if you promote unrestricted Asks. Primary prospect groups for unrestricted support Asks include boards of directors, employees, phonathon prospects, and giving club prospects.

TABLE 10.3
Anticipated Unrestricted Versus Restricted Giving by Source

Activity	Unrestricted (%)	Scholarship (%)	Restricted (%)
Board of Directors giving	70	30	0
Employee annual giving	60	30	10
Phonathon	60	20	20
Giving clubs	90	10	0
Board-inspired giving	70	30	0
Scholarships	0	100	0
Other	50	30	20
In honor/memorials	80	20	0
Grants	20	60	10

Board of Directors Giving

Every foundation board must give with 100 percent participation. Board participation rates are publicized in proposals to foundations and to the staff and faculty during the employee annual giving campaign, and in annual reports to the community. The goal is to realize the maximum amount of support in the most efficient manner.

TIP #28

Kick off the Annual Fund campaign with board of directors giving in the first month of the fiscal year.

Begin the fiscal year with board of directors giving, to "prime the pump" and put some numbers on the board during July, the slowest month of the fiscal year. In our model, board giving comprises between 12 and 15 percent of the Annual Fund goal. The chair of the Annual Fund Committee makes the pitch during a July board meeting. The CDO determines Ask amounts using the guidelines of past giving as well as the overall goal of making board giving meaningful. I like to start with a minimum Ask of $1,000 per member. Board Annual Fund Ask amounts are commonly between $1,000 and $5,000. Any amount above that is all the better.

Thirty thousand dollars plus would be a normal yield from a board of twenty members. In fact, this is a conservative estimate. This is their personal giving, not the dollars members leverage from their companies. It does not matter whether you include or exclude ex officio members in the totals as long as you are consistent in your categories and avoid overlaps. I exclude ex officio staff members from the board totals to include them with employee annual giving.

Here is how to make a group pitch at a board meeting: The Annual Fund Committee chair hands out personalized pledge cards containing a specific Ask amount. The chair explains that board members will have eleven months to fulfill their pledges. The chair requests that board members hand in their pledge cards at the meeting if possible. This will prevent the director of annual giving from having to chase down board members individually for their gifts over the ensuing months. You want to report 100 percent participation as soon as possible. By all means, encourage gifts of securities.

Occasionally you will encounter board members who have made previ-ous multiyear major gift pledges, which may have been accepted without consideration of future annual support. Discuss these cases with the Annual Fund Committee chair. Ask the board member to make a separate Annual Fund gift. If the board member is reluctant to give more, you can request permission to designate a portion of the pledge payment as an Annual Fund gift. You will need to discount the major gift portion of the pledge in terms of its fund designation, but that's okay. Annual Fund support precedes major gift or campaign support. Observing this rule demonstrates your com-mitment to the Annual Fund and to the efforts of your director of annual giving.

Observing the primacy of the annual gift will prevent many problems from emerging in the coordination of efforts between annual giving and major gifts, and later, campaign gifts. At CASE conferences you will often hear presentations from four-year college Annual Fund directors who are wrestling with a seeming competition between the two initiatives. Taking the approach outlined here will prevent that bifurcation from emerging. It will also enhance the sense of team effort between Annual Fund and major officers.

If you have difficulty reaching the board Annual Fund goal, it is some-times an indication that something is wrong at the board level—unless you simply miscalculated the goal. Most likely, the problem lies in not making giving expectations clear. You will need to enlist your Annual Fund Commit-tee and chair to have private conversations with any members who do not understand that it is their obligation to give. If you are serious about the Annual Fund, then you are serious about board of directors giving. Board giving is where college philanthropy begins.

Employee Annual Giving

Employee annual giving is another mainstay of the Annual Fund. Workplace giving has come a long way from the old United Way campaigns in which the byword was, "Fair share or fresh air."[1] As a young development officer starting out in a hospital foundation shop, I dreaded employee annual giv-ing. It was just "balloon season" to me. You see, my supervisor thought employee annual giving was all about "hoopla"—balloons, banners, and thermometers. So every morning it would be my sworn duty to "refresh the balloons" I had placed earlier throughout the hospital. Among the gowns and gurneys, gliding amid concerned family members and busy doctors and nurses, I would go, wheeling my helium tank and holding my Mylar balloons. My early, awkward experiences with balloons led me to conclude that what faculty and staff want is not *hoopla*, but *mission*.

What Faculty and Staff Want to Hear

- That the foundation is 100 percent devoted to furthering the mission of the college
- That the foundation is increasing its support to the college
- That the foundation is investing in critical new labs, equipment, and college improvements
- That the foundation is partnering with faculty members to raise funds for the initiatives that mean the most to them
- That when the dean of student life told the foundation that more money was needed for the student emergency assistance fund, the development staff secured a 50 percent increase in funding for that fund
- That the foundation shares faculty aspirations to increase scholarship funding and has a detailed plan in place to do so
- That the foundation is a good steward of funds raised
- That the board members demonstrate that they care about their work
- That the foundation is not "political"
- That the funds they donated previously were well spent
- That the CDO is their partner
- That the board is their benefactor

Convey this message, in person, to your staff and they will give. How best to do it? Try a single group encounter with the greatest number of faculty and staff possible. Many colleges host an academic-year kickoff event, but any mass gathering will do. The primary ingredient you need is access to the entire employee base, or at least the greatest number possible. Figure out how to accomplish that and half the battle is won.

The CDO delivers the message to the assembled faculty and staff in what will be one of the CDO's most important public presentations of the year. The message must be crisp, clear, polished, upbeat, persuasive, and sincere. Mission is the heart of employee annual giving and the CDO is its driver. Frame the presentation with an introduction by the president stating his or her 100 percent support for the initiative and perhaps a testimonial from a faculty leader or the chair of the scholarship selection committee; but the CDO is the driver and the closer. After all, they, the employees, believe this is what you are there for.

Let's look at some of the mechanics of employee giving. The amount of labor invested will determine your results. In a start-up situation, I have sometimes resolved not to pull out all the stops. Why? Because in a situation where community support has been underperforming, it seems unbalanced to focus the entire fundraising arsenal at my disposal on the *captive* stakeholders of the college. Rather, I would like to maintain a margin for growth in employee annual giving to be leveraged and inspired in the future by the growth of community support. I will present the parameters of a basic campaign, along with some additional suggestions, should a more intensive effort be desired.

Setting Goals

We begin by analyzing last year's campaign. What kind of results did you achieve? Who led it? Did employees perceive the campaign to be a priority of the president? How much did you raise? What percentage of the employee base gave?

Table 10.1 shows a modest goal of $25,000, 10 percent of the total Annual Fund goal. Let's say that you are shooting for a participation rate of 27 percent. This is based on your results from last year in which we'll say 20 percent of your 450 employees gave a total of $16,000. That is a pretty good jump: $9,000 and 7 percent improvement in participation. But it is still anemic. As a rule, make it your first goal to get your participation rate to one-third of your employee base. Then, for an employee base of four to five hundred, shoot for revenue of about $33,000.

TIP #29

Set your sights on a threshold of one-third participation in an early stage employee annual giving campaign.

The following year, shoot for 37 percent participation, raising about $40,000. Then, aim for the 50 percent range and plan to raise $50,000. Fifty-fifty; now you are on the boards. Strategically speaking, employee annual giving is an area of rapid potential growth, which makes it an invaluable product line to have in an Annual Fund campaign. Faculty donors have the potential to become quite generous; gifts of $500 to $1,000 are not uncommon. (Likewise for college leadership.) The trick is to get more faculty members to give. Plan to spend more time achieving more modest results with staff departments in which participation has traditionally been lower. Taking your participation rates to the stratosphere of two-thirds or more will require special measures. It is a rare achievement outside of a capital or comprehensive campaign. We'll cover some of those advanced techniques shortly.

Ongoing Pledges

Ongoing pledges are the secret to running efficient employee annual giving campaigns. Use your brochure to spell out that employee annual giving pledges continue until the employee modifies, increases, or cancels the pledge.

TIP #30

Implement ongoing, multiyear, payroll deduction pledges to build the base of employee annual giving participation.

An ongoing base of giving becomes a powerful engine for growth. At this point in the developmental curve, seeking annual upgrades of pledge amounts is a secondary consideration, though you can accomplish that, too, within the multiyear pledge format. The ongoing pledge arrangement also decreases the accounting workload, where formerly each pledge was entered anew at the beginning of each new fiscal year.

Calendar Year Timing

The employee giving campaign should last about three weeks, with a quiet follow-up phase continuing for another two weeks or so. The timing of the employee campaign is subject to a variety of approaches. There must be some kind of lag between the campaign and the beginning of a payroll deduction cycle to allow for the administrative portion of the workload to be accomplished, and for gifts from stragglers to trickle in.

From the accounting standpoint—and this is not insignificant—time your campaign pledge year to coincide with your college and foundation fiscal year. If you do this, you won't have any receivables to report on your audit. This is a good thing, a big time-saver. If the fiscal year begins on July 1, the campaign should begin somewhere between February and April.

One college president told me I was crazy to run an employee campaign in February, the "dead of winter," when he felt morale was at its lowest ebb. Nevertheless, I persisted. I thought I could do it, and sure enough, that campaign achieved 100 percent participation, an almost unheard of result.[2]

TIP #31

Allow the employee annual giving pledge year to coincide with your fiscal year for maximum accounting efficiency.

If you run the employee campaign in the spring, you will have some change in adjunct personnel to deal with come September. Your two primary windows for payroll deduction cycles are July 1 and January 1. Though you could start a payroll deduction cycle on September 1, you cannot run a campaign in the summer for obvious reasons. Most colleges can't possibly process a pledge made on August 22 to appear on a paycheck dated September 14, so we are still left with the two windows. If you run the campaign in late August, you might have to use the January 1 start date. Of course the downside of this arrangement is that come the following September, you will have to contend with all of the adjunct status changes, so it is not without problems either way. All told, I prefer a spring campaign with a July 1 pledge start date.

Preparation

Pave the way for the employee annual giving campaign with an internal report to the employees. I convey this through a multipage letter from the executive director reporting on the status of the foundation, with particular emphasis on areas of interest to the faculty and staff. This goes out as an attachment to an email sent to all employees about a month before the kickoff of the employee campaign. Base it on the format of a report to the community. Here is a sample excerpt:

> This year, the Foundation disbursed more funds to the College than ever before. The Foundation board approved the disbursement of $300,000 for scholarships and program support during the year. This is a 20 percent

increase over the amount disbursed last year. Highlights included the scanning electron microscope for the biology department; the new $50,000 Trustee Scholars program, awarding renewable scholarships to first-year students; and The John Doe Foundation's support for launching The Learning Center.

The heart of the Foundation mission is to seek support from private sources. The amount of private dollars raised increased by 43 percent over the year. Here's how we tracked our results. . . .

The report to employees establishes stewardship, mission, results, and commitment to the college, and it paves the way for the employee presentation to follow. I follow that up with a letter from the president about a week before the kickoff.

You will need an up-to-date list of employees by department to track your results. The development office prepares a color brochure, printed in-house, that conveys the primary messages of the campaign. This, along with the pledge card and return envelope, is the campaign collateral material. Format the material to fit in a #10 envelope.

The CDO approaches each member of the leadership team one to one in advance of the kickoff to ask—or thank him or her—for the ongoing leadership gift. I explain to those signed up for ongoing pledges that I do not take their gift for granted, but instead prefer to touch base with each of them personally and reinforce his or her support. Some give by check, so you will need their renewed gift commitment. Others might be new since last year. Make personal contact with all of them.

The obvious reason for this investment of time is that we want to announce a 100 percent commitment on the part of the college leadership, together with an amount raised, which, it is hoped, will inspire and challenge employees to give generously. During the meeting, be sure to ask college leaders if you, or members of your staff, can attend their division and/or department meetings for small-group, follow-up presentations. Before I meet with the leadership, I ask the president to say a few words about the upcoming campaign, and the importance of leadership gifts, in a leadership team meeting.

Consider naming one senior faculty member and one staff leader to serve as honorary chairs. Their names appear on the brochure. You might ask one or both to say a few words during the kickoff presentation. Ask them to send a few encouraging emails during the campaign reporting on some benchmark achieved while asking employees to turn in their pledge cards.

The Kickoff "Close"

For large-group kickoff presentations, you need at least fifteen minutes to convey the message if you have three speakers. I encourage the immediate return of pledge cards by offering entry into a drawing for all donors on file within twenty-four hours.[3] The premium might be something like an Apple iPod, or some other gadget of the moment. If employees themselves are not iPod users, their children or grandchildren are. Existing donors need do nothing. Their names are entered based on their preexisting pledges. However, I do remind them to consider increasing their gifts. Many do. Development officers and staff assistants are present at the aisles holding envelopes or boxes in which to collect pledge cards. Each employee, upon exiting, must pass a staff member. The intensive approach yields excellent results. Within twenty-four hours, the director of annual giving tallies up the total of existing pledges, leadership gifts, and new pledges to announce an impressive total—and the winner of the iPod.

The Message

I rely upon a message template I devised back in the days of my hospital campaigns. I have tailored it to suit the academic environment:

> *I invite you to take a moment to stand back and regard the mission inherent in preparing young people to create their own futures. The question is: "Can we invest in our own mission?" Yes!*

> *Donors, foundations, trustees all ask, "Do your faculty and staff support you?"*

> *I ask you to join me to make the answer an emphatic "Yes!"*

> *When we as employees consider a charitable gift to the Foundation, we stand back, look at the fundamental mission of our work, and answer the question, "Does this matter?" No one knows better than you that the answer is "Yes."*

> *You are not being asked to give something back to your employer, you are being asked to stand together to support the mission of teaching and learning—changing the lives of those we serve. Please consider the value of this mission in your personal charitable giving plan.*

Educators care deeply for the mission of their life's work. I ask that they consider their family charitable budgets, and as they allocate resources to support their place of worship, their alma maters, their kids' hockey programs, and their other favorite causes, to see if they can't find a place for the mission that is so close to their hearts.

Follow-Up Meetings

Plan to make division and departmental presentations immediately on the heels of the kickoff. Either the CDO and director of annual giving, or just the director, can conduct these as appropriate and as time allows. Having the top development officer present to answer questions is the best option. At faculty meetings, feature foundation activities that benefit academics, particularly the department you are addressing. Announce the amounts raised for departmental scholarships. I made it a point to be familiar with volunteer leadership activities, big gifts restricted to particular departments, high rates of employee annual giving participation, the names of scholarship recipients—anything that will reinforce a strong, active connection between advancement and their worlds.

One final trick: ask the director of annual giving to contact a couple of loyal allies in the group you are addressing to hand in pledge cards at the presentation. Having a couple of "ringers" in the audience increases the peer influence (we'll stay away from peer pressure for now!) so necessary to a successful campaign. In fact, peer influence is probably the primary driver in employee annual giving campaigns. Resistance to giving is not so much a deep-rooted conviction as it is a habit of not giving. We just need a little leverage to break that habit and participation follows.

In a basic campaign, it will prove difficult to meet with every department. For that reason, divisional meetings are preferable. But if we were in a pull-out-all-the-stops campaign, we would leave no meeting unturned.

Dealing with Reservations

The United Way pretty much wrote the book on workplace giving. Its approach to the workplace solicitation, outlined in a classic pamphlet, *Effective Solicitation Skills for Donor Representatives*, produced by the Bay Area United Way, was notable for the simple techniques it presented for dealing with reservations, or objections.[4] Its premise is that objections are a natural part of the process. The pamphlet outlined four steps for dealing with reservations:

- Listen for objections.
  - Listen actively and thoroughly to objections.

- ○ Encourage the donor to communicate by smiling, nodding your head, and maintaining good eye contact.
- ○ Don't appear defensive.
- Restate the objection.
  - ○ This affirms your interest and shows that you understand the objections raised.
  - ○ Restating the objection prepares the donor for your answer. It also gives you a moment to phrase your answer in a positive manner.
- Acknowledge the objection.
  - ○ Use phrases like, "I understand your point" or "I can understand how you feel that way."
  - ○ Use nonverbal acknowledgment like smiling and nodding your head.
- Answer the objection by supplying relevant missing information.
  - ○ Offer context.
  - ○ Give historical details.
  - ○ Set the record straight with facts (and a smile).
  - ○ Acknowledge that the past is never perfect, but you are doing your utmost to be responsive to the mission and you welcome advice and input.
  - ○ Ask if, for the present purposes, we could set a union gripe aside, but that you hope those concerns can be negotiated successfully by the parties involved.
  - ○ Offer to supply missing details at a later date.
  - ○ Return to the need––the *mission*—and ask if the prospect can make the gift in light of the present conversation.

This may sound strange, but I appreciate the voicing of reservations. It means I am actively negotiating the decision to give. Perhaps it is the result of all those years in the hospital, dealing with fifteen hundred employees, some of whom voiced objections with passion. As long as I was confident in my mission (and in truth, I always was), I was free to give the best good-faith answer I could muster. Sometimes my good faith seemed to prompt a gift despite the objection. I was representing, in this moment, philanthropy, not the administration, and it is proper to distance the two during the employee annual giving campaign.

More Follow-Up

With the permission of the president, show your campaign results by department. Occasionally department heads chafe at this practice, but it can be very effective. Offer a catered lunch with the president to the first department that reaches 100 percent participation. (*Do not accept cash gifts, preventing those who would give a dollar in someone else's name from using that gambit.*) Ten days into the campaign, follow up with another letter from the president commending everyone on the results to date and asking those who have not yet responded to make a gift. Round out the campaign with other promotions and giveaways; put up the proverbial thermometer in a prominent place, and you are on your way to completing a smart, quick campaign.

Declare Victory

Upon conclusion of the campaign, tally up the results and publicize your success. Hang a banner or put the results on the college's electronic bulletin board. Thank all those who helped out. Put a notice in your magazine or newsletter and online. You may want to host an ice cream social or some other thank-you event if your budget allows.

By keeping the campaign to a focused length, you have concentrated attention on the effort. Now your director of annual giving can move on to the next project while contributions continue to trickle in. Prepare your spreadsheet for the accounting department well in advance of the date of the first payroll deduction cycle. Your methodical approach leaves you poised to achieve even better results next year. By that time you will have focused your internal communications over the course of the year on building awareness of how the foundation is meeting the needs of the college.

Advanced Techniques

When participation rates of 60 percent and up are required, it becomes necessary to devote significantly more time to the employee campaign. The secret is to recruit departmental-level volunteers, or team captains, for every subunit of the college. In a college of five hundred employees, you will need roughly thirty volunteers. The role of the team captain is to mobilize the support of the employees in an assigned unit. The team captain participates in group presentations made by the director of annual giving, and then follows up with employees in individual meetings during which the team captain directly asks the employee prospect for a gift.

This approach requires the following commitments:

- a significant commitment of time on the part of the development officer;
- training sessions for the team captains; and

- a significant commitment of involvement on the part of team captains.

Most people do not find asking their peers for charitable gifts to be an easy task. The United Way designed the techniques for dealing with reservations expressly for use by team captains. This material represents an invaluable resource to help them prepare for the assignment. The intensive employee campaign model requires that the campaign chairs play an active role in following up with team captains to ensure that they are getting the job done. With benchmark information on hand, it is relatively easy to forecast the ROI the intensive campaign model might produce. If 30 percent of your employee base is contributing $40,000, 60 percent participation might yield $65,000 to $70,000. You should factor in a decrease in the average gift amount when using the intensive model. If you are willing to commit time and energy to the intensive campaign, it can be extremely effective. In a comprehensive campaign, you will need to use it.

The Phonathon

The term *phonathon* strikes fear into the hearts of development professionals everywhere. The phonathon is one of the most difficult annual giving tasks to do well. It gives directors of annual giving cold sweats, and it is where they prove their worth. The deployment of an effective phonathon is the mark of a strong Annual Fund.

The fallacy that community college alumni don't give is largely due to the ineffectiveness of direct mail as a fundraising vehicle. I am referring to the generic "Dear Friend" letter that goes out to fifteen thousand alumni. I have seen direct mail campaign yields in the .03 percent range. The rule of thumb here is if it doesn't work, stop doing it.

The phonathon is uniquely suited to higher education. Who has not succumbed to the appeal of a perky college student calling from the alma mater? Four-year colleges have refined the practice to a science and deploy it with enviable effectiveness. A remarkable early example of the higher education phone campaign is the 1978 Harvard Campaign Regional Phase "telethon" that reached out to forty thousand alumni in 1982 with the technique known as Open, Engage, Ask, and Close (Owen 1982, 42). The appeal succeeded beyond Harvard's wildest dreams, raising over $5 million by telephone. We are going to borrow a page or two from the four-year college playbook here.

Many community college alumni recognize the debt they owe to the college where they got their start. Charitable giving may honor beginnings, too. Simply make the case to the alumni for supporting the college where they got their start in higher education. True, community college alumni do not give at anywhere near the rate that alumni of four-year colleges do. But who would turn down the opportunity to build, over time, an alumni donor base of, say, a thousand individuals? Even if this represents only 5 percent of your entire alumni database, it still qualifies the phonathon as an indispensable part of your development program.

The key to an effective phonathon is to use well-trained, paid student callers. The student caller is the direct link to the alumni's time spent at the college. When student callers announce where they are calling from, their course of study, and what they hope to accomplish with their education, when they ask alumni a question or two about their own college experience or what they went on to do, it forms the basis of the most compelling Ask you could hope to craft. The Ask is direct, for a specific amount. When the donor pays with a credit card, the transaction is completed on the spot. What's more, amid the clutter of direct mail, donors remember that a student called, did a good job on the Ask, and convinced them to give. Come next October, when the phone rings and the student caller says, "Hello, my name is Amy—I'm calling from Your Community College and I want to thank you for the $50 you gave last October . . . ," the pump, so to speak, is primed.

Planning the Phonathon

The ability to plan and execute a modest phonathon, the variety I am describing here, is the litmus test of an effective director of annual giving. The phonathon is one of the primary reasons you held out to hire a development officer with a background in the collegiate model of development.

The single most important factor to the success of the phonathon is the ability to recruit and train a sufficient number of the student callers. The director will need to recruit twenty student callers for a three-week commitment. The students will be paid $10 an hour, an amount that is sufficient to gain and hold their attention. The foundation may choose to fund this expense.

Recruit student callers via ads in the student paper, posters on campus, faculty announcements, word of mouth, and personal interactions with your director of annual giving. Recruitment for the phonathon can begin at student orientation via an information table staffed by the development office. For programs with a high degree of alumni affiliation, like nursing, ask nursing faculty members to announce the opportunity in their classes. In this case, student callers will be calling alumni from their own program. Remarkable things can happen in these conversations as students and alumni share their personal experiences related to the program. The student caller may even identify an internship or volunteer opportunity through the interaction.

Write out phonathon policies for the students to follow. These include:

- Don't fudge on pledges.
- Show up on time.
- Call if you can't work.
- Write credit card numbers only on the call sheet.
- Document your calls.
- Always be polite and perky.
- Don't touch anything in an office.
- Wipe down everything at the end of the night.
- Know when to seek help.

Schedule the phonathon for an October start. I don't know why; it is just phonathon season, and it works. Your telephone ringing off the hook at home should clue you in to this fact. The three-week rule is highly advised, unless you have two crews of callers (and perhaps two directors of annual giving!). It is important to prevent burnout on both parties' parts. Your student callers may also hold part-time jobs and they are also under pressure to perform academically. Prepare to lose some to other demands.

Mining the Database

The director of annual giving will execute a series of queries on your donor database to yield the desired alumni demographic. With twenty thousand names on file, you can't call everyone. In addition, plan to call parents. Contact the office of research or your IT department early on to obtain an Excel file containing the contact information for this group. With twenty student callers, the director will need approximately five thousand households to call over the three-week campaign.

Laura Curley, writing in *Contributions*, estimates that a good caller can dial twenty-five numbers an hour (1994, 23), but the caller may speak to only seven people out of that group. During the first nights of the phonathon, determine the ratio of dials to "reaches" to get a sense of how many prospects you will need to keep twenty callers busy for three weeks.

The question of which alumni to call depends on a number of factors; there are no hard-and-fast rules. Previous experience with a phonathon will be your best guide. Nevertheless, here are a few demographic considerations for alumni:

- Phone numbers on file
- Cohesive program affiliations like nursing, dental hygiene, culinary arts
- Number of years out of college
- Affluent zip codes
- Donor status: new prospects, current donors, LYBUNTs (Last Year But Not This)

From the parent database select from the following parameters:

- Phone numbers on file
- Parents of students between the ages of eighteen and twenty-one
- Parents of Post-Secondary Enrollment Options (PSEO) students
- Affluent zip codes

Establish a mix of these two groups that gives you the number of prospects you need. Parents will provide a better yield than alumni, but alumni are much more likely to become long-term donors. You can expect most of the parents to lapse once their children have left your college, but don't forget that many have more than one child. The parent segment becomes a rolling demographic that refreshes itself in two-year cycles, while the alumni, if properly nurtured, become long-term donors.

You may experience problems in securing parent information from the college database system. If parental information was not collected previously, the phonathon represents a good reason to do so. This will usually be a system-level decision. The emergency contact field may also contain parental contact information. Some students (for some reason) put their own cell phone numbers down in this field, so you will have to deal with that in some cases.

If you don't have phone numbers for your alumni, you have a more fundamental problem. For a price, you can request a database phone number overlay from a data services company. If this step is needed, begin the process several months before the start of the phonathon. We cover recommended data management practices later on. For the moment, just bear in mind that the lack of phone numbers is a time-consuming obstacle to overcome.

Print out the prospect data on a call sheet (Appendix F) that includes all the data needed for the call and spaces for information to be filled in by the student caller. Print it out on perforated paper so students can write in the pledge amount and a few words of thanks, tear off the top part of the call sheet, and pop it in a window envelope. This step helps to minimize collection loss. Donors who may have said yes just slightly against their will note that the student is highly involved in the transaction. This will encourage the donor to follow through in making the pledge payment.

Managing the Details

You will need a temporary, on-campus phone room. Your development office and adjacent administrative suite may suffice, or you might try the Admissions Office area. (Note to file: next time the college engages in a renovation, request extra phone jacks!) You will need access to at least twelve to fourteen phones to accommodate maximum projected use at any one time. You want an area where the students are not cloistered in individual offices; a partitioned open office area is ideal.

Feeding your callers is an essential part of ensuring that they show up. Find a couple of food vendors who deliver. The menu cannot be pizza every night, and college catering just won't do for three weeks straight.

The Script

I have seen four-year college scripts eight pages in length, with suggested clauses for every possible contingency. That is way too much for our purposes. For a start-up operation with inexperienced callers, the shorter the better. Plan to get it on a single sheet, front and back. The script begins as follows:

- "Hello, my name is Amy. I'm calling from Your Community College as part of the fall telephone outreach project. Do you have a moment?"
- "First of all could I verify your listing in our records? Are you still located at . . . ?"
- "Our records show that you attended in 1985–86. May I ask what your time at YCC did for your education and career?"

- "I'm a first-year student at YCC. It's exciting but it is a challenge to keep up with my studies and hold down a part-time job. How much was tuition when you attended? It's $3,500 a year now. Did you know the state used to fund 60 percent of our budget, but now it's only 35 percent?"
- "Part of the reason I'm calling is to tell you about our new Annual Fund. It supports scholarships for students like me, funds student activities, emergency assistance for students, and a lot of other things, too. . . ."
- "Do you think you could make a gift of $150 to support the Annual Fund?" [Long pause.]
- "I understand. What amount would work for you?"
- "That's fantastic! What credit card would you like to put that on?"
- "You'll receive an acknowledgment note from me in the mail in a few days . . . and next fall you will receive an invitation to our Evening of Recognition. I can't thank you enough; you made my day! Good-bye."

This is as stripped down and straight to the chase as it gets. The call is composed of three movements: bond, ask, and thank. People know why the student is calling, so just use your two top attention getters, the current cost of tuition and the loss of state funding, to bolster the Ask. We won't worry about fancy stuff like dealing with reservations at the outset. We are looking for prospects who will give when asked directly.

Several basic sales principles are incorporated into this pitch. The first is that the Ask amount is higher than you expect to actually receive. The Ask of $150 establishes a *psychological floor*, so the prospect understands that we are looking for more than *go away gifts* of $20.

TIP #32

Establish the *psychological floor* with an aggressive phonathon Ask amount.

A note on this tactic: A student caller once called me from the University of California, Santa Cruz, when my daughter was a freshman there. The perky caller established a warm and fuzzy bond over my daughter's new life and asked me for *$1,000*. Now that is a psychological floor! Maybe her director of annual giving correlated that Ask to my zip code, the fact that my daughter was the recipient of a merit scholarship, or perhaps the student caller just asked every "newbie" parent for that amount. Whatever the case, it got my attention, and the gift I gave was larger than I otherwise would have given. What's more, that amount set my psychological giving floor with UC for the years to follow. I received a call from my own alma mater, McGill University, this year, and the caller asked me for a gift three times the amount I gave last year. So we needn't be shy about this business of the initial Ask amount.

The second sales principle is the *presumptive close* as expressed by the question, "What amount would work for you?" This approach keeps the focus on *how much*, rather than *if*. The final principle is a second presumptive close with, "Which credit card would you like to use?" Again, *which*, not *if*. Payment by credit card cuts collection costs immeasurably, allowing more of the funds raised to support the college directly, so it is worth it to lean a little. Train your callers to explain this if challenged. I hand out a two-sided fact sheet about the college that student callers can refer to in a pinch that includes suggested answers to frequently asked questions.

Training

Conduct training within a week of the launch, preferably within days, so everything stays fresh. Two sessions of ten students each allows for personal interaction with your callers-in-training. Walk your trainees through the phonathon policies described previously. *Emphasize perkiness.* Encourage them to briefly share something about themselves during the call. International students often have compelling stories to share. Explain the bonus plan to the student callers. One technique I like is to hand out dollar bills for qualifying pledges.

Emphasize that no shenanigans will be tolerated. Explain that callers can call their parents to practice. Underscore the agreed-upon length of the work commitment. Following the initial orientation, pair off the students for role-playing calls. Have each student call the director of annual giving or a development colleague as a "final exam." Then offer an encouraging critique. By all means, let callers know they will be encountering a lot of *Nos* and not to take it to heart. As they say in the sales biz, every no is just one more step on the way to yes. Have the CDO present to thank them and offer a few words of encouragement, and take a group photograph to include in the college magazine.

Devise an awards program. Once again, I prefer the iPod, offering it as the bonus for the caller who raises the most money over the three-week

---

TIP #33

Offer an iPod to the top phonathon caller.

---

period. Track this amount and let students know where they stand. Smaller awards offered over the course of the three weeks help to boost flagging morale. Here is how director of annual giving Emily Best handled her incentive program:

> I offered dollar bonuses for credit card gifts. I handed them out as the gifts came in. It allowed for the callers to get instant gratification. Also, to switch things up a bit, on the last two nights of calling I gave them each an individual goal and a team goal and got rid of the other incentives. If they made their individual goal, they got a $10 gift card, if the team made its goal, each member would get $5 cash. They didn't make the team goal either night, but they had really good numbers. Just goes to show that it helps to change up the incentives.[5]

As this director of annual giving suggests, introduce a few gimmicks, and encourage, encourage, encourage to keep morale from flagging.

Showtime!

During the phonathon the director of annual giving should shift his or her schedule to that of noon to 9 p.m. At 5 p.m. on the first day, the food arrives, the students show up (they'd better!), they are briefed while they eat, and it's off to the phones. Segment the call sheets so callers receive a mix of parents, previous donors, and alumni prospects. You may even salt the list with a few people you know will give. It is amazing what a $500 gift will do for morale on the first night. This isn't sneaky when you factor in the importance of early success in building confidence. Confident callers are effective callers. Hand out those dollar bills for successful calls. Get that thermometer on the wall. Pile in the juices and soft drinks. It is going to be a challenging three weeks!

Advanced Techniques

As I said before, credit card payments rule. To encourage them, I made a presentation to a local bank before a phonathon and asked the bank to make a $5,000 matching gift to the foundation, matching every gift paid with a credit or debit card.

TIP #34

Secure a matching gift pledge from a bank
to match gifts made by credit card.

I promised that the bank would be named in each of the thousands of calls we placed. I also offered the bank a sponsorship listing for our recognition event. The bank agreed, and every student caller informed donors that the bank would match gifts paid by credit card until the match goal was reached. Callers informed the donors how many more dollars they needed to raise to redeem the full match. You might offer a prize for the student who happens to be on the phone with the donor who redeems the final dollar of the $5,000 match. As any good phonathon manager will tell you, it's the little things that count.

It may be possible to recruit a phone room manager to run your phonathon. Contact your peers at four-year colleges to ask if they can refer you to any former student callers who may be living in your area. Many four-year colleges run their programs for most of the academic year, allowing their student workers to develop substantial expertise in the nuances of phonathon tactics. These individuals can make excellent short-term employees. They may just turn out to be future directors of annual giving.

TIP #35

Hire a recent graduate with significant experience as a student
caller in a four-year college to run your phone room.

The use of this option may allow a small college, or college branch campus, without the means to hire a director of annual giving to introduce this essential ingredient of an Annual Fund. The option is particularly suited to a public education foundation operating as a one-person shop.

Consider asking your alumni board to organize an alumni phone night. This works best when alumni are calling former classmates from programs with high levels of affiliation and can be a viable option for any applied program. The results may be modest, but the effort will help you to reach a

---

TIP #36

Try an alumni phonathon night during
which alumni call former classmates.

---

few more people. It will also help to reinforce your alumni board's commitment to philanthropy. Technical colleges have an advantage here, because their programs tend to be characterized by a higher level of student and alumni affiliation. In addition, technical colleges may have a little more trouble recruiting student callers. Dunwoody College of Technology has long used alumni callers to good effect, but I still prefer students.

Putting It in Perspective

Let's say you have just successfully completed your first phonathon. Your goal was $8,000 and you actually surpassed that, raising $9,000 (not including the bank match) from 180 alumni and 100 parents. That yields an average gift of $32, which represents only 3.5 percent of your Annual Fund goal, but it was worth it because you acquired nearly three hundred donors at a reasonable cost. What's more, you have proven that alumni give—as do parents—and you are poised to enlist another three hundred new donors by this time next year. So what if that amounts to only 3 percent of your reachable donor database. You have to start somewhere.

A suggested goal for next year might be an 11 percent increase over this year's results, to $10,000. The year after that, go for $11,500. Moving from an initial goal of $8,000 to $11,500 over three years would represent a 31 percent increase. Not bad for starters. The students survived; you had twelve callers still working on your final night; one student won the iPod by raising $845 in pledges; and you, the director of annual giving, are glad it's over.

If at the end of all this you find you are mad about phonathons, consider scheduling one in the spring. During the "off-season," make it a point to learn more about how four-year colleges run their operations. I guarantee you will learn some useful tactics. For example, I attended a CASE conference presentation at which a phonathon manager from a large university

> ## TIP #37
>
> Send a targeted mail appeal and follow-up to the
> prospects who requested additional information or
> said they couldn't give at the moment.

explained that her college tested sending out postcards to prospects before the phonathon. They found that it made no difference to the rate of giving whether the prospect received a postcard in advance. That was good enough for me—no advance postcards in our shop.

One final note: consider a *thankathon* in the spring. Have one or two of your most personable callers call donors to thank them and impart a few highlights on how the college will use the funds raised. Then thank them again.

> ## TIP #38
>
> Stage a *thankathon* in the spring.

Gestures like the thankathon will make your shop a contender in the "mindshare" sweepstakes. Bear in mind that your college is competing with an unlimited number of worthy causes in this sweepstakes. Donors tend to repeat their gifts where they feel their gifts have been valued most. So demonstrate that even a modest gift means more to your college. A thankathon will do just that.

Giving Clubs

A giving club appeal is an appeal by letter, by phone, or in person with the primary aim being to secure unrestricted dollars at levels from $150 to $10,000. I use giving clubs primarily to secure unrestricted dollars, though restricted gifts are also included in this category. These appeals often begin with a personalized letter based on a template (see Appendix G).

You might organize giving clubs as shown in Table 10.4.

TABLE 10.4	
Annual Fund Giving Club Levels	
Founder's Circle	$5,000+
Chairman's Circle	$2,500
President's Circle	$1,000
Dean's List	$500
Honor Roll	$150

More advanced programs might have a $10,000 club level. The point here is to have donors listed in each group. To have a top giving level listed on your annual report with one entry, "Anonymous," is not very impressive.

One of the beauties of a giving club appeal is that it is largely staff-driven. If you know your market, and know when to use an unrestricted operating support Ask (as opposed to a scholarship Ask), you are ready to succeed with a giving club program.

Giving Club Prospects

The first rule of thumb for selecting prospects from your existing donor base is: if you acquired a donor via a letter, renew by letter. If you acquired a donor via a phonathon, renew the donor that way. One exception to this rule might be if you are considering asking for a significant upgrade in the gift amount, in which case you might want to talk to the individual personally.

Who are some viable prospects for the giving club appeal?

- Local businesses with which you have had previous contact
- Event sponsors from your former gala
- Former board members
- Board contacts deemed inappropriate for the board-inspired giving program
- Prominent people who attended a college event
- Former faculty and administrators

This is just a start. Anyone who can give $150 for unrestricted operating support might be a prospect. In addition, use the giving club appeal as a conversion tactic for former gala or golf event sponsors. The prime prospect is a warm prospect, at least in the initial stages of giving club development.

The Nuts and Bolts of Giving Clubs

The giving club appeal is ideal as a calendar year–end campaign. Send the letter out in mid-November to allow time for follow-up. (What good is a letter without follow-up?) The second rule of thumb is to send out the letter in the month preceding the anniversary of the donor's gift last year. Third, use the appeal for a fiscal year–end appeal. In effect, you can conduct giving club appeals throughout the calendar year.

Begin with the letter template (Appendix G); then personalize the template so it doesn't sound like a generic appeal. Mention the last time you saw the prospect; thank the prospect for his or her last gift, noting the amount. Indicate that the gala has been reformatted as a recognition event, allowing more of the gift to support the mission of the college directly. Include a motivational comment by a board member known to the prospect. Ask for a *stretch-gift amount*—an amount that will challenge or inspire without being unrealistic. An unrealistic Ask might indicate that you don't really know the prospect.

Have the Ask originate with whoever knows the prospect best. Candidates might include the director of annual giving, the CDO, the president, or a member of the board. There is one slight advantage in having staff sign the letter. It makes it easier to write, "I'll follow up with you by phone in a couple of weeks. I look forward to talking with you!"

TIP #39

Telephone follow-up is the most important
aspect of a giving club appeal.

That last phrase, regarding the follow-up, is an essential element of the letter. In development work, nothing is more important than the follow-up. It means that this is a serious, personal Ask. If a prospect merits a $1,000 appeal for support, he or she certainly merits a phone call. And by all means, if you say you are going to do it, *do it*—and in a timely manner. It may take several attempts to reach your prospects. After all, they know why you are calling. The follow-up is personal, brief, and to the point. Make sure to ask for the gift. If such focused donor interactions are new to you as a development officer, you might consider some training. If after three attempts, you have not had any luck in reaching the prospect, send a personal note, perhaps handwritten:

> Dear John,
>   I tried to reach you last week but we weren't able to connect. I know the new business must be keeping you busy. And I know you mentioned you had some business out of town this month. The reason I was calling is we are wrapping up our fall appeal and I was hoping you would consider making a gift of $1,000 in place of the event sponsorship gift you gave last year. You are a wonderful friend of the college. I look forward to talking with you soon.
>   Best wishes,
>   Cindy

Enclose a response envelope and you are done. If John does not respond in November or December, put his name on the list for May.

The giving club appeal represents an effective approach to the two most strategic giving levels in an emerging two-year college program: $5,000 and $1,000 gifts.

TIP #40

Gifts of $5,000 and $1,000 are the two most strategically important giving levels in an emerging Annual Fund program.

An Annual Fund director simply cannot do everything, so you have to prioritize your efforts where they will have the greatest impact on the bottom line. A focus on these two gift classes will make the greatest impact. Gifts of $5,000 represent the largest denomination that you expect to receive. Seven to ten of these can account for up to 20 percent of an Annual Fund goal. Gifts between $1,000 and $2,500 represent the most strategic amounts for which you have the expectation of receiving a good number of gifts, say, 35, which would yield about $40,000, or 16 percent of the goal. Between these two gift classes, you see the potential to account for over a third of your annual revenue. A mature program may establish a different pattern, attracting a significant number of gifts at the $10,000 level. For a public education foundation, even a few $5,000 gifts would represent a significant early stage achievement.

Donor Premiums and Benefits

Giving club levels are primarily honorific designations. They dress up our Asks and look good on our annual reports. We are not in the museum business, so we generally do not offer tangible membership-style benefits. Moreover, significant benefits may reduce the tax deductibility of the gift. Nonetheless, here are some benefits to consider:

- Donor recognition event sponsorship (top level only)
- Invitation to the donor recognition reception (standard)
- Invitation to a luncheon with the president
- Bookstore discounts
- Library privileges
- Reduced-cost tickets to sporting or other college events

The first entry, recognition event sponsorship, is worthy of notice. Reward top-level donors with sponsorship status. You may reserve the benefit to top-level corporate donors if you prefer; the status may mean the most to them. Annual operating support in $5,000 and $10,000 denominations is a precious resource; recognize these donors profusely. By the way, this is a way to distinguish between annual operating and scholarship donors. Top-level scholarship donors receive recognition through the Scholarship Recognition Event. Why not create opportunities for your most valued unrestricted fund donors to receive recognition? Be creative. Honorific sponsorships are effective tools.

Tax Implications of Donor Premiums and Benefits

If you are considering offering financial benefits of any type, it is important to understand their tax implications. The IRS considers some benefits, such as rights to purchase sporting event season ticket packages and tickets offered in exchange for a gift payment, as financial benefits to the donor. These types of benefits are offered more commonly as alumni association or athletic booster club benefits, especially when the payment is characterized as membership dues. We won't copy the topic of actual membership dues here, but many of the principles hold for any type of a gift.

The basic rule, according to IRS Publication 526, "Charitable Contributions," is that you can deduct only the amount that is greater than the value of the benefits you receive (Internal Revenue Service [IRS] 2010a). Certain membership-style benefits, however, can be disregarded. If the payment, or gift, is $75 or less, you can disregard frequently used benefits, including:

free or discounted admission to the organization's facilities or events, free or discounted parking, preferred access to goods or services, and discounts on the purchase of goods and services. (IRS 2010b)

In addition, you may disregard admission to events that are open only to members of the organization "if the organization reasonably projects that the cost per person (excluding an allocated overhead) cost per head is not more than $9.60" (2010 amount). The IRS adjusts the amount for inflation annually.

While an Annual Fund contribution is not a membership contribution, it can be like a membership contribution, especially when an alumni association consideration is involved. The examples above offer guidance, but the final one, regarding admission to membership-only events, raises another problem. Many recognition events offer benefits that exceed the cost per head allowed by the IRS. To avoid running afoul of this stipulation, ensure that your recognition event is not a de facto membership event:

- Keep the event open to stakeholders, including prospects, friends, volunteers, and donors.
- Make the invitation contingent on one's status as a friend of the college, rather than the gift alone. You may demonstrate this by inviting LYBUNT donors.
- Do not emphasize a quid pro quo relationship between the gift and the recognition event in your solicitation materials.

Token Items

The issue of token items offered in exchange for a gift is relevant to most Annual Fund programs. Consider this the tote bag and coffee mug clause. Donors can deduct the entire gift amount while receiving a token item if the following conditions are met:

- The consideration is "a small item or other benefit of token value."
- The organization represents to the donor that the value of the item or benefit received is not substantial and that the donor can deduct the full amount of the gift.

To determine whether the premium is below the threshold of "substantial" value, refer to IRS Revenue Procedures 90-12 and 92-49, making sure to factor in an inflation adjustment, which can be found in IRS Publication 1771. If you prefer (and are prepared to wait on the line), you can call IRS Exempt Organizations Customer Account Services at 877-829-5500 for annual inflation adjustment information. Here are the qualifying amounts for 2010:

- For gifts of $48 or more, the donor may deduct the full amount of the gift payment if the organization offers a token item bearing the name or logo of the college valued at $9.60 or less.
- For gifts of a larger amount, say, $1,000 and up, the organization may offer an item or benefit valued at 2 percent of the gift amount, or $96, whichever is less.

So, if a donor makes a gift of $1,000, the value of the recognition item may not exceed 2 percent, or $20.

Donative intent is the prime determinant in this equation. If you create a quid pro quo expectation of conveying a *material financial benefit*, you will have to disclose the value of the benefit and reduce the tax-deductible component of the payment accordingly. A material financial benefit is one that exceeds the limits explained above.

Raffles

Offering entry into a raffle in quid pro quo exchange for a gift is problematic because it negates donative intent. If, however, anyone in the college, the neighborhood, or the universe—all nondonors—can enter the raffle just by submitting an entry form, the quid pro quo expectation is not established. This is how I handled the giveaway of the iPod. Employees had to turn in a pledge card to be eligible, but they did not have to make a gift.

Giveaways can be tricky. Sometimes it is simpler just to keep the focus on the mission. You can offer donors and volunteers recognition items that are delivered in a manner entirely separate from the Ask. You do not advertise these recognition items as related to the conveyance of a gift. Instead, these items may recognize the donor's status as a valued friend of the college. (More on this tactic later.)

While on the topic of IRS regulations, and Publication 526, I should reiterate that you must provide a written acknowledgment for all gifts of $75 or greater when a consideration of any value is given to the donor. The acknowledgment must state whether the item or benefit exceeds the material threshold and reflects the amount of the allowable donation accordingly. For gifts of $250 or more, a written acknowledgment must be issued for the donor to deduct the gift. The IRS allows email acknowledgments as well.

The acknowledgment must include the statement that no goods or services were provided by the organization in return for the contribution when that is the case. When indicated, I include this statement on acknowledgments for gifts of all amounts.

IRS Publication 526 is a useful resource for questions related to the tax deductibility of a wide range of gifts. For the tricky business of valuing gifts of donated property, consult Publication 561. Although the IRS no longer publishes Publication 1391, "Deductibility of Payments Made to Charities Conducting Fund-Raising Events," it remains a useful resource for organizations sponsoring fundraising events. Its contents have been summarized widely on the Web and in publications, including *How Much Really Is Tax Deductible*, published by Independent Sector (1997).

Board-Inspired Giving

Board-inspired giving is a term I coined to describe an appeal that relies on the board's own network of contacts in a personalized approach that requires their direct involvement. This network of prospects is often one that would not be readily available to you without the assistance of your board. It might represent individuals whom you know but who would be cold-call prospects.

Board-inspired giving is well-suited to making quick progress in a start-up situation—if you have board members with clout. The most effective deployment of the model I have witnessed in a mature program is the one conducted at Dunwoody College of Technology, where it was introduced and refined under the direction of the vice president for development and alumni relations, Mark Skipper. At Dunwoody, the model is deployed using a team approach. Teams are organized within the board of directors as well as the alumni association board. Individual members may secure a parcel of gifts totaling $10,000 or more—and the program incorporates nearly fifty volunteer participants.

For our purposes, board-inspired giving will focus on gifts of $500 to $5,000. Each board member is assigned a goal. We'll use $1,500 as a starting point. The first gift received upon introducing this program at Normandale Community College was a gift of $5,000 from a previously unknown donor. But it is important to bear in mind that upon first hearing of this approach, a number of board members may experience trepidation. It is better to exceed a modest goal than to miss an aggressive one.

TIP #41

In introducing board-inspired giving, it is preferable to achieve success with a modest goal rather than failure with an aggressive one.

Here is how it works: Board members, in consultation with the director of annual giving, offer names of peers whom they agree to approach. Business associates make ideal prospects. The director composes an appeal letter template to be personalized by the board member and printed out—on the board member's letterhead if available—by either the development office or the board member's office. The key, as with the giving club, is the follow-up. In this case, *the secret is that the board member makes the call* or performs the follow-up over lunch or golf. Even better, the board member makes the Ask in person and follows up with a letter. In this manner, you incorporate two powerful drivers of charitable giving—the board member's volunteer leadership status and the personal Ask. If the board member cannot be persuaded to make the follow-up call, the task falls to the director of annual giving. Of course, this tends to defeat the whole purpose of the appeal and should be avoided whenever possible. Still, it is better than no call at all.

Board-inspired giving is a time-intensive effort on the part of the development officer and the executive assistant. One must overcome board-member procrastination, a reluctance to surrender names, the logistics of schlepping letterhead around for signatures, the vagaries of simply staying in touch, and the board member's reluctance to follow up. Keep board members apprised of the status of transactions, especially the arrival of gifts, in a timely manner.

The potential payoff of board-inspired giving is huge. The effect is akin to doubling the giving capacity of your board. Our model reflects a goal of $20,000, 8 percent of our annual goal, in the dollar ranges we most value—and all from newly acquired donors. Avoid incorporating existing donors into the program, since they were acquired without the assistance of the board, unless by so doing you increase the chances of obtaining a much larger gift.

The critical factors to success in this program are the support of the chair of the Annual Fund Committee and the experience and talent of the

Annual Fund manager. Introduce the program to the board as a project of the Annual Fund Committee. The support of the board chair and the CDO is also critical. Early success with a few supportive board members can be instrumental in achieving critical mass. As noted previously, these dollars can be largely unrestricted—if you design the appeal that way.

Scholarships

This is the single largest category of appeals in most two-year college shops. Presumably, your development office already excels with this product line. What else, then, can we say about this category? The most overlooked approach to Annual Fund scholarship Asks is that of a personal Ask made during the course of a cultivation meeting. The Ask can be as simple as, "Have you ever considered setting up a named scholarship to help a student every year?" This question can be posed by the CDO; the director of annual giving; a board member; and, most important, *the president*. It reflects a consonance with mission and a seriousness of purpose. So here we divulge a secret of high-functioning advancement operations—even the president is an Annual Fund officer!

When the Ask is personal, we have the opportunity to relate stories of students whose lives were changed by scholarships. This is an invaluable tool. We glean these stories from personal interviews, articles written for the college magazine, and student speakers at graduation and recognition events.

A common mode of scholarship solicitation is essentially that of the giving club—a personalized letter followed up by a personal contact. This is especially true for renewals. The Ask is direct. You make the case in a brief appeal. You highlight the fact of declining state support, rising tuition, and a changing student body that faces greater financial challenges than ever before. You could include an inspirational student story on a one-page insert. This might include a photo and might even relate the story of interactions between a donor and a scholarship recipient. As with the giving club solicitation, follow-up is paramount.

You can expand your scholarship solicitation program by learning to recognize the diverse profiles of scholarship gift prospects. Annual Fund scholarship Asks can range anywhere from $500 to $50,000. Donors who are currently giving $150 might be encouraged to "think bigger." A scholarship commitment may be a perfect family or couple's project.

The largest market for scholarship expansion in a two-year college is the local business community. Everybody in the college community has local business contacts. Local business owners or managers have always been aware of the college, but their donative intent may have been underdeveloped or nonexistent. Offering to feature the business name within the college community may be a key to unlocking that intent, especially if you can help the business tell the story of its local philanthropy. The key to developing this market is sending the director of annual giving out into the community.

TIP #42

In annual giving and, indeed, all giving, there is
no substitute for face-to-face interaction.

Consultant Mark Davy advises the "truck is in the neighborhood approach," as in, "I'm going to be over your way on Tuesday. I was wondering if I might drop by for a few minutes to say hello and tell you about a couple of things that are going on at Your Community College." This approach is based on the rule that there is no substitute for face-to-face interaction.

Memorial and Honorific Gifts

Gifts made in honor or memory of an individual can become a minor staple of your program. Giving appropriate notice in your annual report, using word of mouth, encouraging people close to you (like the president) to give, and having appropriate envelopes on hand can all boost memorial giving. Similarly, gifts made in honor of a retirement, an anniversary, or a special occasion can provide recognition to a special someone and financial support to the college.

Standard practice is to have a simple, attractive card on hand that can be sent to a surviving family member in the case of a memorial gift, and to the person honored in the case of an honorific gift. The card announces that a gift has been made, together with the contact information of the donor so the party can thank the donor directly. (The amount, of course, is not disclosed.)

Memorial gifts are often listed as a separate category in the annual report, again, without reference to a giving level. If you want to recognize the donor at a certain giving club–level gift, list that individual's name a second time in the appropriate category.

Annual Fund Grants

Grant writing is the process of submitting a written proposal, usually in response to a formal set of guidelines. Grant writing is yet another staff-driven element of the development plan. The market is usually that of corporations, large privately held companies, organizations (like Rotary), and private foundations. With these prospects, the primary relationship interface for the grants officer is the foundation program officer or corporate giving officer. Sometimes the formality of a proposal-based Ask will be appropriate with a smaller business as well. Use small, boilerplate proposals with this market to request annual scholarship or operating support grants. While the proposal to a small business may be more or less boilerplate, the cover letter is always personal.

You need volume to excel with small-grant requests. Robust programs churn out multiple grant applications per week. Grant writers who are used to working exclusively on large program grants may need to adopt a new work style to achieve the volume necessary for an Annual Fund grants program.

Sometimes you don't know until after a grant has been awarded whether it is annual (repeatable and sustainable) or a onetime grant. The latter category, even if a multiyear grant, should be counted in the major gift category. In the Annual Fund world, "repeatable" doesn't just mean theoretically so. It means you have an expectation that the grant will be funded again. A sustainable grant is repeatable more than once. Why does it matter? Because the Annual Fund is like a bank account. You need to refill it each year, and in an amount greater than the year before. Some foundations may offer a three-year funding cycle. Think of that as a major gift that is paid off over a pledge period of three years. Once that cycle is complete, it is over, at least for a while. So resist the effort to pad Annual Fund numbers with grant awards. On the other hand, some corporate contribution programs are quite sustainable. Count those in the Annual Fund. With some grants, it makes sense to count the first one as a major gift and the second—presuming sustainability—as an Annual Fund gift.

In a common Annual Fund grant mix, you will find a number of small boilerplate scholarship grants, five to ten in the range of $5,000 to $10,000, and maybe a couple of large ones totaling $50,000 or more. That logic led us in our strategic planning to establish an Annual Fund goal of $90,000 for the grants program. I refer to large annual grant-based donors as *angel funders*. Often, they will be large family foundations that have made a long-term commitment to your institution. The role of the grant writer with respect to these is the same as that of any other development officer. The grant writer must develop the relationship by offering excellent customer service. This service includes stewardship activities, grant reporting, donor recognition, and timely submissions of renewal proposals.

Never take an angel funder for granted. Never miss a reporting deadline, forget to forward student thank-you letters, or neglect to make routine check-in calls to the program officer. Angel funders are the *anchor tenants* of the Annual Fund. They occupy the corner location. They represent significant financial exposure in that if they do withdraw, replacing them is very difficult. So take good care of them and keep an eye out for new ones. In the next chapter, we talk about a concept called *the nth degree*, which helps to reinforce the value of customer service to donors—a value that is essential in maintaining a relationship with this type of funder.

If you do not have a grants market sufficient to sustain a dedicated position, then the director of annual giving must write Annual Fund proposals. A full-time grants officer may or may not be viable for an emerging K–12 public education foundation. Nevertheless, it does merit some research. Remember, counting annual and major grants together, the grant writers need to bring in about four times their salaries to make the investment pay off. I have found, though, that in the case of a grant writer working on the Annual Fund, an expanded research capacity yields funding sources that a director of annual giving would be unlikely to find.

Survey the board to determine whether it has corporate or foundation contacts that can help you secure grant support. As a general rule, the more formal the funder's program, the less effective board connections are going to be. However, it cannot hurt to try, so leverage those connections when you can. Look for more information on grant writing in chapter 13.

Managing the Whole Process

The director of annual giving must master a large portfolio of donors and prospects. Mark Skipper, vice president of development at Dunwoody College of Technology, introduced a remarkable tool, an Annual Fund Chart, with which to accomplish this task. I am not sure of the exact origin of the chart, but I believe the Boy Scouts of America used it.

The chart (Appendix H) includes a number of boxes, each of which represents a potential gift. These are arranged by giving level to form the shape of a pyramid. To the right of the boxes, a list of prospect names appears. The chart is formulated at the beginning of each fiscal year to match the goals of a program or a development officer. Each month, you fill in the blank boxes as gifts are realized. The name of the donor is checked off. The chart effectively conveys a significant amount of detail. Through its use, the director of annual giving can master the details of a campaign and track its progress in graphic form. Board members love it; it reinforces how a single process management tool can focus attention on the things that really matter.

Carnegie Mellon University computes the average Annual Fund gift amount and compares year-over-year results to see how it is doing (Lambrou 2009). It also computes the percentage of alumni participation and benchmarks that against peer institutions. Carnegie Mellon makes this information public within the university and to the public at large. This practice adheres to our adage "What gets measured gets done" and establishes a firm platform for discussing accountability in outcomes.

Sports Stories

A word to the wise for colleges that offer sports: alumni donors to sports programs need to know that academics precede sports. Try to instill the value that an Annual Fund gift precedes a gift to the football team. After all, without the educational mission, there would be no football. And increasingly, if athletes do not succeed in the classroom, there will be no football. The coach needs to be the one who delivers this message to alumni donors, and the president needs to be the one to convey this to the coach. (The development staff will know what I mean.) It seems so simple, yet it goes awry all too often. This inherent tension will be most pronounced at emerging four-year colleges with a history of strong athletic contributions and a weak Annual Fund.

The Annual Fund is the bedrock of your program. As such, it requires the full attention of the CDO, the support of the president, the involvement of the board, and the talents of an experienced director. This concludes the chapter on the Annual Fund, but not the entire discussion. Cultivation and donor relations are an integral part of the Annual Fund, as is the issue of database management. We move on now to cover these topics in detail.

Endnotes

1. Reported to me by an old United Way campaigner from the factories of Detroit.

2. This employee campaign was part of a comprehensive campaign in which employees were asked to make a combined annual and campaign pledge.

3. To stay within the law, employees submitting a pledge card did not need to make a gift to be eligible to win.

4. Adapted with permission from United Way of the Bay Area. 1990. *Effective solicitation skills for donor representatives*. San Francisco: United Way of the Bay Area, 4–25.

5. Emily Best, former director of annual giving and alumni relations at Normandale Community College, personal email correspondence with the author, 2007.

References

Collins, J. 2001. *Good to great and the social sectors*. New York: HarperBusiness.

Curley, L. 1994. Touchtone tactics. *Contributions* 8, no. 2, 23.

Internal Revenue Service (IRS). 2010a. "Certain membership benefits can be disregarded." Publication 526. http://www.irs.gov/publications/p526/ar02.html#en_US_2010_publink1000229650 (accessed February 14, 2011).

———. 2010b. "Charitable Contributions." Publication 526. http://www.irs.gov/publications/p526/ar02.html#en_US_2010_publink1000229650 (accessed February 14, 2011).

Lambrou, K. 2009. Achieving success: Fundraising fundamentals for volunteers. PowerPoint presentation, Carnegie Mellon University 2009 Volunteer Forum. http://www.cmu.edu/alumni/images/vf2010presentations/fundraising.pdf (accessed September 1, 2011).

Owen, D. 1982. State-of-the-art panhandling. *Harper's Magazine* 265 (August), 42.

11

CULTIVATION AND
DONOR RELATIONS

C ultivation and donor relations are two areas that bear on the entirety of your program, so this chapter is a pivot point before we move on to major gifts and planned giving. The essence of cultivation is simple—the development of relationships with donors. This has always been the hallmark of leading-edge programs. David W. Lawrence, senior associate at Demont & Associates in Portland, Maine, said of the development program at the Mayo Clinic, where he served as chief development officer for eighteen years, "What we're about at Mayo is not fund raising but philanthropy—the development of a relationship over time" (Collins 1996, 13).

To the *nth* Degree

Consultant Mark Davy used an advertising slogan borrowed from the former Norwest Bank in Minneapolis to instill in the development officers at Dunwoody College of Technology a strong ethos of customer service. The slogan was *to the nth degree,* as in "we will provide donor service to the nth degree." The slogan worked at Dunwoody and must have worked for the bank, too, since Norwest went on to acquire Wells Fargo. At Dunwoody, development officers were crystal clear in their understanding that donors come first, that no amount of attention to detail in relationship building was too much. This ethos formed the basis of their development culture and became one of their secrets to success in campaigns that have yielded over $55 million for the college.

   Part of the impetus behind this advice was that Mark realized that a technical college does not have the *cachet* of the opera, the symphony, or the university. Therefore, like Avis, we as development officers had to try harder to provide the unique, high-quality, personal cultivation experience that would create a lasting relationship.

Service to the nth degree begins with accountability. Mark recommended at the outset of the campaign that every Monday begin with a brief *Actions Meeting*, during which development officers presented their actions of the previous week for review by the group. Development officers documented their own actions in the donor database and ran their own action reports before the meeting, and we spent only a few moments on each entry. Each development officer was expected to have at least ten contacts for the week, but lists of twenty or more contacts were commonplace.

The president usually attended the meetings, along with the development officers, to present his actions. The fact that the president attended was a powerful testament to the value of direct donor contact and the importance of accountability.

Another feature of the meeting was a quick review of the main donor-related events of the coming week. If Monday was a holiday, the meetings were held on Tuesday. They were never cancelled. The Actions Meeting was a powerful tool in building a culture of accountability in the development office.

TIP #43

Convene a Monday morning Actions Meeting to
review donor contacts from the previous week.

I have found it useful to prioritize the value of different kinds of donor contacts to reinforce their respective roles in the cultivation process. Here is how I describe the hierarchy of donor contacts.

Not All Actions Are Equal: From High Touch to Low Touch in Donor Cultivation

We don't just count the number of actions in assessing our cultivation record; we look at the quality of the interactions themselves. More is not always better—if the contacts made are highly personal, fewer contacts may trump more. As useful as email is, for example, it is a third-tier form of cultivation. Here is how I rank cultivation actions:

High Touch—Most Valued

- Solicitation in person
- Meeting
- Visited contact
- Breakfast/lunch
- Campus tour
- Conversation

Medium Touch—Valued

- Dropped by
- Proposal
- Phone call
- Personal letter
- Note

Low Touch—Somewhat Less Valued

- Email
- Left message
- Fax

Therefore, a visit trumps a phone call, which, in turn, trumps an email.

The Essentials of Cultivation

The four essential elements of cultivation are a Relationship Key, a message, a purpose, and an opportunity. The first, the *Relationship Key*, refers to the personal dynamics of the interaction. Prospects are not automatons. They are living, breathing beings possessed of an endless variety of personal concerns and emotional needs. We know this. So why do we so often bypass the bond-building stage and jump straight to pitching *our* needs? Get to know the donor first. Get the names of family members. By all means, ask about the kids. The former president of Dunwoody, Frank Starke, used to fill his Dictaphone call reports with details about kids. These details formed the basis of real relationships, so every time Frank gave the prospect a call and asked about the kids by name, the contact felt a friend was calling.

Make it a primary objective to learn about the donor's background, interests, involvements, and aspirations. Ask about all of those topics; then listen closely. The sum total of this information forms the Relationship Key that unlocks the donor's personal motivations. Of course, relationships are a two-way street. The development officer should share personal details that serve to deepen the relationship, but the platform is unequal. Our political beliefs, for example, have little standing in the conversation. However, details about our families, the interests of our children, our own experiences in the world can be relevant to relationship development. As development officers, we are always friendly; but only rarely do we become friends with the donor.

The *message* is the heart of the deal for us. Our organizations have needs, but more than that, they have aspirations and opportunities. We are looking for a match between our aspirations and the donor's interests. We have a variety of initiatives that may or may not interest the donor. Often, we lead with the news, those campus developments or breakthroughs that may capture the donor's interest. Then we talk about our aspirations in a manner that highlights success and touches on need. For example, "We served over two thousand students in our success center last year and won a Chancellor's Award for Innovation. This year we hope to extend our services to students with two specific learning disabilities."

Purpose is the third key. In our chapter on major gifts, we delve into purposeful cultivation in a little more detail; here we'll touch on the basics. The reality is that there are many prospects and never enough time, so we must be purposeful with respect to whom we talk to and why. Our primary purpose is, at all times, to foster donative intent. It is a circuitous route in many cases. Yet circuitous does not mean random. This may seem obvious, but, in fact, random cultivation efforts can become a problematic pattern for many development officers. We must be stewards of our own time and effort and follow the donor's cues to ensure that the prospect feels the mission behind our words at all times. We must also consider the purpose at hand. The prospect may be a major gift prospect, but our present purpose may be to close an annual gift over the course of two to three interactions. Present purposes must dovetail with long-term purposes, and development officers must master the intricacies of these multifaceted interactions.

Our fourth ingredient is *opportunity*. We are in the business of creating opportunities. In this case, the object is to create opportunities for direct contact with donors. This is a test of our creativity and our commitment to the nth degree. Whether a news article triggers a note, or a faculty presentation calls for an invitation, we are always on the lookout for keys to involvement. Involvement is the wellspring of giving. Sometimes we feel that people are so busy that we are hesitant to inject ourselves into their lives. Influential people are busier and more harried than ever, and if we haven't built the bridge to interaction through the means of Relationship Keys, we may be perceived as an intrusion. If you want to engage people, appeal to their needs for:

- Prestige—"I am somebody."
- Access—"I am a member of the inner circle."
- Entrée, a way to give something back—"They care what I think."

Here is a handy top ten list regarding cultivation written by nationally known organizational consultant and educator Kay Sprinkel Grace:

1. Cultivation is a partnership involving board members, volunteers, donors, and staff.
2. Cultivation is strategic.
3. Cultivation is systematic.
4. Cultivation should be coordinated.
5. Cultivation shouldn't be limited to large gift prospects only.
6. Not all cultivation involves personal interaction at an event or meeting.
7. Cultivation, with or without strategic planning, can also occur unexpectedly.
8. While it is important to cultivate, know when to ask.
9. Cultivation of corporations and foundations is different from cultivation of individuals in one major respect (there is an established timeline and process for closing the gift).
10. Be sure there is a budget for cultivation.[1] (1998)

Recall this remark from chapter 4: "College president? That's a sales job!" Development officers, too, are the college's sales force. They may not immediately recognize such a designation; however, many tenets of a *consultative sales* practice, such as employed by financial planners and insurance professionals, directly apply to the practice of development officers. The practice of consultative sales focuses on meeting the customer's needs through the development of a relationship, a mutual exchange of information, education, and the presentation of a solution that meets the customer's fundamental needs. Consider the following text from Sales Sense LLC in Plano, Texas:

A short definition of a consultative sales person

A consultative salesperson is one who can resist the temptation to "pitch" their product or solution until they have laid a solid foundation for their further selling:

- They've built a high trust and high credibility relationship with the prospect.
- They've had sufficient dialogue with the prospect to understand their business environment, critical business drivers, and existing high priority business initiatives.
- They've thoroughly validated that their value proposition holds water in the prospect's specific business environment.
- They've discovered that a compelling business case can be built for their solution. (Cooper n.d.)

Now substitute the word *personal* for the first four occurrences of the word *business* in the text and the word *philanthropic* for the final reference. See what I mean? In our case, the product or solution is the mission of our organization. The training, perspective, and experience of consultative sales professionals can help us to better conceive our own work. That is one reason consultative sales professionals can be effective board members. In development, we refer to this type of consultative practice as being *donor-centric*: the focus is on the donor rather than the organization.

TIP #44

Think of the development function as *sales transformed by mission*.

So, what in the end is the nature of our work as development professionals? I like to think of it as *sales transformed by mission*.

Thank-You Visits

Each July rings in a new fiscal year, after the (slightly frantic) round of year-end follow-up calls has been completed and the Annual Fund tally sits, once again, at a big fat zero. I like to get the development staff out of the office in July on a round of thank-you visits. Present your donors and volunteers with some kind of meaningful thank-you gift or premium that relates to the college. You might want to offer gifts to key volunteers and $1,000-plus donors. To schedule the visits we let the donor know that we have a small token of appreciation for him or her and would just like to drop by for a quick visit. It is amazing how easy it is to schedule these appointments!

The agenda is straightforward. Say thanks (several times), say a word or two about what is going on at the college, and mostly talk about whatever the donor wishes, for as long as he or she wishes, be that ten minutes or two hours. These visits can do wonderful things to strengthen relationships. I find myself disclosing a little more about myself during these visits. Donors respond in kind. Some relate the history of how they became involved with the college. Some express the desire to "do more." A few have made an unsolicited commitment to double their gift. One couple made the commitment to put the college in their will—and followed up with a letter from their attorney the following week! With each staff member committing to three visits a week, your office can make twenty-four to thirty-six visits in the course of a month. Ask the president to make several visits, too. This exercise energizes your staff because the calls can be so inherently satisfying and the practice starts your year off on a pleasant, donor-centric note.

TIP #45

Start the fiscal year off with a round of thank-you visits.

Cultivation Events

The "Evening of Recognition"

Cultivation events form the backbone of our group interactions with donors. The premier event in our model is the *Evening of Recognition* donor (and volunteer) recognition (and cultivation) event. We use the donor recognition event to showcase our mission while offering first-class hospitality. Its elements are easy to envision. We provide a setting, such as a lovely off-campus location. We provide hospitality, as in a well-catered buffet dinner. We offer the opportunity for social interaction—the "meet and greet" aspect for which development professionals are renowned. We recognize sponsors. We bestow awards, such as the Outstanding Alumni or the Spirit of Our College Award. *We tell our story.* We tell it in several ways, through the remarks of the president, the chair, a celebrity—and especially through the words of students and donors themselves.

If you have staged a gala—and I know you have—you already have all the tools at your disposal to create a first-class cultivation event. The invitation list might be composed of:

TIP #46

Tell your college's story at the Evening of Recognition event.

- Donors at a certain gift threshold (perhaps $75 and up)
- VIPs
- Award recipients (including their families and/or professional colleagues)
- Advisory council members
- Friends of the board
- Student representatives
- *Individuals you wish to cultivate*

Of these groups, the last one is most commonly forgotten. A recognition event is a perfect cultivation vehicle. Simply have the right person personally invite these guests by telephone. Telephone follow-up to written invitations should be a routine element of the invitation protocol anyway. All members of the development staff, including the executive assistant, may make these calls. Gently explain to board members that attendance at the event is de rigueur. Put it in the job description, and ask your board chair to be the enforcer. This is your big evening of the year and you need a strong board turnout.

September, the back-to-school month, is a good time to hold this event. Get a mayor, a governor, a senator, or a celebrity alumnus/alumna to speak. Showcase student involvement by incorporating students as speakers, servers, greeters, and musicians. Bestow a few awards, allowing the recipients to make brief remarks in most cases. Devise a prestigious award and bestow it on a true leader. Then engage inspiring and compelling student speakers to tell their personal stories. Close with a few highlights of the year delivered by your president. And thank, thank, thank. Your presenters should be on and off the stage in forty minutes. And what have you offered your guests? They've become *insiders*, initiated into your collective organizational life. A sample budget for this event appears in Table 9.3 on page 122.

The Scholarship Recognition Event

This is probably an existing feature of most college donor relations programs. The object, of course, is to bring students together with scholarship donors.

The students receive scholarship certificates bestowed with a bit of ceremony. Students speak, donors speak, and food is served. The goal should be *not a dry eye in the house.* The object is to share student stories with power and conviction.

The event is usually held on campus, and the food comes from your campus vendor. (Try for pro bono service.) Every member of the board should be encouraged to attend. Once again, make personal follow-up calls to invitees. One important detail is a seating plan that pairs scholarship recipients with donors.

TIP #47

Pair donors with scholars at your Scholarship Recognition Event.

The director of annual giving should assume planning responsibility for this event. Events like this need to become a core competency of the staff member in this position. In addition, the audience is largely composed of Annual Fund donors. The executive assistant should assist with event logistics. Spring is a good time to hold the event; wait until the snowbirds are back in town.

Other Events

Other events may round out your cultivation calendar. With the aid of some retirees, you can organize an annual retiree luncheon with a minimum of fuss. Some events may not be annual, such as the naming of a wing or the installation of a president. No potential event should escape the development officer's imagination. Breakfast with the president, or chancellor, a president's council meeting, a holiday party hosted by the foundation chair, all of these may suit your purposes. You can position student showcases and faculty presentations for cultivation purposes. And, of course, those of you who host sports programs know the benefits inherent in a VIP homecoming reception or sports banquet.

Other Cultivation Techniques

Cultivation is as cultivation does. The more you cultivate, the more it becomes part of the fabric of your organizational life, and the easier it gets.

Over time, it becomes more personal, more meaningful, and more productive. High-functioning college programs know this and rarely miss an opportunity to write about a donor, establish a new connection with a donor, or put a donor onstage. An interview with a donor can make wonderful copy for your magazine. Private universities excel at bringing in influential donors as guest lecturers; why not try it at your college? Cultivate faculty members whose programs might be suitable for such an arrangement.

TIP #48

Offer an honorary Lifelong Learning Degree (LLD) to your top donor.

College commencement addresses and honorary degree ceremonies are a tried-and-true feature of four-year college recognition programs. If an honorary AA degree does not possess the cachet you seek, you might consider an honorary Lifelong Learning Degree (LLD). Ask your governing board to create one. The list of cultivation devices is endless, and the more you hang out with college development officers the more new ideas you will learn.

A quick word about advisory committees: they are necessary and appropriate to the life of the college but I do not favor them as cultivation vehicles. They take up too much time and are subject to mission drift, an inherent occupational hazard when pursuing dual-objective goals. Let advisory committees remain the domain of academic departments.

Stewardship and Recognition

David W. Lawrence defines stewardship as "the focused application of recognition" (Collins 1996, 16). Stewardship means keeping in touch after the gift. Formally, stewardship is the exercise of ethical accountability in managing and expending philanthropic gifts.[2] Part of that practice is ongoing communication with the donor. The first rule of cultivation is that it is essential to stay in touch with the donor when you are *not* asking for anything. Simple techniques, such as sending scholarship donors handwritten thank-you notes from scholarship recipients, go a long way toward maintaining that essential ingredient, donor goodwill. Cultivation for the next gift begins with acknowledgment of the last. "All donors to the Stanford Fund, which provides undergraduate financial aid, receive a handwritten note from a student beneficiary. The university is sending the signal that a $100 gift matters," according to a 2006 article in *CASE Currents* (Logue 2007). That sounds like the nth degree to me.

TIP #49

Send donors handwritten thank-you notes from a member of the board for gifts of $5,000 or more.

Beyond recognition in the foundation annual report, consider installing or updating a donor wall of honor in a prominent place on campus. A new donor wall represents a significant expenditure, and significant due diligence should precede the purchase. The college should be expected to pay for the donor wall display. Expect to budget $15,000–$20,000 for a simple installation. The board should register cumulative giving (except perhaps in the case of donor recognition for a specific capital project, like a new building wing).

Purchase a display that allows you to move the names around. In this way, the board becomes a living record of donor activity. No other arrangement will do as an expression of cumulative giving. New plaques or name panels should be available at a modest cost, say $25. Spending this type of money on an attractive, modular donor wall should give you many years of recognition value at a reasonable cost. Recognize your Annual Fund donors with an attractive, framed poster that can be updated every year.

Endnotes

1. Parenthetical text in #9 paraphrased with permission.

2. Rosso and his colleagues define stewardship as "The philosophy and means by which an institution exercises ethical accountability in the use of contributed resources and the philosophy and means by which a donor exercises responsibility in the voluntary use of resources; the guiding principle in philanthropic fund raising" (2003). Reprinted with permission of John Wiley & Sons, Inc.

References

Collins, W. R. 1996. The subtleties of stewardship. *Advancing Philanthropy* 4, no. 3. http://demontassociates.com/our-team/ (accessed February 17, 2011).

Cooper, J. R. n.d. Consultative selling. http://www.sales-sense.com/Consultative Selling.htm (accessed September 8, 2011).

Grace, K. S. 1998. Ten things you should know about . . . cultivating your donors. *Contributions* 12, no. 6.

Logue, A. C. 2007. Away they go? *CASE Currents* 33, no. 4, 6–27.

Rosso, H. A. & Associates; Eugene R. Tempel (ed.). 2003. *Achieving excellence in fund raising* (2nd ed.). San Francisco: Jossey-Bass, 505.

12

MAJOR GIFTS

F irst off, let's define a major gift. A major gift is a significant, onetime gift intended to further the mission of the college. The gift is usually made after a long-term, strategic cultivation effort and is usually for a restricted purpose. In fact, for major gifts other than those given by board members, such gifts will almost always be restricted to a particular purpose, such as scholarships, endowed scholarships, a specific program, capacity development, or capital improvements, including equipment and facilities. In terms of the amount, for a start-up operation, a major gift might be $10,000. The high-end gift, the transformative gift for a two-year college, is probably a million-dollar gift.

When the donor is an individual, the gift will be donated from accumulated assets, rather than current income. These include securities, savings, and property. Sometimes the individual gift may be donated via a family foundation. A major gift may or may not be a "gift of a lifetime," but for colleges in our market, gifts over a million dollars often are. For major gifts under that amount, they may be repeatable, though usually not for a number of years. When that is the case, the amount of the second or third gift is usually larger than the first.

For gifts given by corporations and privately held companies, the gift usually originates either through a formal giving program or through the involvement of a senior officer of the corporation. Formal giving program gifts are often spearheaded by the efforts of the CDO and/or grant writer working through the channels of the company's formal program. Gifts from companies without formal philanthropy programs are often obtained as a result of a corporate officer's presence on your foundation board, or because one of your board members knows the corporate officer. Gifts from privately held companies are often a result of the cultivation or board membership of the CEO or a senior executive of the company; these are often repeatable.

Gifts given by private foundations, especially very large private foundations, usually conform to stated guidelines. As such, they are nearly always restricted. The process becomes that of matching the interests of the college to the guidelines of the foundation. Program development grants would be a prime example. Dealing with large foundations is a top-level strategic function of the major gift program. Major gifts derived from small and midsize foundations are more likely to be derived from a staff-driven effort.

Who's Driving?

Every two-year college has obtained some major gifts. Our goal is to launch a major gift *program,* a systematic, focused effort to create a stable expectancy for big gifts. This will be a primary responsibility of our major gift officer, the CDO. But the CDO will have some allies. Let's look for a moment at some classic advancement theory:

> At the center of the communications effort is the chief executive. He or she personifies the institution and is the one that must visibly carry the message to key constituents, provide direction and motivation of board members, and be involved in most calls for major gifts.[1] (DeWitt 1995)

The Magic of the Headdress

The issue of *personifying the institution* is a fascinating one. I call it *the wearing of the headdress.* It reflects a subtle psychological transformation as the office itself elevates the stature of the leader in the eyes of stakeholders and the public. In the context of philanthropy, some donors just want to talk to the "top dog." Donors perceive leadership attention as validation that their gift is as transformational for the institution as it is for them.

Relying on the direct involvement of the president is not the only way to close a major gift. University major gift officers know this well. Nevertheless, presidential involvement is a primary dynamic of the major gift process. The practice should be reserved for occasions when it will truly make a difference—and must be handled with the nth degree of professionalism.

> So what, then is the role of development officers in the major gifts process?
>   They understand that institutional goals can be met only by a team effort that relies on the involvement and support of the C.E.O. and members of the board, the institution's chief volunteers. They create the plan

of action to raise the friends and funds the institution requires and work with staff and key volunteers in implementing it. They make calls and ask for money, but they know that major dollars are committed with the direct involvement of the right volunteer and the C.E.O. (DeWitt 1995)

First, the board is the third critical partner to major gift cultivation. A two-year college with a modest history of fundraising success is not likely to be well networked in the circles in which major gift prospects are found. The board member's role of ambassador, or door opener, is required for prospect identification and cultivation. Second, the willingness to accompany the CDO on calls and, when the time is right, make Asks is a must. Many two-year college and public education foundation boards were not recruited with these tasks in mind. Board members recruited under the banner of a local, grassroots board may protest that they do not really "know" anybody. If that is indeed the case, the board relations committee needs to spearhead the type of strategic board recruitment efforts discussed in chapter 5.

Development of a major gift program is central to the success of the strategic fundraising model proposed here. Without a viable major gift program, the entire concept doesn't fly because economies of scale based on receiving big gifts are never achieved. A weak board is not an option. We spoke earlier of the ability of board members to *leverage* gifts, which means their ability to leverage gifts from their own companies. This capacity can be a primary driver of major gift programs at two-year colleges. In my experience, in the context of a campaign, it has led to the realization of many six-figure gifts.

Creating a Prospect List

Here is another, even more compelling reason why a weak board is not an option: your board comprises your first and primary major gift prospect pool. As such, these relationships need to be managed wisely and professionally according to several principles that we'll discuss shortly. But first, who else will find his or her way onto the list? Prospect qualification begins with strategic thinking about your donor markets. As a general rule, 20 percent of your donor base will provide 80 percent of your income.

Here is another tip that should also lead to more strategic prospect identification. This rule is especially true of prospects other than your board members. In the four-year college and university market, two-thirds of all gifts will tend to come from individual donors and their family foundations,[2] and one-third will come from corporate, foundation, and other organizational markets. In the two-year college market, that percentage is reversed.

TIP #50

Two-thirds of all gifts to community colleges will come from businesses and foundations, one-third from individuals.

Knowing this helps to focus your prospect identification efforts on the critical markets of businesses, corporations, and foundations.

Look at Linkage

The classic model for prospect identification holds that we evaluate capacity and linkage. In most fundraising markets, there is no shortage of *suspects* (a prospect that is not yet qualified) with capacity. After all, every company has money. And every one of those companies has a CEO. And the number of individuals possessing known wealth is also quite large. In the development universe wealth is everywhere. Accessible wealth, on the other hand, is rare. It is far more important to focus on the linkage than on capacity.

TIP #51

In weighing the probabilities of who will give, linkage trumps capacity.

If you think you can simply have a donor research firm come in and do a *wealth overlay* report on your existing database, think again. That is probably one of the least useful things you could do at this point. The firm may identify any number of alumni who have publicly listed wealth, through either public records of their real estate assets or publicly listed stock holdings in the case of corporate executives. But these screens miss most privately held wealth, and even where wealth is identified, it may not be local. In this case, the capacity of your college to develop strong long-distance linkages from scratch may be lacking. An organic approach based on existing networks is far more realistic at this point.

Look first to your Annual Fund donor base, especially those making larger gifts. Everyone has seen the classic donor pyramid model, with the

Annual Fund donors at the bottom. This is why your Annual Fund is the bedrock of your program; it yields the upgraded gifts that lead to major giving. However, unless you are already raising half a million dollars through your Annual Fund, that database is unlikely to have sufficient depth to generate a robust major gift prospect list.

The second area to examine is that of prospects that have come into your orbit through the activities of the president and the board. You might also review the guest lists from recent events your college or foundation has hosted. Some of these contacts may have significant capacity and have at least some familiarity with your college, even if their donative intent remains largely unqualified at this point.

Corporate donors are probably rubbing shoulders with someone from your network every day, through Rotary, the Chamber of Commerce, vendor networks, faculty spouses, parents, board members, and so on. The CDO should play detective here and track down these linkages. As we said, linkage is key. The first priority is to get in the door, and even a peripheral linkage will help to facilitate that.

Regionally known philanthropists represent an elusive but potentially lucrative donor market. The upside is that they give; the downside is they are on everyone's list. Some of them are already associated with education-related causes. To attract their attention you are going to have to be strategic—I mean best-in-class strategic—about tailoring your initiative to their interests. We'll get to this in a moment when we cover "Marquee Projects."

Assume that your competition has tried and failed a number of times with these same philanthropists, and maybe a few have broken through. Did I say competition? The word has hardly come up before. You focus your Annual Fund campaign on your primary stakeholders located within a defined geographical area, which roughly corresponds to the area from which you draw your enrollment. Even in a metropolitan area dotted with two-year colleges, you rule your home turf. It often includes some major companies, maybe even a few corporate head offices. It includes affluent zip codes. We identified these in constructing our Annual Fund drive. But when you come to the field of major gifts, every organization is your competition. Every zoo, symphony, and university, you name it, has a sharp development staff on the lookout for major gift prospects. Every church pastor, priest, and rabbi knows exactly who his or her prospects are. Every major gift prospect already known to you has several charities that are contenders in the contest for who will receive the big gift. You have to be sharp, you have to be humble, you have to consider the nth degree as you enter the fray.

You increase major gift prospects' giving potential over time through strategic cultivation. What would this person or company be able to give if we involved the prospect in a meaningful cultivation program over sixteen months, three years, or more? The biggest mistake two-year colleges make right out of the gate is to identify a prospect and make the Ask too soon. This is a huge mistake and will label your organization as a transgressor against the established etiquette of the major gift process in the mind of that donor. Hank Rosso weighed in on this topic twenty-five years ago. In examining the question of why people do not give when asked, he said, "They're asked too soon!" (1983). Think of capacity as future capacity, based on linkage and cultivation.

Prospect research in a small shop is a grassroots activity. Major universities have amazingly sophisticated research capacities. They have to. They have already identified the easy-to-spot prospects, cultivated them, and received their major gifts. In a small shop, a few simple techniques will get you going. Corporations and foundations are easy. The Web has made this part of the job infinitely more manageable. All you have to do is look up the corporate contributions page on the web site, read the guidelines, then go to the company foundation annual report or IRS Form 990 and see what gifts have been made and for what purposes. Form 990 is an invaluable tool, almost the only one I rely on when the data are available. The same goes for foundations.

Privately held companies are a completely different universe, and it can be hard to find charitable giving information about them. Sometimes word of mouth is the only way to glean information about their giving history and preferences. Have a board member ask an acquaintance to name the company's favorite charities or develop a relationship with an employee. Check for the board affiliations of the CEO. Google may suffice for this bit of research. Often you will see a university affiliation listed, such as the alma mater of the CEO. Read your local business publications for tidbits on privately held businesses and save clippings in your research file.

Tracking down the giving habits of individuals can be even more difficult. Again, start with Google. When nonprofits publish their annual reports on the Web, their donor rosters become public information. Collect the annual reports of organizations that interest you, ask coworkers to pass annual reports on to you, and ask acquaintances of prospects for information on their friends' charitable interests.

The prospect list for a full-fledged major gift program usually contains sixty to a hundred qualified prospects at the outset. By qualified, we mean capacity and linkage have been verified. For *cold* prospects, we include only those for whom you are capable of constructing a viable cultivation plan or with whom you have a known linkage. Everyone else is just the *universe*— known to you, but for the moment inaccessible.

A prospect list entry might look like the one in Table 12.1. Incorporate the data into an Excel spreadsheet, so you can sort the list by a range of variables. The rating refers to a systematic format to classify donors. The "2b" status in the example here refers to a gift range of $50,000–$99,000, and that the prospect is *warm* where:

- $1 = $100,000 +; 2 = $50,000–$99,000; 3 = $25,000–$49,000; 4 = Below $25,000
- a = ready to solicit; b = warm; c = cool; d = cold

The ratings should be data-based, not guesswork, and documented in your research, so the ranges don't begin to drift higher or lower based on overenthusiasm or "cold feet." The prospect list becomes a living document in the cultivation process, so update it regularly.

Developing Major Gift Initiatives

One precept of consultant Mark Davy is *the bigger the vision, the bigger the gift.* While we have subscribed to a donor-centric approach, it is necessary to consider the larger institutional vision as another important element of the major gift process. Our goal is to develop clearly articulated initiatives. You can apply the Rule of Three here also. Avoid a long wish list when discussing institutional priorities with donors. Think rather of a short menu. Highlight a few strategic initiatives in a manner designed to appeal to donors. Ideally, they will correlate to the college strategic plan. I refer to these few, featured initiatives as *Marquee Projects.* They should be big, important, and compelling.

	**TABLE 12.1** **Prospect List Entry**								
#	First Name	LName or Business	Business/ Contact	Interest	Rated	Group	Stage	Assigned	High	Low
8		ABC Foundation	John Doe	Science	2b	Foundation	Cultivation	CDO	50,000	25,000

TIP #52

Base your major gift program on one or several Marquee Projects.

A Marquee Project should encompass the fundamental aspirations of the college. In Collins's terms, it should be a BHAG. It might describe a new building, a new laboratory, a student success center, the launch of a new program, or a scholarship initiative.

Let's say you choose to make a new science laboratory your Marquee Project. One of the drivers behind this decision might be that your campus is known for its science education. Your science graduates are in high demand as transfer students at universities in your region. Your faculty has been recognized for the quality of its teaching. Enhancing your leadership status in science education is a goal of your strategic plan. Science and technology education is a hot topic, and you think you can use it to raise the profile of your college. Your science enrollment is strong, in fact, too strong. Your laboratory facilities are overused and overscheduled. Students complain about a lack of access.

Lack of access is a barrier to excellence in providing science education. Your analysis of enrollment trends indicates that demand is likely to continue to grow. Though your college system leadership is aware of your college's aspirations, because your needs are not representative of a core deficiency, and this is construed as a renovation rather than new construction, your hopes for timely capital funding are dim. You have worked with your faculty and facilities managers to construct a plan for laboratory expansion that would accommodate an additional four hundred students a semester, and faculty members are excited about the plan. The vision includes cutting-edge technology that students can use in a hands-on fashion. This capacity would outstrip even that of the nearest major research university due to accessibility to the equipment for hands-on use by undergraduates. Your donor market area includes many midsize companies that specialize in life science products. You have a couple of board members with ties to leading technology companies. We add all of this up and conclude you have a first-class Marquee Project.

Flagler College, a private institution located in St. Augustine, Florida, used the Marquee Project approach to raise $30 million, well over its $17 million goal for a new student center and the renovation of its art building, winning a CASE 2010 Circle of Excellence Bronze Award in the process (Council for Advancement and Support of Education [CASE] 2010). The judges report summary indicated that the campaign, with its "growth of total donors from 800 to 4,000, . . . stands as a model from which other institutions with emergent fundraising program may certainly benefit." This is a notable achievement given that the college was founded in 1965, in an era during which many other community colleges were founded as well. Having the right Marquee Projects isn't the only answer, but they often serve as a key element in transformational development efforts.

The type of thinking illustrated previously comes naturally to private colleges as they struggle to differentiate themselves and create centers of excellence, turning need into opportunity in the process. But this type of thinking does not always come naturally to community colleges. Technical colleges seem to have an advantage here. Too many community colleges seem to conclude that (1) our only project is scholarship support, or (2) the state will fund it. Scholarship support is a viable candidate for a Marquee Project, but it is important to recognize that scholarships are not the only game in town. As to the second point, increasingly, the state will *not* fund it.

We cannot count on the state to fund excellence—not now or in the long term. However, by leveraging private funds, a college may induce the state to become a partner in funding excellence. The model of state–private funding partnerships has begun to trickle down from the college and university sector to the community college level. I suspect that the competition for much in the way of future state funding for specific projects will depend on private funding matches.

Once you have identified your Marquee Project, produce a fact sheet or brochure and PowerPoint presentation with which to sell it. Articulate the case and produce a case statement that can serve as the basis for future grant proposals. You do not need an eight-page, color booklet. Major gift cultivation is not based on glitz; it relies more on face-to-face conversation.

While a Marquee Project approach is necessary to a strategic major gift effort, our donor-centric approach requires that we also listen to donors and respond to their giving needs. You may be cultivating a couple whose interest is music. Work to find the appropriate music initiative that might fit. Major gift initiatives are not one-size-fits-all. That is why, in our consultative sales model, we listen before we pitch. Your marquee initiatives should not "trample the field" of responsive donor interaction. Beneath the level of the Marquee Project, a good CDO has a finger on the pulse of ten to fifteen initiatives that would benefit the college if a funder could be found.

Major Gift Cultivation

Begin with the board: in campaigns and focused major gift initiatives, the board can be responsible for as much as 50 percent of campaign revenue. Of the opportunities available to you, cultivating the board is probably the easiest cultivation process to manage. Board members are a captive audience; they virtually have to take your calls. Seek them out for advice and counsel. They learn about initiatives such as Marquee Projects from the ground up, and often sell themselves on the merits of these initiatives in the process.

Try to develop a major gift strategy for each member of the foundation board. If, in so doing, you determine that some members neither are qualified prospects nor can potentially leverage a major gift, you might ask yourself exactly why they are on the board. Perhaps a member is the "spark plug" of the Annual Fund—that is an excellent justification. If, however, nothing comes to mind, the individual may be a prospect for the President's Council.

Purposeful Cultivation

Major gift cultivation is purposeful cultivation. To make the point, we're going to look at elements of a presentation, entitled "Purposeful Cultivation," delivered at the 2005 Region V CASE Conference by Penelepe C. Hunt, vice chancellor for development and senior vice president of the UI Foundation at the University of Illinois at Chicago. In these remarks, Hunt focuses on the cultivation visit. According to Hunt, purposeful cultivation is different from just making friends. In fact, sometimes friendships get in the way of making solicitations. So it is important to set expectations early on—as in, "I'm not here to ask you for money, but I'd like to get your thoughts on what we're planning at the college. . . ."

The first goal Hunt suggests is to gather information on:

- Capacity
- Inclination
- Interests
- Readiness

The second goal Hunt suggests is to build rapport. For the prospect this means:

- Deepening the relationship with the college
- Receiving "information to help with decision making"
- "Awakening to opportunities"

Hunt encourages the development officer to get personal. Remark on a personal memento in the office, ask what the kids are up to, and then get to the connection:

- Have you been on campus lately?
- Did anyone in your family attend our college?
- Have any of your employees benefited from the college?

Next, Hunt suggests share some college news with the prospect. Use your elevator speech. But remember, cultivation is involvement:

- Ask for input or advice.
- Active listening is key.
- "Watch for the spark, then fan the flame."

After every encounter Hunt say to ask yourself:

- What did I hear?
- What did I see?
- What does that suggest?

Use this information to develop your cultivation strategy. Regarding the pace of cultivation, the donor leads, but we as development officers influence the interaction. Where possible, we work to create a sense of urgency or occasion. Hunt advises that questions be our primary tools. "Never underestimate the power of a casual question," she says. Ask leading questions. Ask follow-up questions. Ask about the prospect's charitable activities. Hunt recommends that you ask questions to which you think you already know the answers. You never know which answer will become the one upon which to build your case. The next task is to follow up. The follow-up should occur within three to six weeks.

Major gift programs require a wide variety of prospects. We assume that not every prospect is interested. The trick is to find and cultivate those who are (Hunt 2005). Hunt's perspective demonstrates how precisely some of the principles we covered in chapter 11 can be applied to this end.

Consultant Mark Davy uses one cultivation maxim with all of his campaign clients. He says, "If you want advice, ask for money. If you want money, ask for advice." These words of wisdom bring a smile to many an experienced campaigner's face because anyone who has ever participated in a premature Ask has heard the prospect respond to the effect of:

- "What you need to do is some more research on the subject. I don't think such-and-such is such an effective way to go!"
- "Why don't you hire a PR firm or get somebody to fund an ad in the paper."
- "That was a little sloppy. I know a development officer over at Our Lady of the Bucks Hospital who could really help you tighten this thing up."
- "Why don't you restructure the program so it would serve kids between the ages of twelve and sixteen? Then I think you'd really have something."
- "Why don't you talk to Ned Smith? He likes projects like that."

The list of helpful suggestions can be endless. Mark suggests we go in and ask for meaningful advice up front. Structure the interaction so that we are asking the prospect real questions that elicit real answers. Listen closely to those answers and, when possible, include the donor's feedback in your designs. Soliciting advice offers college representatives a comfortable place to be, a participant in a substantive dialogue. Volunteers and presidents become more comfortable with prospects when they are seeking input; every CDO should master the technique.

TIP #53

If you want advice, ask for money. If you want money, ask for advice.

Major Gifts by the Numbers

For the multitasking CDO the question arises, "How do I know when I'm doing enough?" In thinking about performance metrics as applied to major gift cultivation, it pays to understand how this function is managed in large-shop environments. According to a Benz Whaley Flessner survey reported in *CASE Currents* (Grabow 2006), a full-time major gift officer working in a public or private university is expected to make about 150 to 180 face-to-face visits annually. Major gift officers understand that 75 percent of their contacts should be face-to-face. They may be expected to make between twenty and thirty *gift proposals* per year. According to the article, "Some institutions require detailed written strategies for the top 50 or 75 prospects and less detailed written strategies for all other assigned prospects" (29).

The article concludes that programs that are more systematic in "tracking and applying performance metrics" are more successful. It is interesting to note that public universities have been more rigorous in applying performance metrics than private universities. What can we learn from them? As one CEO I know puts it, "What gets measured gets done." A white paper released by the Advisory Board Company, entitled, *Raising the Bar: Managing Major Gifts Officers to Exceptional Performance*, states: "Very few CDOs are satisfied with how much time their MGOs [Major Gift Officers] spend visiting donors. . . . The most common refrain heard in the research was that gifts officers were 'in the office too much'" (Philanthropy Leadership Council 2006, 6). But wait a minute; you are the CDO *and* the MGO. You are going to have to kick yourself out of the office! Seriously, it will be a challenge to hold yourself accountable to make the calls you need to make.

In the by-the-numbers atmosphere of large-shop major gift operations, it is assumed that a gift proposal will be presented after four to five visits (Philanthropy Leadership Council 2006, 25). Chad Gobel, executive director of the Heart and Vascular Institute at the Cleveland Clinic, proposes for planning purposes a *conversion rate* of one to three (2006). So let's add it up: to close five gifts a year, you need to make seventy-five visits, right? But let's stop for a moment and look more closely at this model. In a large shop like a public university or a prestige hospital, they have something we do not: a seemingly inexhaustible supply of prospects. You might have 75, or 175, prospects on your list, but I predict it will be hard to come up with the next 75. Therefore, we need to adapt the model and invest the time needed to close a larger percentage of our prospects, say, two out of three. Nevertheless, large-shop methods suggest three valuable lessons any small shop can use:

- Get out of the office.
- Make a major gift cultivation call a week.
- Manage by metrics.

TIP #54

Train yourself to make one major gift
"purposeful cultivation" call a week.

The large-shop, impersonal, by-the-numbers approach to major gift cultivation doesn't seem to lend itself to our more grassroots effort, and that may ultimately be to your benefit. If we lean toward a specific model here, it is the one described at the beginning of this chapter: that of the development officer flanked by the president and members of the board, at the ready to engage; involve; and, when the prospect is ready, Ask.

Involve the President

Reading how the pros do it may leave you wondering how much energy university presidents invest in major gift cultivation. The answer: tons. According to *University Business* magazine, "Increasingly, university leaders are under relentless pressure to raise private funds to protect and grow colleges and universities" (Kaufman 2004, 50).

Here is a technique to get your president started down the road to becoming a major gift ace. Give him or her a top ten (or fifteen) list of names and phone numbers on a pocket-size laminated card. These should be some of the most important names on your prospect list. The president's assignment is to contact each person on this list once every four to six weeks and to report on the results of each call. The purpose of some of the calls should be to arrange face-to-face meetings. Review the list of names with the president once a month and make substitutions as necessary to optimize the use of your president's valuable time.

TIP #55

Give your president a laminated pocket card containing
contact information for his or her top ten prospects.

Other things you can do include inviting the president to accompany you on a few of your cultivation visits. A president's luncheon is an ideal way to get several prospects to the table at once. But the luncheon will not serve any benefit if the decision makers send stand-ins, so personalize your invitation strategy with the involvement of the president.

Involve the Major Gift Committee

A standing major gift committee of the board is a rarity, but I firmly believe in its value. Developing a major gift ethos on the part of the committee is job one. This may prove to be a challenge. Once this is developed, though, the committee can become a powerful engine of your cultivation process. First, what the committee is *not*: just another meeting at which you, the CDO, deliver reports about all your stellar work. What it is: a working committee designed to enlist board assistance for the calls you and board members need to make.

One of the most crucial things the committee can do is to have its members ask their peers on the board to make calls. Sometimes, when you ask the board member to make a call, it carries a little less weight; the board member may disregard the request or discount its strategic importance. With some major gift prospects you only get one shot at opening the door. Since a significant part of the CDO's job is creative nagging, it behooves him or her to have some powerful allies in the process.

The subject of donor cultivation is inexhaustible. So many experts have developed effective approaches to the task over the years, so many instructive anecdotes—stories of gifts that seem to have been given spontaneously when the cultivation was so seamless it made the gift a *given*, so many effective little twists and techniques. A development officer should be a lifelong learner when it comes to major gift cultivation strategies.

The Ask

When the cultivation process has been thorough and real, the Ask becomes infinitely easier to manage—though it is rarely a fait accompli. The Ask is in some respects the simplest element of the process. Most Asks can be accomplished in twenty minutes; it's all about execution. Either you close the deal or you don't. And it is surprising how often even very sophisticated organizations botch the Ask. That is why strategizing the Ask is a crucial step in the process. You must determine who should ask, how, when, for how much, and what, exactly, you are asking for.

Strategizing the Ask

The What

It would seem that after engaging in a thorough cultivation process you should know which initiative will interest your prospective donor. This is not always the case. You generally will have a pretty clear idea, but your donor may have a surprise or two in store for you. This happens sometimes because you forgot to consider some element in the discovery process, or it may be—and this is more often the case than you might guess—that the donor has not divulged crucial information during the cultivation process. Prepare for this by not putting all your eggs in one basket, your Marquee Project basket, for example. Plan to engage and discuss the options as the donor reveals his or her thoughts about the proposed gift. Nevertheless, always begin with a specific proposal based on your best analysis. I use a one-page gift proposal that spells out the proposed option in as few words as possible; see Appendix I for an example.

How Much

This aspect of the Ask is never as simple as it sounds. The amount must inspire and challenge, but never insult. The *stretch gift* amount should incorporate your best estimation of the donor's capacity as it relates to his or her linkage to your cause. You should discuss the Ask amount within your inner circle and, preferably, vet it with those who know the donor. Establishing the Ask amount is easier when the donor has a history of giving.

Don't forget to consider the terms of the gift. You will frame the gift as a multiyear pledge in most cases. This offers the organization flexibility in negotiating the gift amount. For example, offer to extend the payment period before reducing the amount of the Ask.

The When

When to ask is a question that tends to reflect organizational culture. Some organizations are more aggressive than others. Larger institutions tend to be more aggressive. Others prefer to "go long," emphasizing exceptional relationship development before the Ask. I prefer the latter course for small organizations, for which finding new prospects is not always so easy. The more aggressive you are, the more outright *nos* you are likely to receive. Those embracing the "go long" strategy may be genuinely surprised *not* to get the gift. Inexperienced organizations sometimes jump the process, coming away empty-handed and demoralized. So devote sufficient time to cultivation before asking.

The Who

After trying nearly every solicitation gambit under the sun, here are two approaches I have come to favor:

- The president asks, one-on-one.
- A board member and the CDO meet with the donor in tandem.

In the case of the first option, the president must have the ability to be the *closer*. Many do not, so you will have to deal with that first. Most presidents of four-year universities can be closers when properly prepped in advance. For presidents of two-year colleges this is not always true. If the president is willing and able, it is the responsibility of the CDO to brief, support, coach, and thoroughly prepare the president to make the Ask.

In the case of the second option, the board member represents the moral authority of the Ask. He or she helps to get the appointment, break the ice, and lay the groundwork for the Ask. In deploying the option, use yet another Rule of Three. In this case it means those present at the Ask include the prospective donor, the volunteer, and the CDO. You can break this rule if the donor is a couple. Having anyone else present will compromise the intimacy of the conversation. A three-way conversation leads to *triangulation*, a four-way leads to *conversation strangulation*! Never ask by committee.

The How

The Ask is face-to-face, of course. Beyond that, the preferred practice is to situate the Ask on the donor's turf, the donor's office, for example, in the context of a brief, focused visit. This would be especially true of the second option. Alternatives, especially for very large gift Asks made by the president to a donor couple, might include dinner in a club atmosphere. Distractions are always a hazard in this situation, which is why universities support presidential mansions. Restaurants are even more of a hazard unless specific measures are taken to control the environment in which the discussion takes place. If your donor prospect cannot hear you, or the waiter intrudes at the wrong moment, all may be lost. Commotion is doom!

I have routinely made tandem Asks with a board member over lunch with the donor, but I don't favor them. Board members, however, often do. Sometimes the donor becomes impatient to get to the point of the luncheon, or the board member slips into a social familiarity that complicates the purpose of the meeting. The focus of the gift proposal is easily compromised in this setting. When this format is the best I can manage, I usually try to hold the Ask until about half to two-thirds of the way through the lunch. Simply shift gears from social interaction to the Ask and make the pitch in the same way you would make it in the donor's office.

The Moment of Truth

Finally, after all your preparation, the moment arrives. It should feel natural and personal. Project a sense of ease and purpose, with the focus entirely on the donor. Eye contact, smiles, and relaxed body language are essential in this high-stakes atmosphere. An Ask is an *occasion*.

The Board Member/CDO Ask

When participating in a tandem presentation with a board member, have the board member establish rapport and provide a brief summary of the context of the Ask. Once that is done, the board member turns the presentation over to the CDO, who calls upon the sum total of his or her training and experience to make a serious, compelling, and brief gift presentation. Then together they remain silent and wait for an initial response.

This rule comes straight from "Fundraising 101": never break the silence that follows the Ask. It may be long. It may seem an eternity. And it may mean your Ask has hit home and your counterpart is seriously considering the things you just said. Hank Rosso defined this moment as one of "pure salesmanship" (1983). Commonly, the silence is followed by questions from the donor on a range of details that could include anything from the nature of the proposed project to the specific terms of the gift.

So begins the second stage of the process: dealing with reservations. You may want to refer to the section "Dealing with Reservations" in chapter 10 in relation to Annual Fund Asks. This part of the process is essentially the same for major gifts.

The gift presentation should be geared toward prompting an immediate answer whenever possible. In most cases, "I'll think about it" is not the desired answer. Yet, sometimes that is the best you can do, for example, if you didn't factor in the need for spousal consultation. But be aware that "I'll think about it" often drifts into the category of "no decision." If the answer is less than yes, but more than no, it is critical to arrange a formal follow-up step with the donor, which should occur within weeks.

Sometimes the donor will say the project sounds wonderful but he or she just can't do it right now. Work that angle with open-ended questions to establish whether this is true or you just need to think about the proposed gift in a more creative way. If it is true, the assertion is not a no. It just means that donors make major gifts on their timeline, not yours. In this case the donor just goes back to the cultivation pool.

Sometimes the donor will just say no, sorry, but he or she can't do it due to other priorities and commitments. In this case, thank the donor for his or her time and say that the organization regards the person as one of its closest friends or it would not have asked for support at this level. Then shift to a more casual mode by, for example, stating your hopes that the person will be able to attend an upcoming recognition event. If the answer is yes, thank him or her in the most heartfelt terms, letting the volunteer lead. Express your excitement (this won't be hard) and then . . . *get the gift terms straight.*

Gift Agreements

Gift agreements are formal documents containing the relevant details pertaining to the gift. Some organizations use them; some do not. CASE recommends them. I don't favor them in this context because in a smaller organization an almost familial feeling begins to insinuate itself into the process. The donor relies on the honor of the *gentleperson's agreement* to follow through on a verbal commitment. The donor may recoil from the legalese of a document. At this moment, you don't want the donor thinking about lawyers. Instead, I recommend taking notes, repeating back to the donor the detailed terms of the gift, and promising a formal acknowledgment letter from the president, containing all of the details of the gift, within twenty-four hours.

I have never lost a gift due to the lack of a formal gift agreement. Even a named gift can be handled in this manner. Two exceptions come to mind, however. In the case of establishing an endowment, a permanently restricted gift in the eyes of your auditors, I propose to the donor that a gift agreement be prepared stating the terms of the endowment. The donor and the president each sign the document. In this case, donors seem to appreciate the formality of the process. Whatever confirmation method is used, don't forget to discuss the donor's preferences for announcing and publicizing the gift. Often donors will say they don't need or want any public recognition. Let them know that appropriate publicity may inspire others to give. If in the end you prefer to go with formal gift agreements, *CASE Management and Reporting Standards* offers authoritative document templates (Netherton 2004).

The other exception is that of certain named gift transactions. If you are proposing to name a building, a wing, or a program after a donor, you need to spell out the exact terms and conditions of the agreement. In the past, naming opportunities were thought to be forever. But what if your college decides to renovate the facility in fifteen years? What if the donor dies without fulfilling the pledge and the heirs decide not to pay it off? Since you never know what the future may hold, it is a good idea to get the agreement down on paper.

When naming opportunities arise, it is advisable to have a named gift policy on hand that spells out the correlation between gift amounts and the opportunities for named recognition. Do some benchmarking with similar colleges that already have such policies in place to determine what might work at your college. Having these policies on hand can sometimes even facilitate the closing of a larger than anticipated gift. Ben Wright, president of Dunwoody College of Technology, told me of a conversation he had with a longtime donor during which the donor asked what kind of gift it might take to name a particular program after him. Ben consulted his handy naming opportunities guide and said, "Half a million dollars." The donor said, "Let me think about it over the weekend." He made the gift.

Variations of the Ask

There are three variations of Ask formats. The first is to have the development officer make the Ask one-on-one. This format is common in four-year university major gift programs. In obtaining the appointment, the development officer should indicate that an Ask is coming, by saying something to the effect of, "I'd like to talk to you about a gift opportunity." Given proper prior cultivation, the development officer should have no trouble establishing rapport and setting the stage for the Ask in the opening minutes of the visit.

The second variation is the major gift obtained by submitting a grant proposal. In this case, the turning point is the invitation to submit a formal proposal. The proposal must spell out the goals, objectives, metrics, and outcomes of the grant-supported initiative. The proposal development process can take weeks or months in the case of large grants. The CDO should monitor the entire process to keep the scope of the work on track. Moreover, the CDO should review and approve the final product before submission.

In considering the proposal, the funder may request more information or clarification of certain aspects of the proposal. Keep the president and board leadership in the loop throughout the process and, where appropriate, get them involved in the final-stage communications with the funder. When you receive the gift, seek the funder's permission to roll out the PR machinery to share the news of its philanthropic largesse with the world.

A third variation is the development of an industry partnership as a component of the gift. This practice is most common at technical colleges or for applied programs such as nursing. Such partnerships are routinely sought in a campaign, but one can also come into play in a major gift transaction. Industry partnerships can be an invaluable asset to the college, but they sometimes lead to problems in gift terms, control, execution, and follow-through on the part of the industry partner or the college.

Here are a few principles to help keep partnerships on track:

- Partnerships are a two-way street.
- Dialogue is the first element of a partnership; the checkbook is the last.
- Education moves more slowly than business. Both parties must negotiate a learning curve in learning to work together.
- Educational institutions can proceed in a businesslike manner without becoming a business.
- Private industry values most the ability to deliver.

A Long-Term Perspective

Engaging in a major gift program inevitably will have some transformative effects on the college. Proficiency in the major gift arena takes time. If early efforts do not yield immediate results, be patient. I have been involved in cultivation processes that took up to ten years to land a major gift. In the end, the only rules that work are those that work with each individual donor. When the course of action is in question, try to put yourself in the donor's shoes. And never give up. Major gifts is an area in which a long-term perspective often contains the key to the ultimate gift.

Endnotes

1. DeWitt is the author of *The Nonprofit Development Companion*, The AFP/Wiley Fund Development Series (2010).

2. In Council for Aid to Education. 2007. *2006 Voluntary Support of Education*, New York: Council for Aid to Education Table 4, indicates that total individual giving comprised 51.7 percent of all gifts to higher education. The report states, "Total personal giving would have been 14.3 percent higher had those [family foundation] gifts been added to other reported personal gifts" (p. 15). These two amounts, when added together, equal 66 percent, supporting the contention stated in this book. The *2009 Voluntary Support of Education* survey states that alumni and other individual gifts account for 45.3 percent of total giving, compared to 51.7 percent in 2006. This decline is probably attributable to the recession of 2007–2009. However, an additional 21.1 percent of imputed personal gifts from family foundations in 2009 yields a total 66.4 percent of all gifts derived from private donors. This further reinforces the durability of the pattern.

References

Council for Advancement and Support of Education (CASE). 2010. 2010 *Circle of Excellence Awards Judges Report.* https://www.casecurrents.org/Award_Programs/ Circle_of_Excellence/2010_Winners/Fundraising_Programs_2010_Judges_Re port.html (accessed September 8, 2011).

DeWitt, B. M. 1995. Letters to the Editor: A better philosophy of development. *Chronicle of Philanthropy* 7, no. 1.

Gobel, C. M. 2006. Major gifts—by the numbers. Presented at CASE V Conference, Chicago, December 11.

Grabow, T. W. 2006. By the numbers. *CASE Currents* 32, no. 3, 25–32.

Hunt, P. C. 2005. Purposeful cultivation. Presented at CASE V Conference, Chicago, December 12.

Kaufman, B. 2004. Juggling act. *University Business* 7, no. 7.

Netherton, Robin (ed.). 2004. *CASE management and reporting standards* (3rd ed.). Washington, DC: Council of Advancement and Support of Education, Appendices C-N, 97–127.

Philanthropy Leadership Council. 2006. *Raising the bar: Managing major gifts officers to exceptional performance.* Washington, DC: Philanthropy Leadership Council/ The Advisory Board Company.

Rosso, H. A. 1983. Fund raising 101 (author's lecture notes). Presented at The Fund Raising School, San Rafael, CA, October 23.

13

DEVELOPING A FULL-FEATURED PROGRAM

The Annual Fund and major gift programs are the alpha and omega of our model, but in this chapter we explore some elements to broaden your program and perhaps launch you in new directions. We consider how to develop a robust grant program, a rudimentary planned giving program, and an alumni relations program.

Building a Grant Program

We have already covered how a grant program can serve the Annual Fund. Here we focus on program grants. Your ability to deploy this activity will depend on your location, markets, and budget. Given the two-year college sector experience in the government grants arena, we can expect to build on some existing grant development expertise.

Prospect Research

Since the ability of your college to sustain a significant private grant program may be an open question, we'll begin by investigating your potential markets. The objective is to identify corporate and foundation sources that fund higher education, scholarships, diversity, and areas of academic and special interest that intersect with your college's core capacities. These may include:

- Immigrant services
- Women's issues
- Disabilities
- Refugees
- Social justice

- Economic self-sufficiency
- Workforce development
- Math and science competency
- College readiness
- Secondary and postsecondary partnerships
- Literacy

These topics often occur as keywords in searchable databases. As with the Annual Fund, our process is quick and simple: check the guidelines, spot a match, see what similar organizations are funded, and determine whether you have a qualified funding source. The free online GuideStar web site (www.guidestar.org) is an excellent source of IRS Form 990s for nonprofit funders. The second element of our research strategy is to review the annual reports of comparable colleges and organizations. You can often find these online, including at GuideStar. The ability to assemble a list of fifty potential funders in your service area would tend to indicate the potential for a viable private grant program staffed by a full-time staff member.

The Foundation Center (http://foundationcenter.org) is an invaluable online resource to identify foundation funders. It maintains fifty Cooperating Collection sites around the country and offers personalized assistance through its Associates Program.

Initiative Development

The next step is an internal review of potential or existing initiatives that might be suitable for grant funding. You might begin by interviewing academic and student affairs officers. These conversations should touch on the college strategic plan and current state of special project funding. But often, the real potential for innovative initiative development is found at the faculty and program director level. The best way to gather this information is through individual conversations.

Knowing which faculty members to interview is often based on one's tenure on the job. Seek out creative thinkers, dynamic program directors, program initiators, holders of previous grants, and others of a similar description. Ask your deans whom to consult. A government grant writer can be an informed source with an existing network of faculty and staff partners.

Use informal interviews to identify your colleagues' academic passions, paying particular attention to interests that coincide with known foundation and corporate sector interests, such as diversity. Pay particular attention to the capacity of your potential faculty and staff partners to execute. Having collected a number of ideas, the grant officer should then conduct follow-up research to see what other colleges are doing in those areas. Next, the grant writer should collaborate with the CDO to analyze the efficacy of potential initiatives from two points of view: the ability of the college to develop the program, and the potential willingness of the funding community to support it. Then identify existing documents that might provide elements of a draft proposal. Draft several proposal templates that make the case for the ideas you think have the best chance of gaining private grant support. This is where the college is dependent on your expertise. The *fundability* of each project is the paramount concern here.

One of the hallmarks of an effective grant program is the ability to get quality proposals out quickly in response to funding opportunities. Effective grant writing is a systematic process of research, writing, direct contact with funders—and volume. It is *not* working until midnight the night before the deadline. The ability to write well is a requisite talent. The ability to state appropriate goals, objectives, outcomes, metrics, mission-based ROI calculations, and timelines is paramount in today's results-oriented corporate and foundations market. We covered most of these topics in chapter 7, in relation to the development of the strategic plan. Remember, the whole outputs versus outcomes discussion originated in the grants world.

Grants must offer value to the funder in terms of *mission-based ROI.* Mission-based ROI begins with bang-for-the-buck and ends the notion that the gift investment advances the mission of the *funder.* Doing good things for people is great. Foundation program officers receive dozens of proposals proposing just that every day. But learning how to align your proposal with the core mission of any given foundation is invaluable expertise in the grants arena. Once a basic alignment of a proposal with foundation program objectives is established, the next thing foundation officers look for is the potential return on investment toward the societal good *they seek.* That is, they have their own mission to fulfill.

My philosophy is to promote programs that serve many beneficiaries—to significant, life-changing effect. Helping a large number of students trumps helping a small number. If the project is going to serve only a few students, then the outcomes had better be nothing less than transformational. I try to highlight these dynamics for program officers so they don't have to figure them out for themselves.

One more thing: to maintain your own integrity as a steward of charitable dollars, never pitch a program that your organization cannot deliver or to which it is not committed. Pitching programs that have insufficient internal buy-in can lead to disaster. The best way to facilitate getting your next grant is to excel in performing your first grant. Conversely, foundation program officers within a given region know each other and a questionable reputation travels fast.

Grant Cultivation

Once you have completed your prospect research and preliminary initiative development, get on the phone with grant program officers. Introduce yourself in a manner sufficiently personal that program officers will remember you in the future. Compliment them on some aspect of their work about which you have become knowledgeable. *Seek their advice* about some question with which you are wrestling. Ask to meet them. They usually discourage personal meetings with grant seekers, but occasionally you get lucky.

Your first goal is to get program officers to listen to your elevator speech about a program that fits their guidelines. Explain that you don't want to waste their time with a written submission about a project that would be outside their area of interest. Often, on the heels of that introduction, they will give you a few minutes of phone time. Hang on to every word of their feedback. Say, "Oh, that's a great point. Give me a second to jot that down so I don't lose it." I know this sounds rote. It sounds stupidly simple—but it works. Having established this basic rapport, you can feel confident that they will remember who you are. Moreover, you have established some degree of credibility with them.

TIP #56

Always talk to a program grant officer about your idea
before writing a letter of inquiry or full proposal.

The second goal is to get an invitation to submit a Letter of Intent, or LOI. Establish the optimal time frame for its submission. An LOI received after a telephone conversation merits more consideration than one that arrives unannounced. I attach a personal note to the formal LOI mentioning how I followed up on an observation the program officer made, or some other detail pursuant to the original telephone conversation.

Cue your follow-up to the LOI to posted review cycles or information you received from the program officer. Follow up by telephone rather than email. Once you receive an answer, it goes one of three ways: up, down, or resubmit in another grant cycle. Up is easy. Complete the full proposal for the earliest possible grant review cycle. Resubmit is easy, too. Just ask when. A "No" is more intriguing. Whenever appropriate, call the program officer and *ask for advice*. What can you do to strengthen the program? What would make the idea more compelling? How well did he or she think it fit the guidelines? Would another funding cycle be better? Can the program officer recommend another funding source?

Writing Tips for Grant Writers

Once you have secured the invitation to submit a full proposal, write as precisely as possible to the published guidelines. The grant proposal is a very specialized type of writing. It helps to make it a *fact-rich environment*. Data, measurement, specificity—these are all prized components in good grant applications. It takes time to build a proposal on data. The research or data upon which the proposal is based is usually the weakest element of grant applications. That's why, once we have decided on our initiatives, we need to build the case for them before turning them into grant applications. Don't assume the funder already knows how wonderful you, as a college, are. So build the case, and then write the proposal. Rule number one follows from this requirement: Don't procrastinate. Grants take time.

The Who-What-When-Where-How format works well in grant proposals, with special attention to the What-When axis of information. This takes us back to our discussion of outputs versus outcomes from chapter 7. To write: "Our goal is to boost our FTE persistence rate by five points, from 60 to 65 percent, by June 30, 20XX," really does win the grant.

Sometimes too much really is too much. Even if you have a boilerplate proposal ready to go, be prepared to tailor it to the preferences of a given funder. For example, don't send a fifty-page proposal to a funder who prefers ten pages. And if you only have ten pages and you imagine they want fifty, don't pad the extra forty off the top of your head. Unnecessary verbiage weakens grant proposals.

15 Tips for Writing Better Grants

1. Remember, short is better. Program officers do a lot of reading. Although a major grant proposal should be perceived as a substantial document, it should never be padded with ineffective writing.

2. Write to the *deliverables.* Focus your writing around the central things you are promising to do if you receive the money. This should become the central organizing principle for your narrative.

3. Keep it simple. Never succumb to the temptation to try out all your old graduate school moves just because you are writing to a prestigious foundation. In their world, clarity is highly prized.

4. Use simple, active-voice sentence structures. Subject-verb-object wins the day for quick readers. Minimize the use of adjectives and adverbs. Rely instead on strong, active verbs. Be specific. Tell them exactly what you will do and when.

5. Devise a powerful, elegant statement of the problem you are addressing. Foundations were invented to solve social problems, so make yours compelling. This means building the case with data, illustrating it with personal anecdotes or experiences, and making compelling conclusions about the situation you are describing.

6. Don't waste time. Get to the point.

7. Cut jargon, even benign jargon. It doesn't make you look smarter. Instead, write things the way you might say them to a person who is outside your immediate orbit. In the outside world a "learner" is still a "student."

8. Explain acronyms and don't overuse them.

9. Never confuse outputs with outcomes.

10. Don't over- or underpromise. Bang-for-the-buck is a huge issue for grant makers. They want to achieve measurable change with each grant they make.

11. Think lean and don't pad when it comes to funding. Perhaps you have an internal policy that you tack on 30 percent overhead for any grant you submit. Consider that such a policy may win you 30 percent fewer grants.

12. Write to the grant form. Provide sufficient detail where prompted. Those questions are there for a reason. Tailor your narrative to the funder's preferences. If the funder wants to know your graduation rate, but your college doesn't count things that way, translate and offer detail.

13. Build a compelling picture of organizational effectiveness by citing achievements, outcomes, and recognition. Include numbers and dates. You may revere your president, but just because your president says something doesn't make it so.

14. Be modest. Express success with facts. It is possible to convey excellence without sounding like you are beating your chest.
15. Be readable. This is a sum-total judgment. Enlist a disinterested party to review the nearly finished product. Don't forget the rules from Composition 101; but remember, this is *business writing.*

Sometimes the prospective funder requires a site visit. Here is a little secret I have learned over many years of grantsmanship: program officers have ego needs. Cater to them a little. That means the same principles apply to the site visit as to any other development cultivation function. Go to the nth degree and marshal all of the resources at your disposal to meet the needs of your visitor. The faculty member or program director closest to the project should be present, the vice president for academics or dean may be involved, and the president may at least stop by to say hello.

Paradoxically, the goal of the college grant officer is to write as few grant proposals as possible. The process of developing a quality proposal takes too much time to waste the effort on a weak concept or an unlikely funder. And sending out scattershot boilerplate proposals is pointless. A good grant writer should know how to achieve a two-thirds success rate on proposals submitted. Being a good writer is less important than mastering research, positioning, and cultivation strategies. As development officers who are aware of the need for an ROI on our time, we must apply all of the relationship-building tools at our disposal to create a relative funding advantage.

For those unfortunate (and we hope, rare) occurrences when a grant is not funded, refer to the recommendations in the discussion on responding to LOI denials. Contact the program officer by phone (never email) to respectfully request more detail on why the grant was not funded. The more deeply you can explore the issue with the program officer, the more you will learn what you need to know to improve the competitiveness of your proposals and your college. Try to discern whether the funder thought you made a compelling case for your project and the mission-based ROI for the deliverables you promised. These two issues are at the core of your competitive standing in the grants arena. College grant officers are privileged to have the opportunity to receive candid assessments from funders—private donors will often withhold the real reason they decline to give. And while it is true that we learn much from our successes, we do, in fact, learn far more from our near misses.

When you do receive the grant, timely, fact-rich reporting is a must. But more important still is the ability to deliver exactly what you said you would deliver within the time frame you promised. Over many years, in many institutions, I have seen this principle honored in the breach. I know: *things happen.* But that should be the exception rather than the rule. The best way to get the next grant is to overdeliver on the first—and to back up your claims of success with hard data.

Government Grants

While the government grant program is often situated within the chief academic officer's portfolio, a few of the principles bear a mention here, if for no other reason than sometimes a single grant writer handles private and government grants. Most government grants to community colleges come from federal and state funders. Government agencies publish guidelines online and colleges respond to Requests for Proposals, or RFPs. Well-known federal programs include Fund for the Improvement of Postsecondary Education (FIPSE); TRIO; and Title III, Part A. These programs are characterized by intense competition for funding. State programs are more varied and address a much smaller universe of colleges. Several principles can aid colleges that seek to be more competitive in this environment.

As one who began his development career in federal grants, winning over a million dollars in funding from the Title III and the former Title VIII programs for a four-year college, I can attest that the research and data organization skills I acquired in graduate school came in handy here. The most important asset a college can develop is to have an experienced grant writer on the staff who specializes in this activity. There is no substitute for specialization here.

That said, four overarching principles determine a good portion of a college's competitiveness in the government grants arena:

1. **Target those programs for which you are best positioned to succeed.** Winning government grants takes so much time and expertise and so many resources that no college can pursue every opportunity. Strategic factors, including geography, student demographics, course offerings, faculty expertise, management sophistication, and other factors, influence the competitiveness of the college in winning government grants. Colleges tend to make the best determination of competitiveness when senior leadership collaborates with an experienced government grant writer to make these decisions. The best decisions take into account a long-term perspective. Such a perspective often includes multiyear or multifunding cycle strategies to build credibility and expertise. Sometimes it takes a full-on effort just to

receive the preliminary reader feedback from the funding agency. Given limited resources, colleges do well to match their prospects with realistic assessments of the productivity of the grant writer. This is not to say that others, such as faculty and institutional leaders, may not be involved with the research and writing, but success usually comes down to having an expert leading a team of experts.

2. **Devote your very best strategic research resources to the effort.** Once you know you are well positioned to succeed, the real work begins. Seeking funding for something like the federal TRIO program to promote student persistence takes a significant amount of research and strategic planning. Internal and external research combine to build the strongest applicant profiles. Internal research involves understanding your capacities for student interventions and pedagogy, along with sophisticated information technology input on issues like student demography. External research involves understanding the guidelines, competition, timelines, expectations, odds, and unspoken rules of the game. The most valuable external research I ever did was to attend a multiday workshop for federal grant seekers to the U.S. Department of Education Title III program. Presenters from the Department of Education offered vital information and perspectives. Fellow attendees revealed much about the nature of the competition and the strategic issues at their colleges through their interactions.

The best analogy I can think of for a successful institutional research effort is the type associated with the reaccreditation team effort, especially the type deployed in support of an AQIP-based accreditation effort. You convene a grant team the same way you do an accreditation team. Areas of expertise are assigned and staged deadline dates all feed into a final output stage where a writer or writers input final text into finicky online application formats. The primary mistake colleges make at the research and planning stage is assuming that programs are "good enough." Given the competition, there is no such thing until proposed programs are firmly grounded in the best education research you can find. Assignment of personnel is never more important than it is with government grants. You can't use placeholders; people need to plan the actual work to construct a compelling narrative.

Program professionals must understand how their student demographic compares on a national stage. This is most important when

---

TIP #57

Government grants should be grounded in the best
research of which your institution is capable.

---

considering programs that seek to involve the underserved. Institutional research must feed into what you intend to do and how and when you intend to do it. And all of it must be oriented to creating a substantial measure, no, a *transformational* amount of change with the dollars you receive. Whether you are strengthening your institution or improving the lives of students, you must be solving significant problems with significant solutions. If you can do that, you are on the right track.

3. **Cultivate complete college buy-in to the government grant effort.** Government grant programs can't be run from silos. A grant writer isolated from academic leadership tends to show up in grant applications. Instead, work to involve the best faculty thinkers whose work touches on the grant initiative at hand, and bolster that involvement with input from your top academic officer and the office of the president. Regular meetings led by the grant writer keep people in the loop and on schedule. For many grants, the cooperation of information technology and institutional research offices is essential to developing competitive proposals. With programs like FIPSE, you need your most innovative faculty minds involved at the ground level. Think of how an accreditation team functions at your college; that should be the model for really big grants.

4. **Write exactly to specifications.** Writing in response to federal agency RFPs is technical writing. Nowhere else do you find a complex scoring system assigning points to each and every detail of a proposal. Though academics are often contracted to assign these scores to applications, the writing that wins the day is almost never purely academic writing, but is instead highly technical, unitary writing that conveys the specific information required by the question or narrative instructions at hand. Writing government grants is like no other kind of writing in higher education. You must know how the rating system weights various sections of the proposal. If you can't slam-dunk the

most heavily weighted criteria, then your brilliant concept will never get a hearing. For example, if the credentials of your project leaders are unconvincing, no one will take the time to give you the credit you deserve for a brilliant implementation plan. For this reason, you can't simply assign sections of the proposal to faculty members and post their work without integrating it into the flow, narrative, and style of the whole. All of this argues for the value of having an experienced government grant specialist leading the team in all its aspects, including the final written product. Don't let hierarchy get in the way of that.

Planned Giving Demystified

Planned giving is the secret weapon of long-established institutions. Wills and trusts can account for significant annual revenue for even a small college with a long history. Planned giving is the means by which such institutional treasures as Harvard's $27 billion endowment are amassed. It used to be called *deferred giving*, but the only deferral I discern in too many nonprofit organizations is the deferral of launching the planned giving program itself. Why is that? I suppose it is because the payoff is not immediate. Other things (the gala) seem more pressing. Yet if Harvard had not built its endowment over the years, there might not even *be* a Harvard today. The twin engines of an active planned giving program and a growing endowment can help to put the wind to your back for generations to come.

Just how powerful can this engine become to two-year colleges? Kirkwood Community College, which launched its planned giving program in 1996 (Mitvalsky and Hawn 2005, 5, 8), administers an endowment of $13.5 million (Kirkwood Community College 2010). Monroe Community College in Rochester, New York, has twenty-three members in its planned gift recognition society (Mitvalsky and Hawn 2005, 13). Dunwoody College of Technology, with its ninety-year history, has over a hundred living members in its legacy society.

Planned giving is a vast field, but we focus on wills, or bequests. Gifts made by will constitute roughly 80 percent of all planned giving dollars raised. For small organizations, that number approaches 100 percent. At times, it seems as if elements of the professional planned giving community have conspired to turn planned giving into a boutique of complicated, tax-driven legal constructions. Much of that complexity is unnecessary. When I was campaign director at Dunwoody, out of the nearly $40 million raised through campaigns during my tenure, we had a grand total of two charitable remainder trusts and one charitable lead trust. During that period, the college received $10 million through bequests.

One of the predictors we used in identifying bequest prospects was the existence of a donor record that included many small gifts made over a

---

TIP #58

Identify bequest prospects by their long history of giving small gifts.

---

period of years. These gifts were commonly in the range of $20 each. Just why this donor profile is appropriate for planned giving is a bit of a mystery, although I have a couple of theories. First, many loyal donors are afraid of outliving their money. Second, many of these donors fit the psychographic profile described in the book *The Millionaire Next Door*, by Stanley and Danko (1996):

> These people cannot be millionaires! They don't look like millionaires, they don't dress like millionaires, they don't eat like millionaires, they don't act like millionaires—they don't even have millionaire names. Where are the millionaires who look like millionaires? (7)

This book is a useful companion text for thinking about planned giving. As we remarked in the prologue to this work, many community colleges are about forty years old now and the first generation of faculty is retiring. These men and women have devoted their careers to your mission, they care deeply about the legacy of their life's work, and they are your first market for bequests.

Here is a list of primary markets for bequests:

TIP #59

Consider retired faculty and senior administrators
as a primary prospect pool for bequests.

- Faculty (current and retired)
- Senior administrators
- Major donors with a long history of support
- Friends of the college
- Long-term board members
- Long-term, low-dollar donors
- Millionaires next door

This is not a large universe of prospects. Perhaps that's why community colleges have overlooked planned giving too often. Yet you are almost certain to find planned giving donors within these constituencies. Here is how I would proceed:

- Identify prospects from the groups.
- Write or purchase a wills brochure.
- Make some exploratory calls on presidents emeriti or longtime board members.
- Send the brochure to qualified prospects, announcing the formation of a Legacy Society for bequest donors.
- Refine the pitch for endowed scholarships.
- Talk up the Legacy Society at a retiree luncheon.
- Cultivate former faculty members through personal visits.
- Close several first-round gifts.
- Hold the first Legacy Society luncheon.
- Publish the story of one bequest donor in the college magazine.

Planned giving is the responsibility of the CDO. By implementing the steps above, you should be able to close three or four bequest gifts during the first year and at least that many every year to follow. If you can do this, congratulate yourself, even if nobody else recognizes your good work. Launching a planned giving program is a huge achievement. It just might be one of the most important things you will ever do for your college. It can become a satisfying aspect of your professional life. You have just launched a permanent program that, with proper stewardship over time, will help to fulfill the mission of the college.

The wills brochure presents the advantages of estate planning and the perils of leaving the estate unplanned and communicates how easy it is to update an estate plan. (The occasion of an update to the plan presents a good opportunity to include one's favorite charity.) The brochure also touches on some of the life changes that can precipitate an estate review. It emphasizes your mission and the wonderful things a legacy gift can accomplish. The brochure contains boilerplate language covering a number of options through which to structure a bequest (Appendix J). You can purchase personalized wills brochures from specialized vendors, but I prefer to write my own. It allows for a greater focus on your own institution's mission. It also allows you to use more familiar, folksier language than vendors tend to use. If you are not a writer, hire one and provide him or her with an example of a brochure you like as a guide.

Distribute the wills brochure via cultivation sessions and visits. Think of yourself engaging a donor or couple over coffee. It may also be distributed via *micromailings* to targeted groups, such as your retired faculty, accompanied by a letter offering to assist with legacy planning (Appendix J1). The brochure is not intended for mass mail distribution. If you try that, expect a miniscule response. In any case, a small print run will do. To develop your planned giving skills further, enroll in a training workshop such as the one offered by John Brown, of John Brown Limited, a noted expert in the field (www.johnbrownlimited.com).

The planned giving call requires developing a unique cultivation style. A planned giving Ask is a *soft Ask*. A prerequisite is a solid rapport with the donor. Planned giving executive Gary Hargroves holds that there are ten steps to the process, from gathering personal information to stewardship, and each one requires a visit (1998, 17). Knowing the prospect well is not required, but it helps. The nature of the interaction should become personal to the degree that the prospect regards the development officer with a high level of trust. The prospect should view the development officer as a long-term steward of the organization. Planned giving is a discipline in which relationship development skills are paramount. Turnover in this position can really hurt your cause.

The legacy aspiration might be considered a new tier at the pinnacle of Maslow's hierarchy of needs. It becomes an aspiration of the most highly self-actualized individuals. Gently guiding the conversation into the waters of legacy thinking is a valuable skill for a development officer to master. One planned giving practitioner I know asks her prospects to *dream with her a little*.

The legacy Ask is sometimes posed in *what if* terms, such as: "Have you ever considered establishing some sort of family legacy at the college?" It's

---

TIP #60

The legacy Ask is a *soft Ask*.

---

soft. It's a mere suggestion. Then listen for the clues that could lead to a decision.

Once a few legacy donors have signed on, organizing the inaugural Legacy Society luncheon is a simple enough affair. Host the luncheon in an attractive, cozy space on campus—your group will be small at first. At the outset, ask the attendees to stand and introduce themselves, to say a few words about what the college means to them. Lunch is served, new members receive framed certificates, a couple of students speak, and the president gives a brief inspirational talk. The president hosts the luncheon.

Tell the personal story of a legacy donor's gift commitment in a college publication. Consult the publications of private colleges and universities for examples of these. Focus on the donor's aspirations for the good this gift will convey and on the satisfaction the donor derived from the commitment of a *gift of a lifetime*.

Charitable Gift Annuities

The exception to our focus on wills is charitable gift annuities (CGAs). CGAs can be a remarkably effective planned giving vehicle for the right nonprofit. Dunwoody College of Technology's use of the vehicle proved to me its effectiveness in a mature two-year college program. For colleges with some history, CGA use should be explored.

According to the American Council on Gift Annuities (ACGA), a gift annuity is a contract under which a charity, in return for a transfer of cash, marketable securities, or other assets, agrees to pay a fixed amount of money to one or two individuals for the duration of a lifetime (ACGA n.d.[b]). During the donor's life, the annuity pays an income stream to the donor, the amount of which depends on the age of the donor when the gift is made. The amount of a CGA can be as low as $10,000. Donors who become comfortable with the annuity concept often purchase additional annuities over time. The ACGA regulates the percentage rate paid on the annuity.

The downside for the sponsoring organization is that it must assume the risk of guaranteeing the income stream throughout the life of the beneficiary. For this reason, the vehicle can be problematic for colleges that have little experience in managing investments. In addition, some states regulate CGAs (ACGA n.d.[a]). Therefore, you would have to research the eligibility of your college or system to offer CGAs. The Saint Paul Foundation in Minnesota has demonstrated one solution to this potential obstacle; it administers CGAs on behalf of the colleges within the MnSCU system whose endowments are managed by the foundation.

Developing an Alumni Relations Program

Alumni relations is a secondary activity in the emerging college program. *In a small to midsize shop, the alumni relations activity must be driven by the development function.* This is a crucial point. Even when Dunwoody College was raising $5 million a year, it retained a strategic focus on sustaining only the alumni relations activities it could afford and justify in terms of cost and future development opportunities. I have seen many community colleges turn this equation around. They seem to think that only by developing an alumni affairs program first could they ever hope to attract alumni support. This is just not true.

In the model I propose, the alumni relations activity is composed of the following components:

- A college flagship publication with an alumni component
- A nominal alumni association
- An alumni association board
- An alumni volunteer activity
- Program-specific alumni events

The College Magazine

My recommendation is to go with a high-quality flagship publication that represents the entire college to the community. Fund the publication partly with college marketing dollars. How do I justify this? *The college would require the publication even if no development program existed.* This is true because the publication satisfies the marketing and image needs of the college. Perhaps 50 percent of the content should focus directly or indirectly on community and alumni involvement and a sense of giving back. The editorial philosophy I recommend is this: *no ideas but in people.*

TIP #61

Adopt an editorial philosophy of *no ideas but in people* for your college magazine.

Colleges tend to like to write about how wonderful they are. But communication professionals and journalists tell us always to tell the story through the experiences of real people. Recruit writers from your English Department faculty—and pay them. Use a four-color format, because this is one publication in which such a format really matters. To afford these luxuries, send your flagship publication to the prime demographic of your database while reserving a thinner publication aimed directly at your alumni for the bulk of your largely undifferentiated alumni database. This segment of the list will largely be composed of younger nondonors. Mail with sufficient frequency to track the movement of your database and augment this strategy with reliance on the U.S. Postal Service's National Change of Address (NCOA) service. One more tip: for a low-cost college foundation annual report, produce it as a four-page, two-color insert in your magazine.

TIP #62

Produce a low-cost foundation annual report by including it as an insert in your college magazine.

The Alumni Association and Alumni Board

Our strategic fundraising philosophy employs a bit of counterintuitive thinking to propose that forming an alumni association board is a more important function than developing a robust alumni association. An alumni association is a loose identification with the alma mater, to no particular purpose except that of a loose identification with the alma mater. Yes, membership in the association may lead to an increased propensity to give, especially in the case of a four-year college or university with an established brand. At its core, the alumni association is a bit of, as Kurt Vonnegut would say, "a *granfalloon*" (1963, 91–92), "a proud and meaningless association of human beings" (Vonnegut 1974, xv). I recommend you extend alumni association membership to alumni who make a gift and be done with it.

An alumni association board, on the other hand, is a real entity, something you can work with. The alumni association board should be the primary focus of the alumni relations program, because over time this body will become an adjunct volunteer engine of service to the development effort.

TIP #63

Focus your alumni relations activities on
developing a strong alumni association board.

The mission of the alumni association board will be to *give back* to the college. Members of the alumni board must donate with 100 percent participation. Offer to restrict their gifts to an alumni development fund if that will help to promote board giving. The board may assist with admissions; student life enhancement; and, of course, development. Its purpose should also be to develop an emerging leadership cadre from within the alumni.

At Dunwoody, longtime members of this group have emerged as an increasingly important source of major gifts. Keep your long-term development objectives in mind as you recruit members to this board. Focus elements of the board's mission from the outset, for example, by organizing a mentorship project. This type of activity is common among alumni volunteer groups. Focus on assisting students who are academically at risk through a kind of Big Brothers and Sisters effort for student success, for example.

Over time, the board will develop a cultural life of its own. It may become involved in an alumni night during the phonathon. It may want to sponsor a golf tournament. If so, I highly recommend that you stay with a cultivation event rather than a fundraising event, for all the reasons already articulated in this book. Beware of *mission drift* in relation to events.

Alumni Events

The primary organizing principle behind program-specific alumni events or reunions is to reconnect alumni with their former programs. Technical colleges have an advantage here. Community colleges also have opportunities in their nursing, dental hygiene, and culinary programs, to name but a few.

Though the college will need to fund a modest budget for alumni relations, alumni events can be largely self-funded through a modest admission fee.

TIP #64

Organize alumni events around academic
programs with cohesive identities.

Organize these events around the involvement of current and retired faculty members, those touchstones of a shared alumni experience. Run a slide show of old photos (alumni love seeing their faculty as seventies hipsters). Share stories that elicit a communal feeling. Alumni leaders can encourage their peers to give to a program-specific scholarship fund initiated through the phonathon. Invite student callers who represented the program in the phonathon to attend.

Continuing education programs awarding continuing education units (CEUs) might work for some alumni groups. In this case host an on-campus dinner, with remarks by the host faculty, students, and alumni speakers, followed by the continuing education program. You can ask alumni attendees to cover the cost of the dinner and the CEU presenter's fee.

For most events, keep the price in the $15–$20 range. Cover any costs over that amount through your alumni relations budget. That's the basic formula. Repeat as necessary to establish a viable alumni events program. In the next year or two, add to your alumni relations calendar events related to additional programs.

Technical colleges (and nursing programs) that have placed an appreciable number of alumni at a particular company may want to try a company-sponsored alumni event, such as a breakfast. This is a wonderful way to align company and college leadership via a fun, easy event that reinforces the value of the relationship between the college and the employer while encouraging alumni cohesiveness. Dunwoody College of Technology has used this technique extensively to great effect.

To identify alumni who might want to become more involved with your college, conduct an alumni survey, requesting personal data and information on careers and interests. Those who respond are sending you a signal that they may be interested in more involvement. You can link this strategy to an exploration of whether your alumni would like to receive an email newsletter, a technique that might be of particular interest to younger alumni. You

TIP #65

Send out an alumni survey to determine who
is out there and what their interests are.

can strengthen your young alumni engagement by developing your relationships with current student leaders. Keep in touch with them through blast emails once they matriculate. Celebrate their successes as an informal cohort. Your interest in their subsequent college careers may be returned in kind when they come back to serve as alumni volunteers and leaders.

References

American Council on Gift Annuities. n.d.(a). The philosophy of gift annuity agreements. http://www.acga-web.org/philosphy.html (accessed February 17, 2011).

———. n.d.(b). What is a gift annuity? http://www.acga-web.org/whatisga.html (accessed February 17, 2011).

Hargroves, G. 1998. How to conduct donor/prospect visits. *The Journal of Planned Giving* 2, no. 2.

Kirkwood Community College. 2010. Condensed balance sheet: June 30, 2010. http://www.kirkwood.edu/site/index.php?p=22180 (accessed January 24, 2011).

Mitvalsky, C., and Hawn, S. 2005. Planned giving: Approaches that work for community colleges. *Community College Advancement Series* (electronic file, CASE item #28253). Washington, DC: Council for Advancement and Support of Education.

Stanley, T. J., and Danko, W. D. 1996. *The millionaire next door.* Marietta, GA: Longstreet Press.

Vonnegut, K. 1963. *Cat's cradle.* New York: Bantam Doubleday Dell.

———. 1974. *Wampeters, foma and granfalloons.* New York: Dell Publishing.

14

OPERATING THE PROGRAM IN A BUSINESSLIKE MANNER

Over twenty years ago, the accounting firm Coopers & Lybrand, now PricewaterhouseCoopers, called on nonprofits to run their development back-office operations more efficiently, citing the need for cost control, the prevalence of undue complexity, and the increasing importance of charitable giving as a revenue source (Segall 1992, 7). With that assessment in mind, I will focus on a few critical areas and potential trouble spots.

Office Functions

Let's start with the basics. Scholarships are not awarded by the foundation. Accounting is handled by knowledgeable bookkeepers outside of the office. Acknowledgment letters go out within twenty-four hours of receipt of the gift. Monthly revenue reports are produced within days of month-end. You can characterize these efforts as objectives in an annual Action Plan:

- Objective 1: Transfer responsibility for accounting to the business office by 9/30/12.
- Objective 2: Lower the cost of fundraising to 32 percent of revenues while increasing the development budget by 10 percent by 6/30/12.
- Objective 3: Complete scholarship process improvement, cutting administration time by 20 percent below the previous year by 6/30/12.
- Objective 4: Introduce a three-step process improvement plan to coordinate college–foundation fiscal coordination by 11/30/12.
- Objective 5: Refine the disbursement process by 3/31/12.

- Objective 6: Adopt new 501(c)(3) accountability guidelines by 12/31/12.

Where you begin depends on where you are. Developing performance metrics for quality improvement is an important element in running the development operation in a businesslike manner. Learn to *compress time* (McCormack 1998, 2D) in the performance of these activities to spend more time with donors.

The Donor Database

Maintaining a clean donor database can be a major factor in the efficient operation of a development office. One principle rules in this enterprise: garbage in, garbage out. You want to avoid this syndrome at all costs. A development officer with hands-on database management experience should provide top-level oversight of the development database. In a small shop, this usually means the CDO. If the CDO does not have the requisite expertise, you should contract out the work of upgrading the database to an experienced development database consultant. If you can't define *Boolean logic*[1] (Cohen 2007), you probably won't qualify as a database administrator.

Many emerging community college operations are plagued by the following problems:

- Thousands of bad addresses on file
- Hundreds of poorly understood, stale data categories
- Inconsistent data file formats based on botched data imports
- An expanding universe of alumni to track

All of these problems stem from a lack of expertise in data management. So the first rule of thumb is "Hands off!" I prefer to have a designated data management "czar," whose approval is required for each proposed alteration of or addition to the database core structure or standard practices. The second rule is to establish the simplest possible chart of accounts and track things at the optimal hierarchical level. For example, rather than establishing a new "Annual Fund" category every year, keep a single fund designation by that name and track gifts by gift date. A hundred examples like this must correlate properly for you to produce essential database queries and reports easily. Which brings us to rule three: get help when needed.

Lost addresses and lack of phone numbers are particularly vexing problems in most emerging programs. Rule number one is to mail regularly and use the U.S. Postal Service NCOA system as appropriate. Your mail house can manage export/import operations related to mailings for a relatively modest cost. As we mentioned earlier, there are commercial name/address overlay services out there to help you track down lost connections. But it is preferable not to lose touch with your alumni in the first place. If you have twenty thousand alumni of record and valid addresses for fifteen thousand, work the fifteen thousand first. When you do add data, such as new graduate data every year, get everything—second addresses, phone numbers, cell phone numbers, email addresses . . . everything. Arrange to store it all neatly and, above all, consistently.

Increasingly, email addresses and cell phone numbers trump postal addresses and landline numbers in importance. In the cutting-edge development operation, email often. Enhance this contact with blast voice mails regarding important campus events of interest to alumni. Check out four-year, private colleges for some especially creative applications of these and other post-postal communications strategies. One caveat, though: if you want your alumni to read your magazine, send a real magazine.

What'll It Be, Raiser's Edge . . . or Raiser's Edge?

A category killer has emerged in the fundraising database world, a Microsoft for our universe—Blackbaud, whose The Raiser's Edge™ software has emerged as the industry standard. Many development officers don't know anything else. The good news, and major reason to consider Raiser's Edge, is that so many development professionals are familiar with it.

Raiser's Edge is a powerful, complex, relational database program that requires a significant training commitment for those who will be using it on a day-to-day basis. Training is especially important for those who will be devising queries and running reports. Complex reports may require Crystal Reports experience. In our model, the executive assistant has primary responsibility for day-to-day database operations, including query and report generation. The director of annual giving should receive formal training because he or she also manages a data-intensive enterprise.

Once your staff members have been trained, they can rely on impressive telephone support offered by Blackbaud as part of the service agreement. Participation in an online Raiser's Edge users' group can help your staff to determine how other organizations solve similar problems. For more comprehensive needs, Blackbaud offers a variety of consulting services as well as a companion accounting package that meets the needs of some organizations.

I am not endorsing this product any more than a person explaining the function of Microsoft Word to a Martian would necessarily be endorsing it. I will share a slight bias with you, though. I do not like *campus-wide integrated higher education solution packages supporting a development function.* The developers of those behemoths do not understand, conceive, or deploy development database applications like the specialists do.

Personnel Management

Training and Development

Despite the availability of a wide array of training and development options, many emerging community college programs don't seem to take advantage of them to any great degree. Regional CASE conferences are an excellent way for practitioners in two-year colleges to broaden their understanding of the collegiate fundraising model while learning from professionals presenting cutting-edge practices from leading institutions. This book has drawn upon many such CASE presentations I have attended.

I have found that CASE conferences offer something to professionals at every level of experience, from the first-year annual giving officer to executives with twenty-five years of experience. The CASE acronym is affectionately known as "Copy And Steal Everything." The ability to share information is one of the miraculous cultural advantages of our profession. So why not celebrate that collegiality by bringing home a few shiny new ideas from your next regional CASE conference? You will find that adapting ideas from four-year colleges is not difficult; all it takes is a little creativity and resourcefulness.

The Council for Resource Development (CRD), an affiliate council of the American Association of Community Colleges (AACC), may be the best-known source of institutional development resources for the two-year college market. Association of Fundraising Professionals (AFP) chapter memberships are a low-cost way to receive monthly professional development and networking opportunities, though the discussion topics will be much more general in nature than those of CASE. Local nonprofit consortiums offer low-cost training series that can be especially useful for the emerging professional. Some law firms have nonprofit or higher education practices that offer special topics series that can yield information on IRS changes, Sarbanes-Oxley-type initiatives, and planned giving. These are just a few of the choices from which to select.

Development officers tend to view professional development opportunities as a highly regarded perk. Too often, they are thwarted in their professional development aspirations by inadequate training budgets. Given our focus on the development of businesslike practices, the CDO is encouraged to review a range of training options before submitting the annual development budget for approval. Every development officer should have a personal development plan that includes one or more annual goals, together with the education required to achieve those goals. The personal development plan is an element to be covered during the annual performance review.

Staff Meetings

Staff meetings can play an essential role in staff development. The trick is to avoid the gravitational pull exerted by administrative trivia during these meetings. When the entire staff is present, rather than just the development officers, the common ground between the administrative and professional staff members is the administrative infrastructure that underlies the development operation. My advice is to push the administrative camel's nose out from under the tent. Schedule administrative procedures meetings when you need them. Staff meetings should be about the development mission. Do not let administrative trivia dominate!

Staff meeting time should provide an opportunity for varied activities to coalesce in a manner that increases awareness of, and appreciation for, the interconnectedness of the elements of the development operation. Discussions of the work at hand allow everyone to see how it all fits together. The full participation of the CDO in these discussions offers the staff insight into their development leader's point of view. Such participation reveals the expertise that supports that point of view. Staff meetings offer an excellent vehicle for the administrative staff to learn the strategic underpinnings of their practice. Discussions of event planning, prospect strategies, awards programs, or the hot development topic of the moment can lead to meaningful dialogue and creative thinking.

I prefer to have the CDO chair the meeting, to keep the tone focused on the leader's view of the team's objectives. The CDO can introduce any number of ideas to reinforce the staff development aspects of the meeting. Ben Wright, of Dunwoody College of Technology, requested that each development officer share a *donor story* at each staff meeting. This practice highlighted the mission and donor interactions in a way that fostered a shared understanding of their deeper meaning. Another technique is to request a presentation based on an article appearing in a professional journal at each meeting to promote awareness of what is going on in the development sector as a whole. Reports on an educational workshop such as one presented at a CASE conference support the same goal. Discussing a shared text such as Hank Rosso and associates' *Achieving Excellence in Fund Raising* (2003) provides a sustained vehicle for thinking about best practices.

Ethics

Use the staff meeting for an annual discussion of ethics. Start with the "Code of Ethical Principals and Standards" published by the Association of Fundraising Professionals (2007). The AFP code has become the industry standard of ethics for the development profession. The document in its comprehensive form is forty-three pages; the code itself is a one-page document. The comprehensive version can serve as the text for a discussion that spans several meetings.

Ethics is more than a rote acceptance of a set of principles. Meaningful discussion should include hypothetical and real-life scenarios that explore the meaning and context of ethical behavior. Consider the topic of conflict of interest at the board level. What if the chair of the finance committee is also an officer of the company with which you invest your funds? Or consider this question posed by Independent Sector:

> A board member who heads the best public relations firm in town is the volunteer chair of your publicity committee, and has a contract for some of the organization's advertising. Is this relationship acceptable and if so, under what conditions? (1991/2002, 22)

Independent Sector recommends that philanthropic organizations conduct a self-evaluation of their ethical practice standards every year. It also recommends that the review address the following questions (2009, 6):

1. Have we articulated and agreed on the values that drive our organization?
2. What steps should we take to integrate our code of ethics into the culture of the organization? Have we ensured that directors, staff, and volunteers are familiar with our code of ethics?

3. How well is our code of ethics reflected in the organization's policies and procedures?

These questions, from *The Principles Workbook*, published by Independent Sector, represent just a few of the comprehensive series of discussion topics and questions posed in *Principles for Good Governance and Ethical Practice: A Guide for Charities and Foundations* (2007) and its accompanying workbook. These are available to download at no cost at Independent Sector's web site. A consideration of these principles in the Independent Sector format should be a mandatory exercise for all nonprofit boards.

I would add to this list an annual review of the AFP code. After collectively reviewing the AFP code of ethics for the first time, I recommend asking each development officer to sign a statement that he or she has read, discussed, understood, and agreed to uphold the code.

Independent Sector recommends an external ethics evaluation every few years. Few nonprofits have adopted this practice, but doing so would qualify as a best practice for organizational ethics and quality assurance.

In my experience, most gray-area ethics issues involving board members sound a little bit like the scenario cited previously of the board member who heads the public relations firm holding a foundation contract. In the most egregious cases, such potential conflicts of interest compromise the integrity of the board, staff, and organization. To complete the circle of ethical accountability, board involvement in ethics reviews should be mandatory. Board members should subscribe to a set of ethics, with explicit reference to self-dealing and conflict of interest. Prohibition of each should be spelled out in a board policy statement or bylaws, and a fellow board member should cover these topics with each new board member during an orientation session.

Organizational integrity begins with personal integrity. Development professionals must model the highest standards of personal integrity in all their interactions. A discussion of integrity and ethics in the communal atmosphere of a staff meeting can be the best way to emphasize the centrality of ethics. Such use of the staff meeting elevates the status and perception of the meeting itself.

Performance Evaluations

I am no expert in this area but I can say that over the course of my career I have seen them botched by the best. Having sat on both sides of the table, I have always wondered: Who dreads the performance evaluation more, the evaluator or the *evaluatee*? To guide my efforts in this area, I developed a practice based on three principles:

- The job description as a performance evaluation reference
- The annual Action Plan as a performance reference
- The use of metrics

The parameters of the job description should establish the field of the conversation. Using our examples in appendices A1–A3, we can refer to the percentage of time allocations to see where the development officer stands on that score. If administrative activities are budgeted for 25 percent of time but consume 40 percent, maybe we need to look at strategies such as *compressing time* or process improvement before we accept allocating that 40 percent to meetings and paperwork. The Action Plan presented in chapter 7 introduces focus and metrics into the conversation. Relying on the Action Plan, the question becomes: Did you make your goal? Did you make the subgoals? If so, let me recognize you for your great achievement in these areas. If not, let's talk about it. Let's take them one by one and review the outcomes.

Regarding qualitative issues such as methods, process, and demeanor, I don't know about you, but where I live, *everybody* is above average. Ratings of "average" or, heaven forbid, "needs work" are grounds for sulking. I prefer to rely on a short narrative, a pithy statement of the issues at hand, rather than a number, a letter, or a grade, but this is not always possible. John Donahoe, CEO of eBay, described the goal of performance review as offering open, objective feedback in a constructive way (Bryant 2009, BU2). That sounds good to me.

Development officers are an interesting breed. They work outside the limelight, without much recognition from the community they serve. Having been denied so often the ego gratification they secretly desire, they can become enormously attached to the work elements within their spheres of influence, elements they wish to own and control. This can create a real minefield in the performance review. My advice is to start with metrics and end with praise if praise is due. If praise is not due, be generous with professional training. There are many excellent resources to choose from. And occasionally we must conclude that development work is not for everyone.

The Audit

Managing the annual audit is a onetime drain that can be managed for efficiency, freeing up time for real work. To help you do this, design the accounting and database systems to generate the numbers auditors need automatically. Have canned reports available for pulling multiyear pledges. Write off bad pledges before the audit. Review the findings from the previous year's management letter early in the fiscal year, so you have time to implement work flow redesigns before the next audit cycle begins. Keep previous-year working file documents organized and handy to prepare the current-year audit trail as efficiently as possible. Doing these things will help to reduce the cost of staff time devoted to the audit.

If you have not sent your audit out for bid in the last five years, benchmark your audit cost with peers. If your cost looks high, send it out for bid. This could save you thousands of dollars.

Postscript: Details Matter

Previously we discussed sending scholarship thank-you notes written by students to scholarship donors. In a discussion of this practice with some community college colleagues, one of them asked, "Well, how do you get the letters from the students?" "We chase them all over for those!" I answered, somewhat amazed. "They don't get the scholarship until we get the letter!" Compared to my colleague's shop, that simple act of interoffice coordination between the development and financial aid offices probably saved enough staff time for my shop to run a phonathon! The colleague continued, "How did you get the financial aid office to agree to do that?" Again, a little bewildered, I said, "I just asked them. They were happy to do it."

Mastering a few of the process improvements described previously can make a huge overall improvement in the efficiency of your office. I encourage development professionals to think about administrative functions in new ways at every opportunity. Systematic process improvement is one of the most powerful tools at your disposal in reshaping the life of the office.

Endnote

1. Boolean logic, which refers to the logical relationship among search terms, is named for the British-born Irish mathematician George Boole.

References

Association of Fundraising Professionals. Code of ethical principles and standards, adopted 1964; amended September 2007. http://www.afpnet.org/Ethics/En forcementDetail.cfm?ItemNumber=3261 (accessed February 17, 2011).

Bryant, A. 2009. Corner office: John Donahoe. *New York Times*, April 5.

Cohen, L. B. 2007. A primer in Boolean logic. *Boolean searching on the Internet.* http://internettutorials.net/boolean.asp (accessed February 1, 2011).

Independent Sector. 1991/2002. Obedience to the unenforceable ethics and the nation's voluntary and philanthropic community (rev.). Washington, DC: Author. http://www.independentsector.org/uploads/Accountability_Documents/ obedience_to_unenforceable.pdf (accessed January 18, 2011).

———. 2007. *Principles for good governance and ethical practice: A guide for charities and foundations.* Washington, DC: Author. http://www.independentsector.org/ principles_for_good_governance (accessed January 21, 2011).

———. 2009. *The principles workbook: Steering your board toward good governance and ethical practice.* Washington, DC: Author. http://www.independentsector .org/principles_for_good_governance (accessed January 21, 2011).

McCormack, M. 1998. Successful people find a way to compress time. *Minneapolis Star Tribune*, December 1.

Rosso, H. A., & Associates; Eugene R. Tempel (ed.). 2003. *Achieving excellence in fund raising* (2nd ed.). San Francisco: Jossey-Bass.

Segall, P. 1992 (July). Fund-raising management: Issues and trends. *Nonprofit Management Newsletter.*

15

A FUNDRAISING FACULTY

Department chairs, faculty members, and college leaders can play an important role in a collegiate advancement program. While department chairs in applied programs like automotive technology, business, culinary arts, information technology, and nursing have an advantage in terms of linkage with a likely pool of prospective donors, chairs in any program can initiate the advancement cycle with a little attention to this aspect of institutional leadership.

Three-Step Process

You might begin with a three-step process:

1 Identify opportunities.
2 Establish linkages.
3 Coordinate with the advancement office.

Identify Opportunities

The first step entails developing a habit of thinking about people you hear of or encounter as potential donors. Prospective donors can sometimes be hiding in plain sight without anyone seeing them as donor prospects. Perhaps what we miss is imagining what a person who is warm to our cause, or who could become warm to our cause, could offer given systematic cultivation.

Begin by making a list of people, institutions, or businesses with whom you might create a linkage to your program. If you know little or nothing about the person, fine; that just makes him or her a *suspect* instead of a *prospect* in development terms. The trick is to move the individual from the former to the latter category. If an individual is an alumnus, or a business has regular interactions with your college, then you've already moved the person up a tier or two on the cultivation grid. Think about ways to convene your faculty around this exercise as a strategic initiative within your department.

TIP #66

Academic and administrative leaders can assist the development mission by evaluating their community contacts as prospective donors.

Establish Linkages

Think about how you can extricate yourself from the office or classroom long enough to make personal contacts with people. It's simple: invite in or go out. Inviting contacts in might include an activity such as a luncheon with students. Inviting local leaders in to engage students directly is one of the most powerful cultivation tools available to faculty members. Initiating an annual alumni get-together is another tool to consider. Inviting local leaders in for tours and inviting them to cultivation events are tried-and-true methods department chairs use to engage the prospective donor community.

Think about ways to reach out to the community as well. Most colleges are represented at local service organizations. Having faculty leaders serve as liaisons to these organizations broadens the base of college perspectives available to the community. Business and professional organizations comprise another field of engagement. Just as the ability to identify potential donative intent in the greater community becomes a habit of mind, the same is true with strengthening community linkages. It comes down to relationship development. Every faculty leader can have a short list of four or five contacts with whom he or she commits to strengthening such relationships.

Development officers are always looking for the next opportunity to interact. Follow their example and commit to asking, "Can I call you next week to follow up on that lead?" or, "Would you mind if I invited you to science project day?" These little entrées are the building blocks of mighty advancement efforts; they all begin with a habit of mind.

Coordinate With the Advancement Office

Here we address the issue of *traffic control*. Advancement departments and chief development officers need to know who is engaging whom out in the community. This becomes a highly focused area of attention in university advancement programs. The first step is to coordinate lists. Ask to meet with your CDO to share your short list of potential donors, and express your interest in engaging them in a cultivation effort. While a donor may be reserved for some established area of giving, or may be identified as a major gift donor, development of multiple relationships within the college community rarely interferes with the advancement process.

Take a moment to reassure the CDO that you will keep him or her in the loop. Brief call notes in an email can go right into the donor record. (And, yes, advancement offices do keep details like that.) Seek advice from the CDO and take care not to get out in front of advancement in terms of asking for the gift. Sometimes, especially with major gifts, the longer you cultivate, the bigger the gift. Your first role with prospective donors is as an ambassador.

Next, ask the CDO if he or she has a few prospects you should get to know. Most CDOs in small-shop advancement offices cannot possibly keep up with the number of potential donors out in the community—or even on their own alumni boards. If you are from a department that does not already have a natural pool of community stakeholders, ask your CDO if you might offer a second, personal gift acknowledgment to scholarship donors whose gifts benefit your students. Offer to sit at a table with students and donors at the annual scholarship recognition dinner as an unofficial *hospitality officer*. This is the type of assignment that junior development officers cut their eyeteeth on, but as a senior leader of the college, you bring an unequaled wealth of experience and knowledge to the task. It may surprise you how responsive donors are to such attention.

Advanced Activities for Department Chairs

Personal, face-to-face interaction is the heart of advancement. When you feel confident about your initial forays with community members, you might want to ramp up your cultivation activities. There are several ways to do this. The first is to remember that *people give to people with a cause*. You can be a prime candidate for this role. First, you need your story—a simple story you can tell in less than five minutes, under the rubric of campus trends and activities. Did you open a new arts or science wing? Are you serving new groups of students? Are your students exhibiting needs the community might address?

Relationship development for advancement is never about just making friends; it is about making friends around your mission. One-on-one meetings are the gold standard for making rapid progress in relationship development. After you have mastered your story, focus on preparing to ask open-ended, *get-to-know-you* questions of your guest. Asking about children is always a great icebreaker. Chapter 12 offers a variety of cultivation tips you can use. Finally, where appropriate, seek advice. This can lead to significant advances when you are dealing with community leaders or business owners.

Always try to think one step ahead about getting the next interaction scheduled. (Yes, it *is* a little like dating!) Sometimes opportunities arise when you meet (a banker wishes to speak about financial literacy to an economics class), and all you have to do is be proactive about following up. Sometimes it helps to have an opportunity or two in your back pocket. Usually, the CDO can help with things like that. The most important point to remember is that the weakest link in this type of cultivation effort is usually the follow-up, so concentrate your resources and attention there to avoid engaging in a series of one-off meetings.

TIP #67

The most important step to effective cultivation is to follow up on personal interactions in a meaningful way.

When you get really good at cultivation, you might want to consider an Annual Fund Ask as part of your cultivation efforts. You should always know whether your prospect is a donor before you meet. When that is the case, you can lead with a personal thank-you. When your acquaintance seems to be demonstrating a desire to give something back, consider including a simple Ask in your repertoire: "You know, Tom, do you think you or your business might consider a $250 gift to the college this year?" Tom always has the option to say he'll think about it and get back to you. Whenever you do include an Ask in your message, make sure to inform the advancement office.

While we are on the topic, always jot down the three most salient points about the meeting immediately upon its conclusion. Formalize those points, and other details of interest, in a three hundred–word call report for the advancement office. They will love you for it.

Gifts In-Kind

Department chairs are uniquely qualified to take the lead in securing gifts in-kind. The first step in such efforts is to develop the relationship before asking for the gift. The next step is to be strategic about what you want—and what you do not want. Finding a match between donative intent and departmental needs is always a delicate dance. You don't want old, cast-off equipment, and your contact in the industry doesn't always want to part with items of current value.

Often, a tour should precede a discussion of gifts in-kind, so your prospect can see firsthand what your real needs are. This step also serves to build the prospect's enthusiasm. In my years in development I have seen many millions of dollars' worth of recent vintage or even new hi-tech equipment donated to my college. These discussions are most like any other major gift solicitation, but I have noticed that department chairs excel in the technical dimensions *and* relationship dynamics of such interactions.

Sometimes, we don't know where to look for the real treasures companies have to offer. When companies move, entire workstation setups, complete with nearly new computers, may become available. Filing cabinets, office furniture, new items for the student lounge, all of these can become part of the corporate in-kind gift package. The key sometimes is just letting a word drop about needs and wants. Again, it is as much a habit of mind as anything else.

Colleges that are serious about gifts in-kind would do well to have gift acceptance policies that address the issues that arise in these cases. For large or big-ticket gifts, you often need to coordinate with facilities managers. Department heads, academic deans, and provosts are well situated to manage the internal process. The bottom line: don't accept anything you can't use.

Grants

Academic leaders are well equipped to partner with advancement grant writers to seek grants from private funders. While grant writers routinely consult with faculty in preparing grant proposals, faculty members possess all the skills necessary to writing compelling grant applications themselves. Larger private foundations, the type staffed by professional program officers, often bring a degree of rigor to their grant making that is familiar to academics. Taking the lead while consulting with the advancement team can be an effective way to improve the competitiveness of your college grants program. When appropriate, collaborate!

Foundation grants often support academic enhancements, particularly for underserved students. Deans of student services can team up with faculty members to write program grants for such initiatives. Advancement grant writers are generalists. When writing is a strong suit, as it so often is for faculty members, why not locate the expertise more directly in the academic realm? While faculty members often claim they do not have the time for such projects, it seems that granting professional development credits for grant writing would be a fair way to underscore the value the college places on such efforts.

At minimum, faculty leaders can research the types of programs that are winning private grant support on the national scene and propose relevant projects for joint development with the advancement team. With grants, the value of a compelling idea supported by data cannot be underestimated.

Actual Fundraising

A few academic departments engage in direct fundraising. Some do it through raffles, special focus events, or student-led efforts. A little grassroots initiative is fine. Quid pro quo efforts like raffles and sales are best left at the margins of philanthropy and in the realm of retail transactions. The art department at Normandale Community College holds an annual soup bowl ceramics sale and lunch that generates goodwill and a few dollars each year. The effort is run entirely within the department, which keeps all the proceeds. It works, and people are content to buy the items without confusing the issue with donations.

Raffles are another story; in general I do not favor them. Academic departments often wish to approach local businesses that are already supporting the college directly with monetary gifts. Some efforts seek to enlist the advancement office to generate letters and receipts. I find it more effective to have departments support existing efforts, such as assisting with special event auctions or taking one night of the phonathon and supplying all the volunteer callers for an evening's effort focused on the department's alumni. Your advancement office will be eternally grateful for such assistance.

Occasionally, a department will come up with its own brand of fundraising that is effective on its own terms. I have seen this in particular with specialized departments such as theater and music. These departments possess expertise with events that can lend themselves to community support. Creativity is the key here. The graduate theater program at the University of Washington sponsors an adopt-an-actor program directed at parents and friends of students. People who have followed the better part of a theater season are sometimes eager to sponsor an actor. Plays offer successive opportunities to engage prospective donors, who can become fans of the program itself. Such efforts require a long-term commitment, branding, and nth degree donor relations to become successful income generators for the program and the college.

Turnover

Most department chairs are elected or selected for limited terms, often one or two years. This potential lack of continuity is a problem you must address when becoming active in advancement. Relationships require time to develop and, once developed, cannot be handed over lightly to a new person. In advancement offices, turnover is one of the primary impediments to success.

But chairs do change, so you want to think about a longer-term plan for the prospects with whom your chair interacts. You could empower former chairs to continue as the primary contacts with donors. If you plan to hand off relationships, the process needs to be intentional and managed with sensitivity to donor perceptions.

It is easier to hand off business relationships than individual donors, who don't always respond well to being "handed off." This becomes a strategic determination—who is the best *fit* with a given donor? Ask your CDO for a little coaching on maintaining relationships in a revolving chair situation.

Involving Students

Recently, I have encountered a number of colleges attempting student-driven options for fundraising. If you encounter an idea by which students are to raise money from other students, I encourage you to think again. There is a wide world of potential community supporters out there. Though students are a tempting captive audience for some, their financial situation is too fragile to see them as a prospect group, despite what they spend on pizza.

I witnessed an interesting exception to this rule after Hurricane Katrina. Student government officers organized solicitations of fellow students and raised several thousand dollars, which the college foundation passed on to an aid organization. These students felt so fortunate in comparison with the devastation experienced by the residents of New Orleans that they felt compelled to organize and contribute on moral grounds. That was an inspiring moment, but it was hardly the norm, and the college was not the beneficiary of these gifts.

Students approaching local businesses can interfere with established relationships maintained by the advancement office, so I would tend to discourage that avenue as well. Students approaching their parents or extended family, on the other hand, can be effective, especially when the purpose of the drive is something students themselves feel strongly about. You might encourage a student government role here. The faculty or administrative advisor should offer guidance on proposed fundraising activities. Solicit input from the advancement office. Not every student idea falls within normal or IRS guidelines for philanthropy, and this goes double for raffles of any kind.

Recruiting students to help as paid callers for a phonathon is another issue entirely. One of the primary barriers to a successful phonathon is the number of callers required. Though I realize this isn't what most faculty members have in mind in considering becoming active on behalf of advancement, it is assistance that is sorely needed and greatly appreciated.

The Role of Deans, Provosts, and VPs

Senior administrators and officers of the college are ideally suited to representing the institution with donors. They share longevity, specialized expertise, and deep knowledge of how things really work within the organizational culture. While many are peripherally involved with major donors, both individual and corporate, assuming greater primary leadership roles would be a natural progression for them.

A good way for senior administrators to begin is by coordinating their contacts with the president. The president can handle only so many interactions personally. Expanding the circle with the involvement of senior leadership is an ideal way to increase effectiveness in cultivation and donor relations.

If the advancement office is already preparing a Top Twenty prospect list for the president, add a second tier of names that officers of the college can divvy up. Just a few names each will make a difference. Then manage these relationships the same way the advancement office co-manages those cultivations with the office of the president.

Another role senior leaders can play is to become *stewardship officers* of the college. Presidents and CDOs must continually be on the lookout for the next big gift to close. But donors appreciate attention *after* making the gift. Why not divvy up a list of influential donors whose gifts bear some relation to a particular department or administrative unit of the college and develop the relationship further? Tours, interactions with students, telephone invitations to college events, inspection of works in progress, and high-level briefings solidify the VIP insider status donors covet. The primary impediment to such interactions is a sense of *busyness*, as in "We're just too busy, our calendars are too full" for such activities. Yet, if a legislator requests attention, we drop everything and attend to his or her needs. Reinforcing the direct connection among cultivation, stewardship, and funding will strengthen the entire external focus of the college in a variety of ways.

Raising the Profile of the College in Coordination with Advancement

Taken together, faculty and administrative leaders maintain extensive networks of professional and civic affiliations. Instead of moving in separate spheres of influence, why not coordinate information derived from these memberships for the benefit of the entire external relations program of the college? Every conference has sponsors, keynote speakers, or participants who may be of interest to the advancement team. Faculty members routinely encounter presentations or research underwritten by foundations. Knowing which programs interest which funders can be invaluable to the advancement officer. Sometimes this information even comes with personal linkages and context provided by the faculty member. It is not that such connections are trade secrets unavailable to development professionals; rather, small-shop advancement programs with limited research capacities may overlook such tidbits of information.

Even a short follow-up email or phone call from a faculty member can provide the impetus to strengthen a linkage. Consider that informed linkage in contrast to the results that could be expected from a cold call from a development officer. It all comes down to sharing information. Any development officer will tell you how valuable this habit of communication is to successful prospecting.

You might even consider taking ten minutes out of your college leadership team or academic dean's meetings for a little *community connection* brainstorming. Often, when one faculty member describes an interaction with a business or organization it sparks ideas from peers. Note these ideas in your minutes or just invite a development officer to join you for the last fifteen minutes of your meeting. Big ideas count in development work, but sometimes little ideas count even more. And every idea or connection needs thoughtful follow-up to count for much in the long run. A little *proaction* goes a long way!

The Attraction of New Ideas

It helps to orient faculty members about the proper role of donations in the college funding hierarchy. Chapter 1 presented the notion that philanthropy provides funding at the margins, funding new initiatives and approaches to academia. It is frustrating to presidents and faculty alike, but you cannot expect donors to rush in to support programs whose state funding has been cut or whose tuition revenue is in decline.

The confusion about the relative attraction of new ideas versus *funding the gap* is found in even the most sophisticated academic settings. A faculty study group at the University of Virginia—a national leader in advancement—concluded that "donors to the University are attracted by 'new ideas,' not the 'bread-and-butter,' day-to-day work of the faculty" (Kelly 2007). Professor Deborah Johnson, chair of the Department of Science, Technology and Society and member of the UV faculty senate in 2007, said, "We have to figure out how to package that to appeal to donors" (Kelly 2007).

Indeed, packaging the daily "bread and butter" in a way that appeals to donors becomes the $64 million question on many campuses today. But I encourage faculty members to engage in the kind of visioning that surpasses repackaging of core activities and instead puts the donor at the center of the equation, asking, "How can we astonish and delight our donors with the amazing work we are doing?" This approach leaves a certain amount of "bread and butter" off the table. But it does lead us in the direction of engaging donors with stories of good works—great works even—because that is what inspires them. And we must inspire them if we want them to make significant investments in our mission. There is no reason why these stories cannot come directly from faculty members (and their students), thus locating teaching and learning at the center of the equation. New ideas are the driver for that process.

Within academic departments, chairs can help to set appropriate expectations about what works well and not so well in advancement appeals. The heart of this is the donor-centric approach advanced in so many development texts today. This recognition reinforces that proper—and ongoing—orientation is a necessary component of the partnership among faculty, administrators, and advancement. In situations where advancement professionals are new to the academic milieu, that orientation must work in both directions.

The needs of academic departments are not always apparent to donors; in some cases, with a little education a fit can be found, but not always. In this respect, the cultivation process in an academic setting is a delicate maneuver. Mutual respect and understanding between the advancement and academic spheres provides the foundation of an effective strategy in educating prospective donors and finding a meaningful balance between institutional need and donor interest. Of course, the donor always speaks last in this dialogue. You just want to create a process by which the donor's final word is "yes."

A Little Recognition Goes a Long Way

The currency of recognition has long been recognized in academia. In situations where compensation and career advancement can be somewhat stationary, awards speak volumes about the values of a college. The University of Arizona Foundation established the Faculty Fundraising Award to honor "faculty members who have shown leadership in fundraising for the University" (2008). The first of the annual awards, which was initiated in 2008, went to Professor Soyeon Shim, who spearheaded a $25 million campaign. "Faculty program directors need to be involved; it's not just the Foundation's job," said Dr. Shim upon receiving the award. Although your dollar and engagement threshold may be slightly lower than that of the University of Arizona, the principle will serve you well.

Innovation at the University of Arizona doesn't stop there. The Deans Plus Development Committee (so named because it includes nondeans) has been a tradition at the university for over twenty years. Its mission is "to encourage active fundraising involvement at the college and unit level." Its members have raised tens of millions of dollars over the committee's twenty-year history.

Faculty Members on Foundation Boards

Rather than appointing faculty members to ex officio or pro forma seats on the foundation board, why not reserve the honor for high-performing faculty members or deans? When faculty advancement efforts begin to make the kind of difference that University of Arizona professor Soyeon Shim makes, the honor has been earned. While the dollar amount raised will probably be less than $25 million in a two-year college setting, the relative importance of faculty leadership could be even more striking.

The secret to success here is to keep the bar high. You might add a clause to your foundation board bylaws indicating that faculty membership is permitted based on the merits of the nominee. In fact, you may replace an ex officio clause with an actual voting membership. While you may limit the number of seats available to faculty to one or two, you should also feel free to hold these places open until faculty involvement reaches the bar. What kind of activity might merit foundation board membership in a two-year college? Strong leadership of an employee annual giving campaign—the type of leadership that results in significant dollar increases—might be one example. Another would be a history of securing major gifts.

Departmental "Advisory" Committees

Some academic departments, especially those of technical and business programs, convene advisory committees composed of established and emerging business leaders in the field. Alumni can be especially effective members of such committees. I put "advisory" in quotes because a better model for advancement would be a departmental *support* committee—with a stated mission to support the department it serves.

The problem with advisory committees is that too often faculties use them as a captive audience for overlong, self-serving reports. Better to assume they know what good work you do, condense the reports, and adopt a project-based mission. One or more projects should be related to securing needed resources for the program. A mix of cash, gifts in-kind, and internships would be entirely appropriate. Adopt financial goals, select leaders, and meet quarterly or, better yet, bimonthly to recruit, engage, and cultivate movers and shakers in your field. I have seen these groups work well with automotive, printing, graphics, culinary, business, and hospitality programs. Why not add yours to the list?

Faculty Advisory Task Forces as Part of Precampaign Planning

The next chapter examines elements of precampaign planning, but we can cover one element of it here. The faculty advisory task force is an intrinsic element of precampaign planning. Just as asking for advice leads to gifts, asking for advice leads to buy-in, and there is no substitute for faculty buy-in to an institution-wide campaign.

Organizing faculty input within a task force allows an advancement office to convene a group that will develop a significant level of shared resources over a three- to six-month period. Here are some of the issues a faculty task force might consider:

- Suggesting campaign initiatives
- Researching and vetting campaign initiatives
- Prioritizing campaign initiatives
- Linking initiatives to accreditation and strategic issues
- Serving as a sounding board for advancement approaches
- Serving as a communication link to the greater faculty
- Suggesting corporate and other prospects
- Building support for the campaign within the college

The faculty advisory task force assumes a broad and comprehensive mission in precampaign planning. Its role is more proactive than any standing or administrative committee's. The task force is charged with partnering with advancement to strengthen the relationship between the two divisions of the college.

Kicking off the first several meetings with the involvement of the president will set the correct tone in terms of the importance of this charter. It will also enable direct interaction between the president and faculty representatives. As to who should be invited to serve, you can't go wrong with faculty members and officers who have supported advancement in the past. Even in situations in which the college is engaged in a formal strategic planning process in preparation for a campaign, the faculty advisory task force remains an invaluable ally in an effort that ultimately involves faculty solicitation of campaign gifts.

References

Kelly, M. 2007. Future of the university, fund raising, faculty's role in developing new schools and programs among topics discussed by faculty senate. *UVA Today*, April 3. http://www.virginia.edu/uvatoday/newsRelease.php?id=1806 (accessed January 14, 2011).

University of Arizona Foundation. 2008. Soyeon Shim receives faculty fundraising award. *UA News*, November 26. http://uanews.org/node/22782 (accessed January 14, 2011).

16

CONTEMPLATING CAMPAIGNS

The subject of developing and launching a campaign is not the subject of the work at hand, though it may one day become the subject of a companion volume to this book. We will limit the discussion to an overview of the topic—complete with a few advisories and a presentation of some of the basic principles that apply to the business of campaigning. Let's begin with a definition: a campaign is an organized, multiyear effort to fund long-term goals through a concerted fundraising effort that goes beyond the normal parameters of the development function.

A college can mount a campaign for a single purpose, such as to build a new building, or you can design a campaign to support a small number of coordinated initiatives that serve a single overriding purpose. You can launch a campaign dedicated to a larger parcel of projects or initiatives designed in their entirety to take the college to the next level. All are valid options; it depends on the institution and its intrinsic needs and opportunities.

TIP #68

Consider the idea of a *comprehensive campaign* to allow
for the announcement of a transformational goal.

The term *comprehensive campaign* is used to signify a fundraising effort that will *count everything* to serve the needs of the entire institution. For example, you count the Annual Fund as a component of such a campaign. The purpose of the comprehensive campaign is to achieve a transformational degree of fundraising success. Large numbers inspire. Think *billion-dollar campaign*; that is a transformational number. Billion-dollar campaigns are comprehensive campaigns. In the two-year college sector, announcing a $10 million goal—and achieving it—may be transformational.

Of course, many community colleges have engaged in campaigns of one sort or another, some of which have been notably successful. Larger, well-established, well-funded two-year colleges have tended to form the vanguard of this group. However, the number of two-year colleges that have engaged in a major campaign comprises a relatively small percentage of the sector as a whole.

Institutional Readiness

In contemplating a campaign, institutional readiness is the first test you must confront. Sometimes college leadership will be champing at the bit to launch a campaign soon after a few major gifts are lined up. For emerging colleges, the response is this: you have to walk before you can run—especially run a marathon such as a campaign.

Stated broadly, the indicators of institutional readiness for a campaign are:

1. A history of significant development activity
2. Demonstrated development staff expertise
3. A functional donor database
4. A robust Annual Fund
5. A history of upgrading gifts
6. Major gift activity
7. An awareness of what it means to engage in a campaign
8. A viable pool of campaign prospects
9. The commitment of the college and board leadership to the campaign
10. Board capacity and willingness to give
11. Committed volunteer campaign leadership
12. Sufficient resources to launch and sustain a campaign
13. A willingness to engage campaign counsel
14. The ability to transform college needs into opportunities for giving
15. A compelling campaign case

Each of these indicators comprises an area of significant precampaign planning. A development audit is a requisite first step. An experienced CDO may be able to perform a portion of the development audit in-house. In

---

TIP #69

Before planning a campaign, conduct an institutional readiness
assessment with the help of outside counsel.

---

an emerging program, however, outside counsel can offer an experienced
perspective on even the most fundamental issues. Focus most on items 1–8
of the list. The consultant will make recommendations regarding staff
deployment, training, and hiring and will evaluate fundraising performance,
systems, and current capacity. Nearly always, the consultant will point out
that the development team needs to spend more time on direct, person-to-
person cultivation and donor development.

Next, turn your attention to leadership, resources, and the case; items
9–15 on the list. You need the perspective of an experienced fundraising
consultant to arrive at an objective assessment here. These are complex,
interrelated issues, which we do not have the space to cover in depth here.
The questions themselves should signal the need for a disinterested perspective. For example, it will be necessary to communicate to the president a
necessary time commitment to the campaign. Typically, this might be 15 to
20 percent of the president's time. However, the demands could be much
higher. Robert C. Keys, president of Rockingham Community College in
North Carolina, estimated that he devoted 70 percent of his working hours
to advancement as his college geared up for a $9 million capital campaign
(Gose 2006a, B5).

You will need a board commitment to form a campaign cabinet. During
the Dunwoody campaign, a remarkably dedicated group of board members
met monthly for *five years*. That practice was a huge factor in the outstanding
results the college achieved. Then there is the issue of securing a campaign
chair or co-chairs. We are not talking about an honorary chair here—some
prominent person willing to lend a well-known name to the effort. We are
talking about a real commitment of heart and soul (and maybe a little blood,
sweat, and tears) to making calls, marshaling the troops, raising the flag, and
staying the course.

Fundraising consulting firm Jerold Panas, Linzy & Partners advises:
"**Evaluate your board with excruciating candor. The buck starts there!** If
your directors don't have the muscle, influence, and financial resources to
mount a campaign, you have problems" (Panas n.d.).

Before engaging a consultant to assess institutional readiness, it would be prudent and instructive to conduct an informal, in-house development audit. Involve the CDO, president, and board leadership to get a sense of where you think you stand from an internal perspective. Think about *why* you are considering a campaign. Is your consideration driven by need? Exhortation by an influential volunteer? Because a persuasive campaign consulting firm contacted you? Because the college down the road is launching one? Because the chancellor said each college in the system should launch one? Any one of these reasons may contain some validity. Nevertheless, may I suggest that you ask yourself: Is our mission driving this campaign? If we engage in a campaign, will it help us to further our mission significantly? What would that be? Will it better enable us to change lives?

Strategic Planning

A smart way to begin is to consult the college strategic plan. You might think this would be automatic, but a survey conducted by consulting firm Marts & Lundy reported that 43 percent of respondents "said they did not participate in strategic planning before launching a campaign" (Matthews 2007, 33). By engaging in strategic planning before mounting a campaign, a college is more likely to arrive at a slate of projects that corresponds to the real needs of the institution. Getting external stakeholder input is invaluable in this regard. Likewise, faculty and staff input validates the mission of the campaign. Later this translates into support for the campaign case.

Adding precampaign considerations to a college-wide strategic planning process is a two-way street in that it promotes dialogue about the marketability of college aspirations within the private sector. If the college desperately wants to launch an endowment to fund scholarships, but the foundation board is not likely to sign on as donors for that goal, a serious up-front discussion should probably ensue. If the college views a campaign as a laundry list of items that it would be nice to have if "someone" would fund them, perhaps a presentation by a campaign consultant would be in order.

Over the course of a campaign, donors will take you in some directions you may not have anticipated during the campaign planning process. Funny thing about donors; they make big gifts based on *their* needs, wants, and aspirations. You will sometimes need to think on the fly, to consider options that did not originate on your drawing board. Some of these occurrences can become miraculous accidents; others have the potential to become train wrecks. You must build a fluid campaign leadership capacity that allows the college to navigate between these two potentialities while the campaign is in progress. Some potential donors may want you to launch programs or organize industry partnerships with which you have little or no experience. Occasionally you just have to walk away from a gift. I would advance—you may disagree—that the ability to consider issues like these is not innate to the deliberative process of community colleges.

Recognize that campaigns take years. Mark Davy says a campaign is a marathon, not a sprint. A lot could change during that time. The current president could retire. A leading board member could leave the board. You may go through several board chairs. Your enrollment outlook may shift. The state funding picture could change. A recession could occur. To some extent, the campaign case you are about to develop is immutable. It must be as compelling to the community at the end of the campaign as it seems now. That is why we rely on strategic planning to get to the things that really matter.

Campaigns require patience. Campaign pledges may take up to seven years to fulfill. And the campaign itself could require five years. In the meantime, the college must strategize how it will manage cash flow to pay the costs of a campaign at the same time it begins to launch projects the campaign funds. If there was ever an aspect of college advancement that called for prudence and deliberation, campaign planning would be it.

Campaign planning also requires the willingness to take significant risks. This may be your first campaign. You are probably seeking a far greater number of big gifts than you have ever attracted in the past. And once you commit, you must remain committed to your case. So align the campaign with your mission through institutional strategic planning to remain on course in uncharted waters.

TIP #70

Align the campaign with your mission through
institution-wide strategic planning.

Considering the Case

Once you have established a sense of where the college wants to go, where does a campaign fit in? Does it meet the criteria necessary for success in terms of the mission and of the campaign itself? What makes for a compelling case? These are some of the thorniest strategic issues a college will ever face. What's more, it is possible to make mistakes during this phase of precampaign due diligence. Ideas often begin to take on a momentum of their own. Think of it as the primary phase of a presidential campaign. Early leaders run into opposition from established stakeholders. Fresh, appealing, populist appeals strike the stakeholders' collective imagination; dark horses emerge; and boutique initiatives bloom and fade. Initiatives that mean the most to the college turn out to be nonstarters to the potential funding base.

One temptation is to say, "Why can't we vote for them all?" Into this flux, we might introduce the Rule of Three to impose a little order. What are the top three initiatives? Do we have a contender for the title of Marquee Project? These are the questions that require the guidance of experienced campaign counsel. Eventually, your consultant will have to road test these contending initiatives through a campaign feasibility study. The more robust your planning process, the greater confidence you can have that the vision you have constructed will appeal to prospective donors.

Private colleges and universities have established norms and traditions regarding the nature of viable campaign projects. Capital expenditures are always appropriate for consideration. For two-year colleges, though, the issue of what constitutes a viable case is less clear. Capital brick-and-mortar expenditures have traditionally been seen as the exclusive provenance of state funding. Some argue that moving outside that framework undermines the rightful claim of a community college to those public dollars. Furthermore, given the amount of hard work necessary to raise, say, $6 million for a capital project, that amount really doesn't go very far given the costs of construction. There are no hard-and-fast answers to these questions.

Public-private partnerships are an increasingly viable option, but it is probably not appropriate for private dollars merely to supplant anticipated public funding. Instead, consider using them to enlarge the scope of proposed projects—according to the dictates of a compelling vision based on expanding capacity and fulfilling the mission of the college. Either that or devote private dollars to projects for which public funding is not likely to be forthcoming.

Capacity building is a major area of opportunity for two-year colleges; but there are so many potential directions—which capacity to choose becomes the question. Try posing the question in two ways: (1) what would make the biggest impact on the lives of students? and (2) what would have the greatest transformative effect on the college? If a project can address both questions at once, so much the better.

Scholarships are the perennial candidate in the capacity-building category. Every college wants to offer more scholarships. They represent a noble goal, to be sure, but given the price point community colleges occupy in the marketplace, one has to question whether they fulfill the criteria of greatest impact and transformational value. After all, in the mix of costs two-year college students face, the cost of tuition is far less than basic living expenses. And colleges aren't rushing into the breach to fund those.

One area of capacity building you might consider is student persistence, retention, success, matriculation, or graduation—in short, outcomes. Donors crave positive outcomes. One of the primary conclusions I drew from my work as a campaign director is this: *nobody wants to fund the status quo*. In designing donor initiatives within the framework of a large campaign, I always tested proposed ideas to determine how they would advance the college beyond the status quo.

Other development professionals have formalized the process in some unique ways. Tom Mitchell, vice chancellor of advancement at the University of California, Irvine, followed the example of universities receiving the largest gifts in the United States to introduce the following process. Mitchell has created six teams of about eleven people each, including faculty and staff members and deans. Each team is exploring a general theme linked to the goals of the institution and to larger societal issues, such as "nurturing a diverse community," "developing models for health-care delivery and discovery," and "developing leaders for the local and global community." Mr. Mitchell says, "We have found that those who give very large gifts want to see very big ideas that can solve important and significant problems." "So we're going to figure out what the problems are that we're already trying to solve and which ones we're prepared to solve" (Strout 2007, A21–A22).

Here is an example of how this type of thought process might play out in a community college. If we look at the effectiveness of community colleges today, we might look at the way they see their students as consumers of education. They traditionally view them as free agents: free to enroll in classes for whatever purposes, some for personal enrichment, some to fill an academic niche, some to complete a certificate program and enter the workforce, and some to complete a two-year course of study and transfer to a four-year college. But the college has no idea which students subscribe to which goals.

To better realize the promise of higher education, community colleges should identify those students who aspire to earn a college degree and hold themselves accountable for their part in the ultimate educational outcomes of those students. Do they graduate from college? This is, in Collins's words, a BHAG and worthy of becoming a campaign vision. Which leads to my final observation: campaigns require transformational thinking. In chapter 12 we encountered the precept of consultant Mark Davy: "the bigger the vision, the bigger the gift." This holds doubly true for campaigns.

TIP #71

In planning a campaign, consider the axiom
The bigger the vision, the bigger the gift.

Considering the Board

I woke up one morning to read in the paper about a really big gift that had been made to the University of St. Thomas in St. Paul, Minnesota (Furst 2007, B1). The gift was a whopping $60 million. The donors were a couple, Lee and Penny Anderson. Lee Anderson is CEO of APi Group, a Twin Cities holding company worth $900 million. Three notable details struck me about this gift. One, the amount. Two, the nature of the business: a privately held fire protection systems company—not a glamour name. I had never heard of it before that moment. Three, Lee Anderson was a trustee of the university. Now the picture comes into focus. A deep-pockets individual from an underrecognized industry, serving as a committed volunteer trustee for a university about which he and his wife care deeply, makes the gift of a lifetime. This is a classic pattern—one of the most common in the annals of big gifts to universities.

In some colleges, up to 50 percent of the receipts of a campaign may come from board gifts. In analyzing your prospect base, take serious stock of what you find close to home. As your board gives, so your campaign will go. Board members undergo the same cultivation cycles as external prospects, so if your board is weak in terms of capacity, you should practice strategic

TIP #72

Consider the board as your primary group of campaign prospects.

board recruitment well before you launch a campaign. This is one reason for the significant attention devoted to board development in chapter 5. You can see based on this evidence just how fundamental a robust, deep-pockets board is to your anticipated campaign.

One other point in terms of timing: if you are considering engaging in a campaign in the next two years, you might want to hold off on board major gift Asks, saving them up for an initial round of even larger gifts. Early stage gifts are crucial to establishing momentum in a campaign. CASE reporting guidelines do not allow gifts to be "grandfathered in" (Netherton 2004, 79–81), so a little planning is advised. You can discuss this strategy directly with board members who are immediate major gift prospects. Board members like to kick off campaigns with their gifts.

Identifying Campaign Prospects

Colleges new to campaigns tend to overestimate capacity. There seems to be a bias toward estimating that the universe of suspects who have been oblivious to the message of the college will miraculously be brought on board once a campaign is announced. This is simply not true.

TIP #73

In setting the campaign goal, consider the implications of the fact that 90 percent of campaign gifts will come from your known universe of suspects.

I have seen feasibility studies prepared by campaign consultants that list every large corporation and foundation in the region as a prospect. That is dangerous—and sloppy—thinking. Each one of those corporations and foundations has its own well-established priorities of mission and self-interest. Your campaign may or may not fit with its goals. Furthermore, even if a potential fit exists, the potential prospect may be too far out of your sphere of influence to qualify. One purpose of the feasibility study is to put some parameters around what might be considered reasonable expectations in this regard.

Of course, you expect to expand your sphere of influence to new stakeholders via the campaign. That, after all, is one of the primary goals of a campaign. But, to paraphrase Nietzsche, the college must "will to capacity" (and not beyond) in this regard. Where no established linkage exists, you must implement a strategic cultivation process to move beyond the barriers of geography, lack of linkage, and past philanthropic practice with regard to these prospects. The same rules apply for corporate and individual donors. Inexperienced organizations tend to aim too high, go too fast, and close too soon.

Every *marquee donor* is on every organization's list. We discussed this in relation to major gifts in chapter 12 as expressed in tip #51: *In weighing the probabilities of who will give, linkage trumps capacity.* In analyzing your potential prospect base, don't forget to look to your alumni. Northampton Community College in Bethlehem, Pennsylvania, raised $14 million in a three-year campaign; 20 percent of the gifts came from alumni (Gose 2006b, B7). As early as 1978, Harvard University development professionals recognized that 95 percent of the Harvard Campaign receipts would come from just 10 percent of all donations, and 75 percent of all receipts would come from less than 1 percent of their donors (Owen 1982, 36). These dynamics are still at work today.

The Communications Piece

Positioning the college for a major advance requires a strategic look at its capacity to communicate the message. The primary role of the communications piece is to expand your sphere of influence. Consultant Mark Davy often identifies external communications as an area in need of work at emerging colleges. Davy points out, for example, that public awareness of the college can be "a mile wide and an inch deep" when the communications capacity is lacking. This expression, instructive in itself, refers to the fact that everybody knows where the college is located, they all drive by it all the time, someone they know has attended the college, the college is known for such and such, and it provides a college education. That's about it. This level of awareness is never sufficient to motivate philanthropic support, so it becomes crucial for the college to tell its story to the greater community as never before.

The first step is to compose the story. Colleges tend to see themselves as potentially all things to all people. The typical mind-set is, "Oh, we do that. We do this other thing also. Oh, and that, too." That's good, and it is probably true. But a good story must incorporate elements of the college's essential *mission* (whom do we serve, and how?), its *challenges* (what we must do to survive and thrive), and its *vision* (this is how we see our mission; this is where we want to go).

Assembling a communications work plan for the campaign goes beyond the scope of this book; let me say just a few words about what it is *not*. It is not producing expensive publications that either sit in a box or are mailed out to the community through a mass mailing. While a campaign requires collateral material, a few high-quality pieces will cover your needs.

Campaign communications should be visionary, bold, even daring. To dream, to build, to achieve, to strengthen: these are the verbs that build a campaign. Content is king. The design and the photos should serve that end. Too often, prospective donors receive materials that are long on production values and short on message, which leaves them wondering how much you spent on the piece.

High-quality campaign materials must inspire. Their content can help get college leadership *on message* and donors tuned in. Nevertheless, the primary impetus in a campaign is always person to person. Campaign communications must be broadcast to the community through multiple channels. The effort is largely viral. People take the message to people. In groups, forums, and one to one, on campus and off, day in and day out, for weeks, months, and years; this is the business of a communications effort.

A communications plan incorporates press releases, invitations to the media, articles, and publications, but keep in mind that the early phase of a campaign is its *quiet phase*. You seek no media headlines during the quiet phase. If this seems paradoxical, that's okay. It's not really. Campaigns begin with quiet conversations, saving the fanfare for later. The task is to sell the vision quietly to influential prospects while big gifts are being closed quietly. The purpose of the quiet phase is to demonstrate to the wider community that the campaign is serious and capable of meeting impressive goals quickly. The strategy goes back at least as far as the 1978 Harvard Campaign mentioned earlier (Owen 1982, 38). Meanwhile, the communications piece is about selling the essential mission, challenges, and vision of the college to those who should have known, but didn't.

Personnel Considerations in a Campaign

To accomplish all of the goals discussed previously, you will need to consider hiring additional staff. It could be professional staff, or, if your shop is large enough, administrative staff, or both. Yet hiring staff should not be an automatic assumption. At first blush you might think, "Well, my time is fully occupied. I can't possibly run a campaign, make actual Asks, and do my regular job, too." The solution to this quandary is that the nature of your regular job must change. This is true of the CDO and the president. If the scope and proposed activities of the campaign require hiring another staff member, your campaign counsel will be able to help you to arrive at an optimal use of precious personnel dollars.

You are going to be coordinating a vast amount of volunteer and staff effort, so you will need to think about *clearing the deck for development* at a whole new level. Database, administrative, and professional functions will have to be coordinated at a higher level of focus and efficiency. Campaigns are driven by the internal capacities of the college; nobody will come in and do it for you. Outside consultants never come and make the Asks for you, though institutions occasionally push them hard to do just that.

The nuts and bolts of a campaign require a great deal of planning expertise by the CDO. What level of activity, for example, justifies hiring a database manager? In addition, if one is hired, the position is likely to become permanent, part of the administrative machinery of the office. If the Annual Fund campaign is racking up revenues in the area of $700,000, it might be time to consider hiring a database manager. In a small shop, this generally would be considered a healthy Annual Fund. Large colleges should certainly be raising an amount in this range before they consider themselves ready for a campaign. The number of transactions required to raise that amount requires the dedicated focus of a database specialist to track it all and provide reports that allow the data to serve the needs of your development officers. A campaign will demand it.

What other personnel might be needed? A major gift officer or a campaign director are two likely choices. The job of a campaign director is to marshal the resources of the entire institution while serving as a major gift officer. I have been surprised to see $60 million campaigns launched by established organizations reach their goal under the direction of just the CDO, with the addition of one or two experienced development officers. I caution against making quick assumptions about what is required to reach a goal of $15 million in a two-year college campaign. An emerging organization might have to work ten times harder than an established institution to reach an equivalent goal.

Resources Required

You can fund an enhanced development operation with campaign revenues only if a sufficient quantity of unrestricted gifts is anticipated. Foundations, for example, are often quite strict about how their grant awards are used. Generally, campaigns are very efficient in terms of cost of fundraising percentages, which routinely fall into the 8 to 15 percent range. The cash flow of these funds, however, can be complex. Most campaign gifts are pledges whose payoff windows may vary from three years to seven (ten is discouraged [Netherton 2004, 80]; five is common). So the college must have a plan in place to fund the cash flow requirements of campaign costs, especially start-up expenses.

To the extent that the efforts of the CDO, executive assistant, and grant writer are devoted to the campaign, campaign revenues may fund development costs related to their positions. But don't forget that costs are rising in the precampaign phase as well. For example, campaign consultant bills need to be paid up front, before any campaign gifts are received. So plan on amassing a campaign war chest to fund your anticipated precampaign costs. Do not borrow from future receipts. Take my word for it and avoid the nasty consequences of negative balances in campaign accounts. In paying for campaign operations, pay as you go is the way to go.

Setting the Goal

The question of the amount of the goal is usually the one that gets the most attention in precampaign deliberations, though, in fact, it should be only a logical outcome of those deliberations. The amount of the goal should arise from a logical, reasoned analysis of the feasibility study's findings. Before the study is completed, you can consider the question only in a hypothetical way. By engaging in a robust due diligence process, you will arrive at a campaign goal that is at once satisfying, impressive, and challenging.

Take Your Time

Follow this fundamental rule in considering if and when you are ready to launch a campaign: *respect the process*. Jumping the process, hot-wiring the car, and driving off in all directions at once is a recipe for disaster. The last thing you want is the ensuing difficulty of a stalled or, worse, failed campaign. The advantage of taking the slow road to a campaign launch is that the endeavor itself becomes much easier in the doing. As momentum builds, the effort becomes almost machine-like; that is an impressive feeling to attain at a college on the verge of a breakthrough. So take your time, kick the tires, and make sure your fundamentals are well in hand before dreaming of campaigns.

References

Furst, R. 2007. St. Thomas gets private donation of $60 million. *Minneapolis Star Tribune*, October 25.

Gose, B. 2006a. At a growing number of community colleges, fund raising is no longer optional. *The Chronicle of Higher Education* 53, no. 10.

———. 2006b. Coming to a community college near you: The alumni phone-athon. *The Chronicle of Higher Education* 53, no. 10.

Matthews, B. 2007. First seating. *CASE Currents* 33, no. 4.

Netherton, R. (ed.). 2004. *CASE management and reporting standards* (3rd ed.). Washington, DC: Council for Advancement and Support of Education.

Owen, D. 1982. State-of-the-art panhandling. *Harper's Magazine* 265, August.

Panas, J. n.d. How to make certain you have a winning fundraising campaign? Chicago: Jerold Panas, Linzy & Partners, Inc. http://www.panaslinzy.com/pages/freeMaterial.htm (accessed February 17, 2011).

Strout, E. 2007. What's the big idea? *The Chronicle of Higher Education* 53, no. 22.

17

BRINGING IT ALL BACK HOME

C ommunity colleges serve nearly half of the undergraduates in the United States, yet receive perhaps 2 percent of private gifts to higher education (Summers 2006, B22).[1] This fact cries out for change. Such colleges straddle the gap between high school limbo and degree majors for millions of students. They have more state funding than high schools, but less than state colleges and universities. Their doors are wide open to the community. They strive to serve whoever reaches minimum standards, such as a GED.

Open enrollment has come to mean serving students regardless of college readiness, while these students, upon matriculation, must meet the same rigorous standards as those applied to students in the four-year system. Though community college capacities are vast and growing, and these colleges' expertise is great, they are ill equipped by virtue of a lack of resources to deal with the tsunami of underprepared students they are called upon to serve.

Community colleges specialize and excel in the business of teaching and learning. The community at large, however, underrecognizes their contributions, especially concerning the special classes of students they serve. Immigrants and new arrivals to the United States are exposed to a world of seemingly boundless opportunity, if only, and only if, they can successfully negotiate community college as a gateway to a further higher education, or complete a tertiary degree program within the two-year framework. Due to the underpreparedness of a significant number of the students they serve, community and technical colleges are increasingly serving students for periods that exceed the traditional two-year window for which they are known. Many students fall by the wayside due to underpreparedness and overwhelming external difficulties, especially financial need, and the system does not know their ultimate fates.

Community colleges are the new melting pot of America. They are, above all, the gateway to a college degree. This means they are, in all their forms and aspects, the gateway to the middle class and beyond for millions of Americans. Despite all this, the nation's two-year colleges are under-recognized and underfunded.

The case for support to community colleges is as great and compelling as that of support to all of higher education. Despite this fact, they receive almost none of the support enjoyed by their senior educational counterparts. They are condemned instead to sit at the proverbial children's table amid a feast of philanthropic generosity the likes of which the world has never witnessed. Yet, no one seems to notice, save for those dedicated practitioners themselves, whose knees can barely squeeze beneath the tabletop.

The rule in philanthropy is that philanthropists give to those who help themselves. This includes those who plot their future, market their case, promote their successes, and diligently ask for support. Two-year colleges have not accomplished this effectively as indicated by their paltry share of the support garnered by all of higher education. Even now, the leaders of some two-year colleges act as if they are asleep at the wheel, while others press ahead with aggressive visions. Institutions that are not busy growing are slowly dying, withering away in the face of greater need and scarcer resources. It's a slow drift, almost imperceptible to many observers, but it is the same slow drift that high schools were on fifteen years ago—before so many of them went over the falls. Even if the falls are still over the horizon for our nation's community colleges, the fundamental equation is out of whack.

Private funds cannot replace the need for public support. Nevertheless, the public university sector, generally pronounced to be in excellent health, the envy of the world even, has proven that private support yields and sustains excellence.

Two-year colleges have it within their reach to make significant advances in the arena of advancement. To do so, they must first change their perception of themselves. They must change the routines by which they operate and their expectations of themselves. Structurally, they are ready to succeed. They have capable presidents; they have well-intentioned foundation boards; they have established, if underperforming, donor markets.

The collegiate model of advancement, properly adapted and managed, provides the optimal model for rapid improvement of two-year college development operations. The ultimate potential of widespread adoption is unknown, but its cumulative effect, in time, most likely would be counted in the hundreds of millions of dollars. Yet, it is not clear that the model will ever be adopted to the extent that it has been by public four-year colleges and universities.

Assertions have been made—"Alumni don't give to community colleges"—that do not hold water. To the extent that such common misconceptions do describe actual barriers, they nevertheless do not prevent the sector from achieving success in the marketplace for private dollars. If two-thirds of private support to community colleges comes from organizations, and one-third from individuals, appropriate strategies exist, as proposed here, to realize the resources that are within reach. This month, next month, and every month, some philanthropist with an intrinsic connection to a two-year college will make a six-figure or larger gift to a community college because of his or her identification with its mission. In the end, we must conclude that if donors aren't giving, it is because they aren't being asked.

Community colleges find themselves at a turning point today. One option is business as usual; the other is greater achievement funded by private resources. The course of excellence requires those resources. It is up to college leadership and its volunteer stakeholders as stewards of the public trust to decide upon a course of action in the face of knowable and achievable results.

In development work, all three parties—leadership, staff, and board—are accountable. No one may be holding them accountable, but in the last analysis they are the collective stewards of the public trust. Independent Sector refers to this dynamic as "Obedience to the Unenforceable" (1991/2002, 22).[2] Ultimately, it takes commitment to the mission and a strong sense of personal stewardship to find a way through the fog of everyday distractions. That is why it is so crucial to raise the mission at every opportunity as if it were a beacon.

Two of the most regularly used terms in this book have been *mission* and *focus* because they are two of the three key ingredients to a successful development program. The third is *commitment*. Start with *mission*. *Focus* on the task. Make a *commitment* to succeed. This is the final Rule of Three. Jim Collins describes the first three "inputs of greatness" as disciplined people, disciplined thought, and disciplined action (2005, 8). This arc of this work parallels those three simple, sturdy concepts in its attention to mission, focus, and commitment.

Obstacles Along the Way

The primary anticipated failure point in using this book as the model for two-year college advancement is that of adopting the model without the necessary institutional commitment. The dynamic will come into play, especially when the driving forces for the campaign originate externally or from an isolated constituency without the necessary internal embrace of the requisites to success. A second instance would be that of the model being pushed by a faction of the board, president, and CDO, without thoroughly engaging the requisite consensus-driven, decision-making process.

Top Ten Reasons for Lack of Success

1. Nominally adopting the plan without its requisite fundamentals. The most critical element is that of institutional commitment, ideally that of making development a *top three* institutional priority.
2. Adopting the plan without committing the necessary resources.
3. Introducing bureaucratic hurdles to the process, such as barriers to getting the right people on the bus.
4. Resistance to the plan or its critical elements by the president.
5. Resistance to the plan by the board.
6. Having an unqualified CDO in charge.
7. Having an unqualified staff charged with carrying out the plan.
8. Lacking focus on major gifts.
9. Faltering in the institutional commitment to the plan over time.
10. Developing the "wrong" strategic plan—wrong, that is, from the point of view of the mission, resources, and overall positioning of the college.

Admittedly, the potential pitfalls are numerous, and it may require successive efforts to succeed with the model. Development-friendly cultures do not readily "take" in every nonprofit environment. If they did, there would be no need for the myriad development resources that exist in the marketplace today. But armed with a sense of urgency, with commitment and expertise, some degree of success can be realized in every case.

In cases where the foundation board and the president lend passive rather than active support to the development initiative, the result is likely to be a *staff-driven* program. Though not the end of the world, this outcome will fall short of the expectations for charitable support engendered by the approach this book outlines. In the case of a weak commitment to the imperatives of development, the two areas most likely to suffer are board involvement and major gifts. A passive board simply will not do.

With regard to major gifts, a staff-driven program will yield revenue results that are perhaps 50 percent below the institutional potential. This, of course, would be regrettable compared to the major gift numbers required to sustain a viable program. Such a record may still represent a significant improvement over baseline performance at some colleges. For the Annual Fund, weak board/presidential participation may depress revenues to 75 percent of potential, especially with regard to board-inspired giving and larger annual gifts. So, while the Annual Fund is affected to a lesser degree than the major gift program, the overall effect will be a program that limps along without reaching its potential. Avoid a staff-driven program if at all possible.

The Plus Side: Top Ten Indicators of Success

I emphasize the converse, the plus side, to underscore that this is a construct of positives in the face of significant challenges.

1. A commitment to the mission
2. A vision of where you want to go
3. A strategic plan to guide the way
4. A shared commitment to the plan
5. A focus on the things that will make a difference
6. The right people on the bus, in the right seats
7. A relentless focus on execution
8. The accumulation of expertise and experience
9. The ability to learn from mistakes
10. The celebration of success

To summarize the basics of the collegiate development model: the Annual Fund is the rock upon which the development program is built. Donor cultivation enlarges your donor universe and renders your audience receptive to your message. Major gifts are the stepping-stones to greatness. Planned giving represents the engine of the future. A successful development program runs like a machine. The culture of development becomes a living, breathing thing that helps to project the influence of your mission into the decades to come.

A Final Encouragement

The most meaningful encouragement is informed encouragement, encouragement that acknowledges the risks, obstacles, and hidden barriers to success. This is the encouragement of the teacher to the graduating student. A

TIP #74

Take a colleague out to lunch and tell him or her about your plan.

---

personal message underlies this kind of encouragement: *I know you can do it.* I know it can be done.

The success I envision is not necessarily spectacular, though in your case it may be. The success I envision is real, bankable, and mission-affirming. It is the incremental monthly increase in the Annual Fund, rising 10 percent above the amount of the previous year's fund. It is the thrill of the first $250,000, or $500,000, or $1 million gift. It is the opportunity to face a room and announce the completion of a major new initiative, funded through the generosity of committed stakeholders.

Development professionals toil in the shadows of the success. They live vicariously through the good works they engender. They serve as stewards, making sure the doors are locked, the lights are dimmed, and the confetti is swept up at the end of the party. They can be invaluable partners in the drive to success, but only if a community of committed leaders and stakeholders supports them. As hired guns, they are ineffective. As administrators, they are sometimes miscast. They are motivated by success. Success is their currency and serves to supplant the material rewards they forgo in their chosen careers. Their world is that of *sales transformed by mission.* My advice to the institutions that engage them is to support them wisely and motivate them well.

So why not begin now? Share this book with a colleague. Bring it up at a meeting. Take a board member out to lunch. Great things begin with the power of a suggestion. And follow the rule that every development officer knows so well: never do tomorrow what would best be done today. *Good luck!*

TIP #75

Share this book with a colleague.

Endnotes

1. Read Prologue note #4 for an extensive discussion of this contested claim.
2. This text was used as course material in the Executive Leadership Institute of the Center on Philanthropy at Indiana University in 2000.

References

Independent Sector. 1991/2002. Obedience to the unenforceable: Ethics and the nation's voluntary and philanthropic community. Washington, DC. http://www.independentsector.org/uploads/Accountability_Documents/obedience_to_unenforceable.pdf (accessed January 18, 2011).

Summers, D. C. 2006. Why are community colleges so slow to jump on the fund-raising bandwagon? *The Chronicle of Higher Education* 53, no. 10.

APPENDIX A1

JOB DESCRIPTION: DIRECTOR OF ANNUAL GIVING AND ALUMNI RELATIONS

Objective

To manage the Annual Fund and alumni relations program with a primary focus on Annual Fund solicitation activities. Activities include cultivation and recognition events, donor recognition, stewardship, prospect research, donor relations, and community relations. Administrative responsibilities include pledge payment oversight, data reporting and documentation, information management, and web site content. Includes hands-on use of database software to manage donor records. The position entails intensive interactions with diverse stakeholders. This position reports to the chief development officer (CDO).

#	DUTIES	%
1	**Manage annual giving solicitation program**	50%

    1. Implement Annual Fund solicitation program as described in the Action Plan.

    2. Make regular in-person and telephone contacts to cultivate and solicit donors.

    3. Manage the phonathon, letter appeals, board-inspired giving, employee annual giving, and other solicitations in all formats for scholarships and general operating support.

    4. Identify prospects.

    5. Generate goals, objectives, projections, reports, and transaction documentation.

    6. Produce collateral materials.

2   **Donor relations**   20%
  1. Monitor, document, and ensure daily acknowledgment of gifts received.
  2. Communicate with donors, alumni, and prospects with a minimum of ten donor contacts per week.
  3. Manage Annual Fund donor stewardship activities.
  4. Staff donor recognition and scholarship recognition events.
  5. Conduct prospect research.

3   **Database functions**   10%
  1. Organize and manage data for effective donor cultivation, solicitation, and stewardship for the Annual Fund.
  2. Document regular contact with donors and prospects.
  3. Report monthly Annual Fund revenues.
  4. Generate reports and database-related documentation.
  5. Identify data needs and develop quality improvement processes for data management, data entry, updating records, reports, and gift tracking.
  6. Coordinate data entry with the executive assistant.
  7. Perform data entry as needed.

4   **Develop and manage an alumni association**   15%
  1. Develop an alumni association board.
  2. Develop and manage alumni association board fundraising activities.
  3. Implement alumni relations events.
  4. Implement a plan for the growth of the alumni association.

5   **Development team activities**   5%
  1. Staff the board Annual Fund Committee.
  2. Participate in development team meetings.
  3. Participate in college and community meetings and activities.
  4. Represent the CDO at events and meetings.
  5. Manage donor recognition activities.
  6. Provide backup to the executive assistant on Annual Fund transactions.
  7. Assist in the development of content for the college magazine.

Interactions

Regular communication with the CDO, the development team, faculty, staff, and the public. Contact with board members, donors, alumni, retirees, prospects, volunteers, students, organizations, and businesses.

Knowledge and Skill Set

- Excellent people skills
- Demonstrated skills in staging cultivation events
- Ability to plan and implement a variety of simultaneous projects and activities
- High-level analytical, organizational, managerial, administrative, communication, writing, and sales skills
- Ability to establish and maintain good working relationships with colleagues
- Highly self-motivated
- Strong public relations and volunteer leadership skills
- Experience with board processes and interactions
- Skills in the development of collateral materials
- Database and computer software knowledge and experience, including management of donor database system
- Process management and quality improvement expertise
- Highly motivated to achieve advancement goals and objectives
- Ability to solve problems effectively and creatively
- High level of creativity in developing purposeful relationships and activities with diverse groups
- Demonstrated high levels of energy and enthusiasm

Qualifications

Three years' minimum successful experience in implementing a fundraising program, including phonathon, solicitation with volunteers, personal solicitation, letter appeals, and proposals, preferably in an academic setting. Demonstrated program implementation experience and abilities. Demonstrated capacity in problem solving, project management, and public relations. Demonstrated proficiency in writing. Demonstrated proficiency in working with a donor database. Experience with alumni relations programs preferred. A record of professional development activities and formal development training. BA required.

APPENDIX A2

JOB DESCRIPTION: GRANT WRITER

Objective

The grant writer is responsible for a high volume of proposal submissions to corporations and corporate and private foundations. The position includes prospect identification, research, proposal development, and writing, sometimes with faculty and staff, and accurate and timely production of final proposals. This position is responsible for monitoring the status of funded program grants and preparing reports to funders. This position is charged with developing personal relationships with program officers and staff members at corporations and foundations. The position reports to the chief development officer (CDO).

#	DUTIES	%
1	**Prospect identification and relationship development**	25%

1. Research foundation prospects.
2. Monitor the grant-making field for opportunities.
3. Develop purposeful personal relationships with corporate and foundation representatives through regular personal communication.
4. Communicate grant opportunities to faculty and staff.
5. Maintain files related to institutional donors.
6. Host a minimum of eight funder site visits per year.
7. Make a minimum of ten qualified funder contacts per week.

2	**Proposal development**	50%

1. Use college and foundation strategic plans to align grant proposals with institutional goals and the advancement Action Plan.
2. Evaluate opportunities for alignment with mission, goals, return on investment, and capacity.

3. Consult with the CDO on proposed grant projects.
4. Assist administrators, deans, and directors in responding to grant opportunities.
5. Enlist staff and faculty as active partners in proposal development.
6. Develop and refine the case for Annual Fund support.
7. Develop case and supporting data and write compelling program grant narratives.
8. Complete and submit proposals developed by others.
9. Submit, track, and follow up on grant proposals.

3   Database functions   5%
1. Organize and manage data for effective donor cultivation, solicitation, and stewardship for the grants program.
2. Enter contacts with donors and prospects.
3. Report monthly grant revenues.
4. Generate reports and grant-related documentation.

4   Grant compliance and accountability   15%
1. Prepare reports for grantors in a timely fashion.
2. Implement formal grant-reporting procedures, compliance standards, and operating guidelines consistent with college policies.
3. Maintain central files on grant applications, awards, reports, and supporting documents.
4. Negotiate appropriate grant terms with funders.
5. Ensure grant compliance through documented interactions with grant program directors, deans, managers, and staff.
6. Gather data to ensure compliance with funding agency reporting requirements.
7. Prepare an annual report of private grants activity.
8. Provide donors with superior stewardship and customer service.
9. Maintain an annual calendar of grant-reporting deadlines.

5   Development team activities   5%
1. Participate in college and community meetings and activities.
2. Participate in development team meetings and activities.

Interactions

Regular communication with the CDO, the development team, faculty, staff, and the public. Contact with board members, friends, and volunteers. Frequent contact with representatives of corporations and foundations.

Knowledge and Skill Set

- Demonstrated excellent written and oral communication skills
- Demonstrated expertise in writing proposals, letters of inquiry, and grant reports
- Expertise in formulating goals, objectives, actions plans, and budgets
- Ability to work cooperatively with corporate and foundation executives, program officers, faculty, and staff in designing compelling, competitive proposals
- Expertise in project management and documentation
- Ability to plan and execute a variety of simultaneous grant proposals and projects
- High-level analytical, organizational, and administrative skills
- Knowledge of and experience with development-related processes and interactions
- Skills in the development of collateral materials
- Database and research experience
- Process management and quality-improvement expertise
- An understanding of the role of grant writing in higher education
- Highly motivated to achieve advancement goals and objectives
- Ability to solve problems effectively and creatively
- Personal attributes required: self-starter, dependable, conscientious, sociable, and attentive to detail
- Ability to work well under pressure and to meet deadlines

Qualifications

Three years' minimum successful experience in grant writing required. Demonstrated research experience and abilities. Demonstrated capacity in problem solving, project management, and public relations. Demonstrated proficiency in writing. Demonstrated proficiency in working with a donor database. Experience with Microsoft Office. A record of professional development activities and formal grant-writing training. BA required.

APPENDIX A3

JOB DESCRIPTION: EXECUTIVE ASSISTANT

Objective

This position supports the advancement program by providing administrative expertise in a dynamic office environment. Provide executive-level support and assistance to the chief development officer (CDO) for internal and external relations, office management, communications, correspondence, data management, and financial transactions. Carry out complex projects, including database management. Key functions of this position include meeting and event coordination, contact with the public, gift acknowledgment, database entry, office management, clerical functions, supervision of student workers, and fiscal and budget administration. The position reports to the CDO.

#	DUTIES	%
1	**Support the chief development officer**	20%

   1. Provide executive-suite level of customer service to handle reception responsibilities for the advancement office, including phone calls and visitors.

   2. Meet all administrative needs of the CDO. Display independent, self-starting initiative in project management and problem resolution for matters not requiring the CDO's personal attention.

   3. Meet reporting requirements and deadlines, internal administration requirements, and protocol and maintain donor and board communications.

   4. Schedule and organize meetings with volunteers, board members, staff, and committees.

5. Prepare correspondence and PowerPoint presentations.
6. Attend development functions and events as required.
7. Manage interoffice relations.
8. Manage the professional presentation of the advancement office.

2   Office management   25%

1. Handle administrative support needs for development staff and activities.
2. Prepare error-free correspondence and donor acknowledgment letters using expert Microsoft Word skills, including mail merge applications.
3. Prepare spreadsheets and reports using expert Microsoft Excel skills.
4. Coordinate printed communications including regular mailings, fundraising communications, newsletters, and magazines.
5. Maintain office files.
6. Provide interoffice coordination of scholarships with financial aid office.
7. Assist in formulation and attainment of administrative goals and objectives according to the Action Plan.
8. Upgrade office systems using continuous quality-improvement techniques.

3   Database and financial functions   30%

1. Provide gift entry and generate reports using the donor database.
2. Provide database maintenance and upgrades.
3. Optimize use of data for effective development operations.
4. Administer development office side of payroll deduction records.
5. Supervise student workers in data entry functions.
6. Coordinate accounting functions with bookkeeper and board Finance Committee.
7. Coordinate budget and fiscal transactions, including accounts payable and pledges receivable.
8. Prepare bank deposits.
9. Maintain fiscal records.
10. Meet deadlines for fiscal reports and documentation.

11. Coordinate and organize documentation for annual audit of the foundation.
12. Train development staff in departmental fiscal operations.

4   **Donor relations activities**   20%
1. Provide administrative support for development and board committees, meetings, and activities, including notices, agendas, media, and collateral material.
2. Prepare donor listings for the annual report.
3. Schedule visits and meetings.
4. Document meetings in files.
5. Take minutes as assigned.
6. Handle logistics for all development events, including on-site support.
7. Maintain an annual calendar of advancement activities.

5   **Development team activities**   5%
1. Participate in college meetings and activities.
2. Participate in development team meetings and activities.

Interactions

Regular communication with the CDO, the development team, faculty, staff, students, and the public. Extensive public contact in person, through email, and by telephone, including extensive communication with executives and organizations, with a particular focus on board members.

Knowledge and Skill Set

- Strong people skills
- Knowledge of nonprofit standards and practices required to manage the office in compliance with applicable regulations and procedures
- Knowledge of basic accounting principles and software applications
- Demonstrated written communication skills
- Knowledge of office systems software, with demonstrated expertise in Microsoft Office applications
- Database skills
- Project management skills

- The ability to collect and analyze data to solve problems and improve administrative processes
- Organizational and administrative skills
- An understanding of the advancement function in higher education
- Knowledge and experience with development-related processes and interactions
- Skills in developing collateral materials
- Personal attributes required: self-starter, dependable, conscientious, sociable, and attentive to detail
- Sound judgment in solving problems independently and with discretion
- Ability to work well under pressure and to meet deadlines

Qualifications

Minimum three years' successful experience in an administrative role, preferably in a development office. Demonstrated written and oral communication skills. Demonstrated high-level capacity in database functions and moderate capacity with basic accounting and bookkeeping functions. Experience with Microsoft Office. A record of professional development activities. Two years of college or AA required.

APPENDIX B

BOARD EFFECTIVENESS CHART

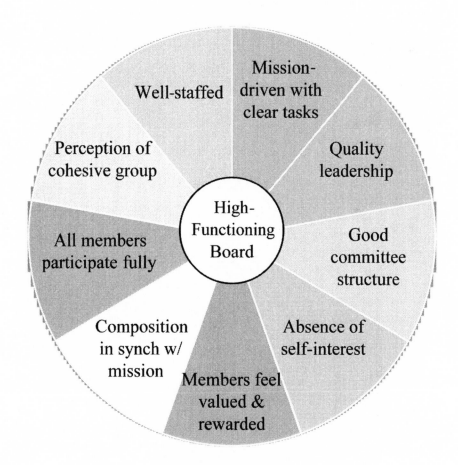

APPENDIX C

BOARD MEMBER POSITION DESCRIPTION

Objective

The Board of Directors is responsible for governing the foundation and securing private resources.

Responsibilities

- Serve a three-year, renewable term on the board.
- Establish foundation goals and policies.
- Provide board-level oversight of foundation activities.
- Serve on a board committee.
- Serve as a college ambassador to the community.
- Make cultivation and fundraising calls.
- Assist with board membership recruitment.
- Lend professional expertise to the college.
- Use business expertise to improve foundation performance.
- Assist and motivate staff members to achieve excellence in fundraising performance.
- Attend board meetings and development-related events.

Interactions

- College president, chief development officer, college leadership, and foundation staff
- Volunteers
- Community

Time Commitment

- One to four hours per month, on average
- Quarterly committee and board meetings
- Periodic phone calls, meetings, and events

Qualifications

- Willingness to serve as a volunteer leader
- Leadership role in business, community, or philanthropy
- The ability to lead and inspire top performance

APPENDIX D

BOARD COMMITMENT MENU

As a board member, I would like to assist the college and foundation in the following ways:

_____ With a personal gift (all members)

_____ Personal or telephone contact with donors

_____ Recruit board members

_____ Enlist the help of friends or business acquaintances

_____ Identify new donors

_____ Make calls to corporate or foundation prospects

_____ Make calls to elected officials

_____ Solicit gifts

_____ Help develop a major gift program

_____ Help develop a planned giving program

_____ Serve on a committee—special interest, if known: _____

_____   _____
Signed   Date

APPENDIX E

ANNUAL FUND
PERFORMANCE CHART

ANNUAL FUND PERFORMANCE

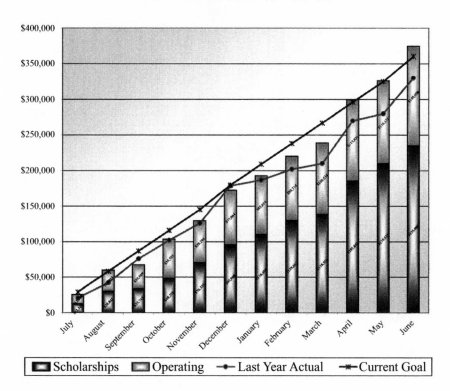

Courtesy Dunwoody College of Technology

APPENDIX F

PHONATHON CALL SHEET

Phonathon Call Sheet

Dear _____   Date: _____

**Your Community
College**
Development Office
Street Address
City, State Zip

Thank you for speaking with me about Your Community College and for your
commitment of $_____ to the Annual Fund.

_____
Phonathon Caller

«FNAME» «MI» «LNAME»
«ADDRESS_1»
«ADDRESS_2»
«CITY», «ST» «ZIP»

Please make checks payable to Your Community College.

ID: «ID» «FNAME» «MI» «LNAME» «ADDRESS_1» «ADDRESS_2» «CITY», «ST» «ZIP» Home Phone: «HOME_PHONE» E-Mail: «EMAIL»				Class Year: «CLASS» Program: «PROGRAM» Job Title: «POSITION» Employer: «BUSINESS»
DATE	CALLER NAME	RESULT	CALL BACK DATE/TIME	**ANNUAL FUND GIVING HISTORY** Last Gift Date: Last Gift Amount: Largest Gift: Largest Gift Date:
				PLEDGE INFORMATION
				Pledge Amount: $_____
				Send Pledge Reminder: Month _____
				Matching Gift: Yes ____ **No** ____
____ Do Not Call Again ____ Bad Phone Number ____ Do Not Solicit ____ Address Change ____ Deceased *(Check all that apply)*				**Credit Card:** ☐ Visa ☐ Master ☐ Discover Card #_____ Exp. Date _____
COMMENTS:				

Courtesy Dunwoody College of Technology

APPENDIX G

GIVING CLUB LETTER

Date

Mr. John Doe
Chief Executive Officer
General Business Corp.
Street Address
City, State, Zip

Dear John:

[*Personalize*] It was a pleasure to get together with you and Jane Smith at your office last July. That new project you told me about sounds exciting; I'd love to get an update from you next time we get together. I hear great things about it from Tom Brown when I see him at board meetings.

I am writing to ask that General Business consider a gift to the college at the level of the Chairman's Circle, with an Annual Fund gift of $2,500. I know this is a significant annual commitment—and I do not ask your support lightly.

[*Personalize*] The Annual Fund provides our students with the kind of critical support that helps them stay in school—I know you and I talked about how that was an issue for community colleges.

Annual support provides scholarships (over $190,000 last year), emergency support grants, and textbook assistance and helps to support the Student Learning Center, where students can go from 8 a.m. to 8 p.m. every day for personal help on the subjects they find difficult. These are just a few of the critical benefits the Annual Fund provides.

We are doing all of this at a time when state support to the college has fallen to just 40 percent of our annual budget. That is a decrease of more than 20 percent over the last five years! As a businessperson, you can appreciate how that kind of revenue decrease might threaten the health of an organization. Janet Jones, chair of the foundation board, has said that she doesn't want to see an undue burden placed on the backs of our students. That's why unrestricted contributions to our Annual Fund are important as never before.

Our students work hard to maintain the balance between academics and the part-time jobs that so many of them hold to pay tuition and living expenses. I am sure their stories would win your respect and your admiration for their perseverance.

There are also some good business reasons to give. For example, the majority of our alumni remain in the community—one survey indicated the number was higher than 60 percent—to launch their careers as well-educated employees in businesses such as yours. I have included a fact sheet on some of the other specific benefits Your Community College offers to the community.

Given the funding challenges we face, Your Community College is committed to taking community support of this remarkable institution to a new level. I hope you will help us increase our Chairman's Circle membership to twenty-five donors this year. We only need five more members to reach that milestone. Honestly, I cannot think of a better investment in the community.

We will recognize your support in a variety of ways, including sending an invitation for you and your guests to join me at the Community Circle Donor Recognition Event scheduled for September 25.

Thanks for considering this gift, John. Believe me, it means a lot to the students we serve. I have enclosed a contribution envelope—and I am happy to answer any questions you might have about making a gift to the college. Just give me a call at 555-555-1000. If you don't mind, I would like to follow up with you by telephone over the next couple of weeks. Thank you for giving this request your serious consideration.

With warm regards,

Linda Lang
Vice President for Advancement
Enclosures

APPENDIX H

ANNUAL FUND CHART

Annual Fund Chart CONFIDENTIAL
$300,000 - Gift Range Table
$66,800 Shown on Chart to X/XX/XX

Gift Range	% of Goal	Gifts / Pledges Needed		Prospects		$ To Date
$50,000	17%	☐ 1/$50,000		1. Prospect 2. Prospect		
$25,000	17%	☐☐ 2/$50,000		1. Prospect 2. Prospect		
$10,000	7%	☐☐ 2/$20,000		1. Prospect 2. Prospect		
$5,000 +	13%	■■■■☐☐☐☐ 8/$40,000 Average = $5,000		1. Donor Name 2. Donor Name 3. Donor Name 4. Prospect 5. Prospect 6. Donor Name		$20,000 4 gifts
$2,500 +	12%	■■■☐☐ ☐☐☐☐☐ ☐☐☐☐ 14/$35,000 Average = $2,566		1. Donor Name 2. Prospect 3. Donor Name 4. Prospect 5. Donor Name 6. Prospect 7. Prospect 8. Prospect 9. Prospect 10. Prospect 11. Prospect 12. Prospect		$7,700 3 gifts
$1,000 +	15%	■■■■■■■■■■ ■■☐☐☐☐☐☐☐☐ ☐☐☐☐☐☐☐☐☐☐ ☐☐☐☐☐☐☐☐☐☐ ☐☐☐☐☐☐ 46/$46,000 Average = $1,165		1. Prospect 2. Prospect 3. Prospect 4. Prospect 5. Donor 6. Prospect 7. Prospect 8. Prospect 9. Prospect 10. Prospect 11. Prospect 12. Prospect 13. Prospect 14. Donor 15. Prospect 16. Prospect 17. Prospect 18. Donor 19. Prospect	20. Prospect 21. Prospect 22. Prospect 23. Donor 24. Prospect 25. Prospect 26. Prospect 27. Prospect 28. Prospect 29. Donor 30. Donor 31. Donor 32. Prospect 33. Donor 34. Donor 35. Donor	$13,980 12 gifts
$500 +	8%	■■■■■■■■■■ ■■■■■■■■■■ ■■☐☐☐☐☐☐☐☐ ☐☐☐☐☐☐☐☐☐☐ ☐☐☐☐☐☐☐☐☐☐ 50/$25,000 Average = $642		1. Donor 2. Prospect 3. Donor 4. Donor 5. Prospect 6. Prospect 7. Donor 8. Donor 9. Prospect 10. Prospect 11. Prospect 12. Prospect 13. Prospect 14. Prospect 15. Donor 16. Prospect 17. Donor	18. Donor 19. Donor 20. Donor 21. Donor 22. Prospect 23. Prospect 24. Donor 25. Donor 26. Donor 27. Donor 28. Donor 29. Donor 30. Donor 31. Donor 32. Donor 33. Donor 34. Donor	$14,120 22 gifts
$250 +	4%	■■■■■■■■■■ ■■■■■■■■■■ ■■■■■■☐☐☐☐ ☐☐☐☐ 44/$11,000 Average = $305		1. Prospect 2. Donor 3. Prospect 4. Donor 5. Donor 6. Donor 7. Donor 8. Donor 9. Donor 10. Prospect 11. Donor 12. Donor 13. Donor 14. Donor 15. Donor 16. Donor 17. Donor 18. Donor 19. Donor 20. Donor	21. Donor 22. Donor 23. Donor 24. Donor 25. Donor 26. Donor 27. Donor 28. Donor 29. Donor 30. Donor 31. Donor 32. Donor 33. Donor 34. Donor 35. Donor 36. Donor 37. Prospect 38. Donor 39. Donor 40. Donor	$11,000 36 gifts

Courtesy Dunwoody College of Technology

APPENDIX I

SAMPLE GIFT PROPOSAL

Proposing a Gift Investment to Support the Student Learning Center

A multiyear leadership pledge of $100,000 would fund Phase 3 development of a Student Learning Center. Your support will help to renovate the facility, double its capacity, and integrate all of the college's tutoring and learning support services into a single, state-of-the-art center. We anticipate that the center will become the new heart of the campus.

This is a critical moment in time for Your Community College as we launch our first major gift initiative to create a new center of excellence funded entirely by private philanthropy. To date, we have raised $1 million of the $2 million project budget.

The goal of the initiative is to create a new center of student activity focused on individual and small-group learning methods that have proven to be most effective in keeping students experiencing academic challenges in college and on course to achieve their goals.

A $100,000 pledge could be funded by five annual payments of $20,000. We hope you will consider this leadership gift in light of your long-standing history of support for Your Community College.

Respectfully submitted for your consideration by president John Doe. Thank you for your consideration!

_____   _____

Signed   Date

APPENDIX J1

SAMPLE BEQUEST LANGUAGE

A charitable bequest is a legacy gift made through the inclusion of enabling language into a will or *codicil*. A codicil is an appendix or supplement to a will. Specific types of charitable bequests include the following:

- **Specific bequest:** a specified amount of money, securities, or other assets
- **Property bequest:** a bequest of property
- **Proportionate bequest:** a specific percentage of an estate
- **Residual bequest:** the remainder of an estate after all other obligations have been fulfilled
- **Contingent bequest**: a bequest that takes effect only if certain conditions are met, such as circumstances related to other beneficiaries named in the will

Sample Language

Specific bequest: a bequest of a specific dollar amount
"Upon my death, I give and bequeath the sum of $_____ to Your Community College Foundation, a [state] nonprofit corporation located at _____, to be used for the general purposes of the organization."

Property: a bequest of property
"Upon my death, I give and bequeath [name the property: artwork, auto, real estate] to Your Community College Foundation, a [state] nonprofit corporation located at _____, to be used for the general purposes of the organization."

Proportionate bequest: a bequest of a specific percentage of an estate
"I give _____ percent of my net estate to Your Community College Foundation, a [state] nonprofit corporation located at _____, to be used for the general purposes of the organization."

Residual bequest: a bequest of the remaining balance of an estate
"I give and bequeath to Your Community College Foundation, a [state] nonprofit corporation located at _____, all the final remaining balance, residue and remainder of my property, real, personal, or mixed, of whatsoever kind and wherever situated of which I die possessed, or which I own or have any interest in at the time of my death, including any property over which I have a power of appointment, which power or powers I expressly exercise (referred to here as my 'residuary estate'), to be used for the general purposes of the organization."

Contingent bequest: a bequest contingent upon the survival of another individual or some other contingent event
"If my [spouse, child] does not survive me, I give and bequeath [indicate one of the types of bequests listed] to Your Community College Foundation, a [state] nonprofit corporation located at _____, to be used for the general purposes of the organization."

In all of these cases, a restricted purpose, such as a gift to an endowment fund, may be substituted for the words "to be used for the general purposes of the organization."

This language is provided only for planning purposes. Consult with your attorney to determine the exact language required to ensure that your intentions are reflected properly in your will.

APPENDIX J2

LETTER TO ACCOMPANY
A WILLS BROCHURE

Date

John and Mary Doe
Street Address
City, State Zip

Dear John and Mary:

I'd like to share a new college brochure with you. The brochure, entitled *Your Will, Your Way*, is a quick reference guide to help you keep your estate plan up to date, so that it fully reflects your intentions in light of any recent changes in your family circumstances or other interests.

Of course, if you don't already have a will, I encourage you to read the section on how states decide where assets will go when no will is in effect.

The brochure points out that the simplest way to keep your will current is through the addition of a *codicil*, an attachment to your will that addresses any changes in your estate plan. For example, the birth of a grandchild may change your thinking, or recent charitable interests may have caused you to think about including a favorite charity in your will. Circumstances like these can be addressed via a codicil. The brochure also contains some specific language you can use to frame your charitable gift intentions.

I am sending the brochure in connection with the launch of the Your Community College Legacy Society. The Legacy Society is composed of friends of the college who have decided to name the college in their wills or made arrangements for some other form of planned gift. Members of the society convene once a year for a luncheon hosted by President Smith. At present, we have seven members who have named the college in their wills. We are particularly honored that several of them are longstanding faculty members who have decided to commemorate their life's work with the "gift of a lifetime" for endowed scholarships.

Over the years, I have been honored to help many families fulfill their charitable dreams in this manner. If you would like to consult with me regarding gift planning, please give me a call at the number below whenever the spirit moves you. And if you have already named the college in your will, please let me know so that Your Community College may honor you as members of the Legacy Society.

Thank you for your family tradition of support to the college.

Sincerely,

Linda Lang
Vice President for Advancement

ADDITIONAL RESOURCES

Alexander, G. D. 1995. Ten ways to tell if your campaign is in trouble. *Fund Raising Management* 25, no. 4.

Association of Fundraising Professionals (AFP). 1994. Donor bill of rights. AFP, AAFRC, AHP and CASE. http://www.afpnet.org.

Bennett, P. 1973. *Up your accountability*. Washington, DC: The Taft Group.

Carver, J. 1992. Time to junk the old formula for boards. *The Chronicle of Philanthropy* 4, no. 22.

Drucker, P. F. 1990. Lessons for successful nonprofit governance. *Nonprofit Management & Leadership* 1, no. 1.

Edles, P. L. 1992. Predicting your campaign's success. *Contributions* 7, no. 2.

Felton, R. W. 1992. *Starting a development program*. Novato, CA: Buck Center for Research in Aging.

Fleishman, J. 1998. To merit and preserve the public's trust in not-for-profit organizations: The urgent need for regulatory reform. Presented at The Future of Philanthropy in a Changing America, sponsored by the Indiana University Center on Philanthropy and the American Assembly, April 23–26. Reprinted as a 2000 Executive Leadership Reading, Indiana University Center on Philanthropy.

Fletcher, K. B. 1992. Effective boards: How executive directors define and develop them. *Nonprofit Management & Leadership* 2, no. 3.

Greenleaf, R. K. 2002. *Servant leadership* (25th anniversary ed.). Mahwah, NJ: The Paulist Press.

Grønbjerg, K. A. 1998. Financing the U.S. nonprofit sector: The role of market and government. Presented at The Voluntary Sector in the Nordic Countries–Democracy, Integration, and Welfare, August 29–31. Reprinted as a 2000 Executive Leadership Reading, Indiana University Center on Philanthropy.

Jay, E., and Sargeant, A. 2004. *Building donor loyalty*. San Francisco: Jossey-Bass.

Koblin, H. 2001. It's all in the plan: Tie your campaign fund raising to long-term campus goals. *CASE Currents* 8, no. 2.

Lawson, D. 1995. Asking successfully for major gifts. *Fund Raising Management* 25, no. 5.

Lipman, R. F. 1997. The constituent life cycle. *Advancing Philanthropy* 5, no. 3.

Lippincott, S. M. 1999. *Meetings: Do's, don'ts and donuts* (2nd ed.). Pittsburgh, PA: Lighthouse Point.

Peterson, C. 1994. Fund raising's 20 biggest and most costly mistakes. *Contributions* 8, no. 2.

Selby, C. C. 1978. Better performance from "nonprofits." *Harvard Business Review* 56, no. 5.

Stukel, C. 2007. Billionaires: Please consider community colleges. *The Chronicle of Higher Education* 54, no. 8.

Wood, E. W. 1996–1997. The art of securing major gifts. *Advancing Philanthropy* 5, no. 4.

WEB SITES

American Council on Education, http://www.acenet.edu

Community College Times, http://www.communitycollegetimes.com

Continuous Quality Improvement Network, http://www.cqin.net

Council for Resource Development, http://www.crdnet.org

Grassroots Fundraising Journal, http://www.grassrootsfundraising.org

Higher Learning Commission of the North Central Association of Colleges and Schools, http://www.ncahlc.org

Institute for Community College Development, http://www.iccd.cornell.edu

League for Innovation in the Community College, http://www.league.org

The Council for Advancement and Support of Education (CASE) is the professional organization for advancement professionals at all levels who work in alumni relations, communications and marketing, development, and advancement services.

CASE's membership includes more than 3,400 colleges, universities, and independent and secondary schools in 61 countries. This makes CASE one of the largest nonprofit education associations in the world in terms of institutional membership. CASE also serves more than 60,000 advancement professionals on staffs of member institutions and has more than 22,500 individual "professional members" and more than 230 Educational Partner corporate members.

CASE has offices in Washington, D.C., London, and Singapore. The association produces high-quality and timely content, publications, conferences, institutes, and workshops that assist advancement professionals perform more effectively and serve their institutions.

For more information, visit *www.case.org* or call + 1-202-328-2273.